SOFTWARE TESTING TECHNIQUES:
FINDING THE DEFECTS
THAT MATTER

Software Testing Techniques: Finding the Defects that Matter

Scott Loveland

Geoffrey Miller

Richard Prewitt Jr.

Michael Shannon

CHARLES RIVER MEDIA, INC.
Hingham, Massachusetts

Acquisitions Editor: James Walsh
Cover Design: The Printed Image

CHARLES RIVER MEDIA, INC.
10 Downer Avenue
Hingham, Massachusetts 02043
781-740-0400
781-740-8816 (FAX)
info@charlesriver.com
www.charlesriver.com

This book is printed on acid-free paper.

Scott Loveland, Geoffrey Miller, Richard Prewitt Jr., Michael Shannon. *Software Testing Techniques: Finding the Defects that Matter.*
ISBN: 1-58450-346-7

Library of Congress Cataloging-in-Publication Data
Software testing techniques : finding the defects that matter / Scott Loveland . . . [et al.].
   p. cm.
Includes bibliographical references and index.
ISBN 1-58450-346-7 (pbk. : alk. paper)
1. Computer software—Testing. 2. Computer software—Reliability. I. Loveland, Scott.
QA76.76.T48S645 2004
005.1'4--dc22
                2004018169

Printed in the United States of America
04 7 6 5 4 3 2 First Edition

CHARLES RIVER MEDIA titles are available for site license or bulk purchase by institutions, user groups, corporations, etc. For additional information, please contact the Special Sales Department at 781-740-0400.

Contents

Acknowledgments

We are grateful to the IBM z/OS Solution Evaluation Test management team for their encouragement and support of this venture. We also appreciate the guidance and professionalism of Bob Diforio, our literary agent, and everyone at Charles River Media. A special thanks to Shelly Loveland for her tremendous editorial suggestions. This book was enriched by the insight, technical contribution, and text review of Karen Rosengren, James Whittaker, Wayne Morschhauser, Jim Mulder, Romney White, Arvind Mistry, and Rachel Reisman. Rich Prewitt would like to extend a special thanks to Dave Stilwell for his continued test leadership and guidance. Finally, many thanks to our wives, Shelly, Cindy, Beth, and Pat, without whose support and patience this book would not have been possible.

Preface

Computer software runs the world. If it crashes, even briefly, the impact to a company's bottom line can often be measured in millions. But crash it does. Well-publicized failures from both industry and government have underscored the need for mission-critical software to withstand harsh conditions. Before it sees the light of day, software must prove its reliability under a white-hot beam of rigorous interrogation. It must be poked and prodded, squeezed and stretched, trashed and torn. In other words, it must be tested.

If you are reading this book, then you are probably already interested in software testing. Perhaps, like many testers, you learned how to write programs, but found you had more fun breaking things than creating them. We did too. So we kept at it, fighting in the trenches to kill software bugs before they could escape into some unsuspecting user's system. We wouldn't have it any other way. To a tester, there's nothing quite as satisfying as ripping into databases, crushing transaction monitors, blasting Web application servers, or forcing operating systems to their knees.

This book will help you succeed in your own hunt for bugs. We've distilled decades of experience across a spectrum of test disciplines into concrete guidelines, recommendations, and techniques for test practitioners. For newbies, it's a practical guide to the fabulous world of software testing. For veterans, it offers additional perspective and new ideas, and may challenge some long-held beliefs. Additionally, there is useful information included for beleaguered test managers and those intrigued by test processes. But at its core, this book is a survival guide written by testers, for testers.

We will zoom in on approaches that have demonstrated their effectiveness over time. The book's concepts are aimed at testing the kind of software that companies bet their business on. Key methods and techniques are illustrated through case studies of actual product tests drawn from a software development laboratory.

These case studies reveal how software is tested on what many consider to be the gold standard for reliable, robust computing: the mainframe. But this is by no means a mainframe-specific book. The techniques described are applicable to testing *any* general-purpose software that must stand up to the rigors of industrial-strength computing.

We will show you how to take your testing assignment and run with it. You will see the ins and outs of both low-level functional testing *and* the kind of system-level testing that is critical for server-class software. You will learn how to gain necessary insight into the software you have been assigned to test by analyzing it from multiple angles, and how to use the best tool available—your intellect. You will also discover how to thrive in an environment where the software is so complex that no single person can thoroughly grasp it all. The importance of load/stress testing will be emphasized, as well as how it differs from (though is sometimes confused with) performance testing. Rarely covered subjects will also be discussed, including techniques for writing effective test programs, tips on how to use old test cases to uncover new bugs, approaches for emulating customers in test environments, and suggestions for when it's better to buy a test tool or build one yourself.

You will also discover how to probe the software's ability to recover from failures, and explore approaches you can use for debugging (and why you should not always leave that task to developers). You will find out about opportunities testers have to influence product design, both for the benefit of customers and the simplification of their own jobs. Testing for data corruption will be discussed, as will writing a data integrity monitor. We will take a look at some specialized approaches, such as artistic testing and algorithm verification testing. We will also examine the testing advantages of a world that's old hat to mainframe folks but is now exploding in other computer systems: virtualized environments.

This book will also go beyond purely technical topics to discuss how you can build both your technical credibility and career path within a software development organization. You will see how to maintain your sanity in the throes of a chaotic test, turn the drudgery of tracking test status to your advantage, and estimate the time needed for testing. You will also learn approaches for continuous improvement, and how to tell if you really have what it takes to be a good tester.

We are confident this book will help you to become a more efficient and effective bug seeker. We also expect it will open your eyes to some new ideas and expand your vision of what's possible in the world of software testing. Most of all, we hope you have as much fun testing as we do.

Part I

Testing: Why Worry?

Someone once said that if you don't know what you want, you'll probably never get it. Likewise, unless you understand the nature of industrial-strength software and the environments in which it operates, your testing may miss the mark. That's because computers are no longer just tools for making organizations more productive and efficient. The use of computer technology has evolved to the point where small businesses, corporations, and governments simply cannot *survive* without computers and software. But with that dependence comes a certain fear: that a software bug will strike at the worst possible moment and cause a devastating outage. Fortunately, one brave group stands between enterprises that rely on software and bugs that lurk within it. They are called testers.

This section looks at why we need to worry about testing. It starts on the people side of the equation, and explores why different personalities play different roles in the software development process. It examines the attributes of people willing to take on the testing challenge and the mindset needed to be successful. The section then turns its attention to technology and puts a microscope on the kind of software that has become so ingrained in business and government that it has fostered such dependence. It studies the software's characteristics, the nature of the computing environments in which it must survive, and the tremendous challenges involved in its testing. The next two chapters set the stage for the rest of the book, and will help you base your testing on insight, rather than guesswork. Now let's get started.

1 The Testing Challenge and Those Who Take It On

In This Chapter

- The challenging nature of software testing
- Why test tools do not supply the complete answer
- Typical users of large-systems software
- Personality traits of good testers

As a software tester, the fate of the world rests on your shoulders. This statement is not an exaggeration if you accept the dual premises that computer software runs the modern world and that all software has bugs—then you will quickly reach the inescapable conclusion that unless the most disruptive bugs are removed, the world as we know it will grind to a halt. You are the one in the software development process that has the role of unearthing those bugs.

Ensuring that software is production-ready is the goal of testing. That sounds easy enough, because after all, anyone can test—it's just an annoyance a software developer has to put up with at the end of a product development cycle. If you agree with this, you have demonstrated one challenge testers face. On the surface, testing seems to be such an easy concept to grasp that performing it "must be simple." However, most software is not simple. It is complex, the demands placed upon it are immense, and the breadth of the environments into which it is deployed is tremendous. Once you see this, you can begin to understand the scope of challenges faced by those who choose to toil within the test discipline.

SOFTWARE ENGINEERING EVOLUTION

The testing challenge stretches beyond software complexity. It reaches into the very nature of the software engineering discipline.

Software Development

Over time, there have been many improvements to the process and tools needed to develop software. High-level programming languages have evolved to where they can greatly ease the burden of developing code. Design modeling techniques have matured, code generation tools have grown and expanded, and many other software development tools have appeared and been refined. Much effort has been spent, and continues to be spent, on making software developers more productive. This means developers can generate more code in less time with less effort. Unfortunately, it does not mean they are writing it any better. To the tester, more code simply means more bugs.

Software Test

During this time of wide-ranging improvements in software development tools, not nearly as much research or effort has been spent on similar improvements in test tooling. Perhaps this is because it is a much more difficult problem to solve. One can quickly grasp the requirements and approaches to improve a software developer's ability to create software. On the other hand, it is not trivial to even understand what a tester needs, let alone create test tooling to facilitate it.

Test Execution Tools

Many tools are available to help automate the execution of tests against software, but they are a relatively small piece of the testing puzzle. Examples include those commonly referred to as *capture-replay* tools which are available from a variety of vendors. These tools give testers the ability to move some Graphical User Interface (GUI) testing away from manual execution by "capturing" mouse clicks and keyboard strokes into a script, and then "replaying" that script to recreate the same sequence of inputs and responses on subsequent tests. There are also load/stress tools (sometimes known as performance tools) that provide the ability to simulate large numbers of clients or end users. Testers can use this type of tool to drive heavy load volumes against the software and servers under test. System testers and performance testers could not be successful without load/stress tools. However, none of these test execution tools assist the tester in *defining* what tests to execute. Automated test execution is highly recommended, but not the total answer to the testing challenge.

Test Creation Tools

Many attempts have been made to automate test creation. One approach requires a formal design specification written in a compilable language. Some success with this approach has been demonstrated, but its usefulness lasts only as long as design and development agree to write formal specifications, and write them in the language required—not a common occurrence in most commercial software projects.

Another approach is to generate test cases from a tester-defined software behavior model known as a *state transition diagram*. Such a diagram identifies all of the software's possible states, and the permitted transitions between those states. But in large software products, the total number of potential states is huge by any measure. Attempting to cover all potential states is not cost effective or even desirable since it would waste precious time by generating many uninteresting tests. As a result, this approach doesn't scale well. The challenge for the tester to define and create the most appropriate tests is still there.

Code Coverage Tools

Code coverage tools are available that support a variety of programming languages. These tools give developers an excellent way to ensure the testing they perform against their own software, known as a *unit test,* has successfully executed all new and changed lines of code. They can also be very helpful in determining what areas of the software are driven by which test cases—making test case selection for regression testing easier. However, there is a whole category of software problems that code coverage tools can never help find. Timing and serialization bugs tend to escape code coverage tools since the determining factor is not *if* a line of code gets executed, but *when*. Also missed is consideration of the content on which those lines of code are executing (e.g., limits, interface values, volumes), as well as the environment in which they are operating and their intended effects on that environment. In other words, code coverage tools can never address the *context* in which any line of code is executing, and context is critical to correctness.

The Testing Paradox

The apparent inability of testing tools to keep pace with those on the development side, combined with constant business requirements for improved time to market, create one of a tester's many challenges. You could make the argument that, as each day passes, it becomes easier to develop software but more difficult to test it.

A TESTER'S TRUE GOAL

All software has bugs. It's a fact of life. So the goal of finding and removing *all* defects in a software product is a losing proposition and a dangerous objective for a test team, because such a goal can divert the test team's attention from what is really important. In the world of general-purpose, large-scale, business-critical software, it is not the goal of a test team to find all of the defects. That is a practical impossibility. Rather, it is to ensure that among the defects found are all of those that will disrupt real production environments; in other words, to *find the defects that matter.*

Trivial Example, Nontrivial Challenge

Let's use one of the most trivial of examples of a defect to help illustrate just one challenge testers face. Many years ago, a program with one line of code was developed and shipped. The program's function is to simply return to its caller. Its nickname is "BR14" because that is just what it does—branch to the address contained in register 14. This terminology comes from the IBM assembler programming language, but knowledge of assembler is not important for the purposes of this example. The BR14 program is basically a no-op (a term used to describe no real operation or function) but can have many uses. One is to act as an aid for performing a unit test on programs by providing a stub routine to fill in for a program that has yet to be developed. Another use is to supply a program that can be called in a batch job to give a user an easy way to drive functions via the batch process (for example, allocating a new file). Here is the entire program:

```
ASTUB   CSECT
        BR    14              Branch back to the caller
        END
```

Is there a bug in this program? It meets its requirement of returning to its caller. Any invocation provides 100% code coverage—and a code coverage tool can prove that testing did in fact exercise this single line of code. It will not abnormally terminate or cause any system or application crash. Since it does not obtain any storage, it can not have a memory leak. It does not obtain any locks or update any fields, so it does not have any serialization concerns. Multiple invocations of this program can simultaneously execute on different processors without any ill effects. Since it does not read or write data, it cannot cause any data integrity problems. Looks good; we are done.

Not so fast: this program does indeed have a bug. There is nothing wrong with what it does. The problem is what is *does not* do. The program does not set a return code prior to returning to its caller. There are a few reasons why this is a bug. One is that the behavior of this program is not consistent. By assembler language convention, register 15 contains a return code. Upon exit from this program, the content of register 15 is unpredictable. It is common practice to examine the return code of programs to determine success or failure. A program with an unpredictable return code that gives no indication of success can cause other programs such as automation routines, to behave incorrectly. So the failure of this program to set a return code is indeed a bug. Furthermore, the fact that this bug might cause other software using it to fail, and conflicts with common practices surrounding its intended use by customers, means that it could impact customer production environments. That makes it a defect that matters.

The fix:

```
ASTUB   CSECT
        SR    15,15           Set return code
        BR    14              Branch back to the caller
        END
```

It is hard to imagine a more trivial example of a program, a bug, or a fix, but the test challenge it illustrates is indeed complex. Testers need to go beyond testing per requirements, testing for code coverage, and showing that abnormal termination or system crashes are not present. Finding what is missing from a product based on a thorough understanding of common practices surrounding its use, or its expected use, by customers is a nontrivial, but important challenge testers need to address. Unfortunately, there is no test tool that will automatically find this type of bug. It takes a good tester with the right mindset, proper preparation, and in-depth knowledge of the software and how it will be used to find and destroy these types of defects that matter.

WHAT IS A USER?

The requirement of understanding the expected customer use of the software under test has already been mentioned. But, as with the nature of testing itself, this is not as simple as it seems. In the world of large, mission-critical systems that keep major companies in business, the term "user" does not necessarily mean "end user." Large systems that run on large servers support tens of thousands of end users (or even more, in some cases) who rarely interface directly with the large-systems software. Instead, they interface with an application or set of applications running on the servers. The true users of large-systems software are a set of IT professionals whose job is to support a production environment.

System administrator is a common term for an IT professional who supports a server at a departmental level. However, large production environments need more than a single system administrator. Typically there is a multitude of support skills and positions involved. Some examples of users of large-systems software are:

Systems Programmers: Install, setup, configure, customize, and maintain software. The term programmer is included in the title due to their typical tasks of writing scripts, customization exits, etc.

Operators: Handle the day-to-day monitoring of the systems.

Database Administrators: Manage database optimization, backup, and recovery.

Performance Analysts: Monitor and tune the performance of the systems.

Capacity Planners: Analyze system growth and project future requirements.

Storage Administrators: Manage data placement across a number of external disk storage devices, data backup, and the storage devices themselves.

Application Developers: Create specific applications that give their business a competitive advantage.

Security Administrators: Protect data and other system resources, control user IDs, and manage security databases.

All of these users have different needs, requirements, and expectations. Systems programmers are particularly interested in the Reliability, Availability, and Serviceability (RAS) characteristics of the software. In other words, systems programmers expect software to recover from failure, be configurable to avoid any single points of failure, provide ways to dynamically make changes to the systems, and provide diagnostic data when a problem occurs so the root cause can be determined and fixed. Remember, when thinking about mission-critical software, the term reboot and what it represents is not an option. Operators are interested in the software's ability to alert them accurately to situations they may need to respond to—and doing so in real time, before it is too late. They are also interested in ease of automation of routine operations. Database administrators are interested in the transaction logging, forward recovery, data integrity, and dynamic change capabilities of the software. Other system support professionals have their own set of requirements and expectations. The entire system support staff makes use of the software to provide very high levels of availability to their business's mission-critical applications and the end users of those applications.

The point is, testers must understand the expectations placed upon the software they test. Testing to remove defects defined in the traditional sense (e.g., logic flaws, abnormal termination) is just the beginning. Testing is also required to prove such things as systems management capabilities, system longevity, and system recovery from failures. Almost all existing test tools, research, and academic study is geared toward removing the "traditional" defects. This is very important and a requirement of any software development project, but it is not the total answer. The other testing needs described are a challenge because they rely on the knowledge and skill of the test professional. The demands upon this knowledge and skill increase as customer production systems become more and more complex.

Different Objectives, Different Tests

You can now see why there is more to testing software than just finding bugs. Many facets of the software need to be exposed. The demands placed on the software are strenuous and customer expectations are high. No single test and no single test team is able to achieve all possible test objectives, so they need to be divided among different teams. The most successful tests occur when the test team has the proper scope and focus. Placing too many objectives on a test team actually reduces effectiveness and efficiency. In Chapter 3, "The Development Process," we will review how different development models address this issue. The merits of any process can be debated, but regardless of the software development process used, the importance of properly focusing a particular test effort cannot be stressed enough.

Software testers have a responsibility to validate that the software they test is production-ready. This means removing bugs, testing to requirements and specifications, verifying appropriate RAS characteristics, ensuring data integrity, proving operational capability, demonstrating acceptable performance, showing systems management capabilities, confirming ease of migration, and so on. A daunting task indeed. What type of person accepts this challenge?

TESTERS, WHAT MAKES THEM SPECIAL?

Good testers enjoy breaking things, especially developers' software. They delight in identifying likely vulnerabilities and devising attacks to expose them, including generalized categories of attacks that can be applied to a wide range of software products. The testing personality is different from that of most other software professionals, who view defects as annoyances to be avoided—"bumps in the road" toward their goal of seeing things work. Having this "breaker mentality" is a crucial trait for those testing software developed to support continuous operation [Loveland02].

Why Do We Need Testers?

Developers are well suited to performing the initial unit testing of their code. But beyond that, testing software products is best left to the professional whose career is devoted to the test discipline. Developers do not have an outsider's perspective on their code. They likely will not consider tests that attack areas outside those they handled during the code's development. Their testing tends to prove that the code works, while testers seek to prove the code doesn't work. It's human nature. Because the developer wrote the code, he believes it works. It is not a good idea for the software developer to be its sole tester, except in the rare case when the only user of the software is the developer himself.

Tester Traits

Testers are a special breed for a variety of reasons. Certain personality traits are required to be a successful, happy, long-term tester. The "anybody can test" myth is exactly that—a myth. Let's consider some common personality traits shared by testers.

Curious

Good testers consistently demonstrate high degrees of curiosity. "Why" and "What if" are common questions they contemplate. They want to know about the function they're testing, the rationale and requirements that instigated the development of that functionality, and how the software will behave when they get a chance to put it through its paces. Testers are not shy about asking questions.

Skeptical

Testers are natural skeptics, and relate easily to Missouri's motto: "Show me." They ask questions and read specifications, but are not satisfied until they experience things for themselves and draw their own conclusions.

Restless

Successful testers are rarely completely satisfied with their work. If a bug escapes from test into production, a tester does not argue facts or become defensive—he takes the problem, analyzes it in detail, and determines what can be enhanced or added to the test to find the same kind of problem in the next test iteration. Good testers always strive to improve, realizing that any problem found by a customer that makes that customer unhappy is automatically considered a defect that matters.

Upbeat

Another trait exhibited by successful testers is the ability to stay positive in a negative environment. Testers do not consider a defect a negative as do all others involved in the software development process. Testers are always under time constraints, frequently asked to take risks beyond their better judgment, and often challenged to defend their view of the product. It is not easy being part of the end phases of a long development process. Testers routinely get squeezed from both ends—late delivery of code combined with an immovable delivery date. Good testers relish addressing this challenge—understanding the importance of both supporting their business and protecting their customers.

Diplomatic

Diplomacy is another important trait possessed by good testers. Good developers have strong egos—it's often one of the things that makes a developer good. The tester needs to be able to be the bearer of bad news and, at times, be prepared to tell a developer that his "baby is ugly." This must be handled in a way that elicits the correct solution without causing contention. To be a successful tester, you need to cultivate excellent relationships with developers, understanding that everyone shares the same goal of delivering the highest-quality products to the marketplace at the right time. For more on this topic, see Chapter 4, "The Test and Development Divide."

Insatiable

With an unquenchable thirst for knowledge, testers want to fully understand the technology they work on, how it is used in real-world environments, and the real concerns of their customers. They enjoy seeing the big picture, understanding complete systems, and working on different problems. A major challenge for testers is keeping up with new and changing software technology *and* test techniques. The life of a tester is never dull.

Generous

Testers are also educators at heart. No one person has the knowledge and ability to understand all aspects of very large systems in detail, so testers frequently rely on each other. They teach each other about different aspects of systems and share information about various software components. Also, since it is testers who get the initial view of new software and systems technology, how it behaves, and what should be avoided, they make very good customer educators. Testers see a broader picture than developers do and can share that perspective and wealth of experience with their customers.

Empathetic

Another invaluable trait is empathy. One of the most important roles a tester plays is that of customer advocate. A good tester continually thinks in terms of his customers, what is important to them, and what he needs to do to "protect" them. Without a working knowledge of customers and their businesses, testers do not have much chance at being successful at finding the defects that matter most. They should have a complete understanding of how their customers use the software, how they deploy that software, and the day-to-day activities of the software support staff. Good testers jump at the chance to interact with their customers through discussions, working to re-create problems they uncover, or spending time at their site. Testers are happiest when their customers are happy and successful when their customers are successful.

Resilient

Resiliency is also important. The customer (either another test team or an external customer) is bound to find a bug or two with any new software. These customers are not privy to the many defects already removed. They only see the tester's failures, not his successes. Many times (actually all times if the test was a good one) the ratio of problems found by the tester is disproportionate to those found by the customer. Testers must be resilient and thick-skinned when after they remove hundreds of defects from a product, a customer installs it, finds one problem, and asks, "Didn't you test this?"

SUMMARY

There are no hard and fast answers when addressing many of the challenges faced in the software test discipline. The testing of complex, critical software is not made up of one thing, accomplished with one tool, or even conducted by one test team. This book identifies and describes some proven approaches to addressing these challenges.

In Chapter 2, "Industrial-Strength Software, It's Not a Science Project," we'll look at another side of the testing challenge, namely the monster that testers must wrestle to the ground: large-scale, general-purpose software. We will identify its characteristics, typical environments in which it is required to perform, and some examples of the demands placed upon it.

2

Industrial-strength Software, It's Not a Science Project

In This Chapter

- Characteristics of industrial-strength software
- The nature of production environments
- Examples of mission-critical software in action
- A Case Study

What do we mean by "industrial-strength software?" A calculator program ships with Microsoft® Windows® software, which makes it part of a commercial product that is used by millions of people every day. That counts perhaps, but we're thinking bigger. When we say "industrial-strength," we're talking about the kind of software that makes the world work. The kind that companies depend on to run their businesses. The kind that enables people to withdraw money from an ATM or have their credit card approved by a salesperson at any time, anywhere in the world. The kind that gets an overnight package to the right place on time. The kind that controls a corporation's pension plan and allows its employees to manage their 401(k)s. We're talking about software that can be absolutely relied on to handle important, complex tasks for today's businesses.

In order to understand the issues with testing such software, you must first understand the nature of the software itself. This chapter will describe the characteristics of enterprise-class software and the complex information technology (IT) environments in which it is deployed. It will also examine the nature of computer servers upon which such software runs, and look at examples of how mission-critical software operates.

INDUSTRIAL-STRENGTH SOFTWARE

There are a number of characteristics of industrial-strength software that make it different from, say, a program written as a high school class project. For starters, there is its size. Of course, commercial programs are written in widely varying lengths, but the software we're discussing consists of at least one hundred thousand lines of code (lines of code may be an imperfect measure, but it will suffice here), although it will often stretch to a million lines or more. That's a lot of code, and each line is a potential bug—but we'll get into that later. Programs of that size are rarely developed by a single individual, but rather by teams of programmers, often broken into subteams responsible for different sections of the whole. Those sections must communicate with each other through well-defined interfaces (i.e., more bugs). Programs of that size also have many things going on at once. As a result they are typically multithreaded and run on large servers with more than one CPU, and require some sort of serialization to synchronize their parallel activities (i.e., some really good bugs).

Commercial software often manipulates huge volumes of data and must do so without making a single mistake and without corrupting the very data it is manipulating. It needs to be robust, meaning that it must do everything in its power to detect, report, and recover from any errors that do arise (and because it's created by human beings, errors will always arise). The data involved is often sensitive in nature, so security precautions have to be deeply ingrained (a little hacking, anyone?).

In a classroom environment, getting a program to run once is often the end game: once it works, you hand it in and celebrate. In commercial environments, once a program seems to work, the game has just begun. That program will often be called upon to run for days, weeks, months, or even years at a time without error. It cannot suffer from so-called "memory leaks" (a.k.a. bugs) that would cause it to slowly degrade over time until it collapses. It must be able to operate at extremely high throughput levels that put the server upon which it is executing under high levels of stress—for a retailer's system, crashing during the holiday rush is not an option.

Because this class of software is by nature sophisticated and complex, if not designed properly it could be almost impossible to use. It needs good usability characteristics, such as an intuitive user interface and meaningful output messages. It also requires extensive documentation (context-sensitive help, hard-copy manuals, or both). While it may sound obvious, that documentation must match and correctly explain the product it is describing (in other words, the bugs keep coming).

Finally, a development team does not write a massive program like this once, and then move onto something else. They rarely get all the desired features incorporated into the product the first time within the allotted time frame; and even if they could, requirements are always evolving and the program will continually need to be adjusted to adapt to those changes. In some sense, this is similar to how San Francisco's Golden Gate Bridge is kept golden. A paint crew starts at one end and works its way to the other; when the painters finish, they start over again. Commercial programs go through multiple release cycles. Each new release must be compatible with the prior one, and allow users to migrate to it easily. A smooth migration means the data is not corrupted and the functions that worked in the previous release continue to work (bugs, bugs, everywhere).

In short, it's a mine field out there. There is no getting around the complexity inherent in this class of software, and layered on top of that complexity is the human element. All the controls, processes, and audits that a development team may put in place can't change one thing: software is written by people. And people make mistakes.

PRODUCTION ENVIRONMENTS

In the IT world, putting a piece of software into *production* means deploying it on an enterprise's computing systems so that it can actually run some portion of that company's business. The intent is not to test it, not to experiment with it, but to rely on it. When a program is past development, through test, beyond beta, and ready to face the cold, cruel world, the place it lands is someone's production environment.

Test-sensitive Characteristics

What is the nature of these environments? There is no single answer to that question. That simple fact alone causes headaches for software testers, especially those working on programs that will eventually be sold as commercial products, because it's impossible to predict (or emulate) every environment in which the program will someday run. In fact, it's not uncommon for a tester who reports a defect to hear a developer deem it a low priority because the tester found it by emulating an "unrealistic environment" in which no customer would ever run—only to have that very same problem become the first customer-reported product defect. Guessing what every customer will or will not do with a piece of software is about as easy as predicting the rise and fall of the stock market. However, there are some typical characteristics we can examine.

Heterogeneity

First and foremost, production environments are *heterogeneous*. It is the rare enterprise that utilizes a single make and model of server across its business, let alone software from only one manufacturer. Unheard of might be a more accurate description. Rather, most large enterprises have a broad mix: servers ranging from small Intel® processor-based workstations to blade servers to midrange boxes to mainframes. Collectively, these processors run such things as Microsoft Windows, UNIX®, Linux®, IBM® z/OS®, and IBM z/VM® operating systems. The networking infrastructure likely supports multiple speeds of Ethernet and perhaps one or more less-common technologies, such as asynchronous transfer mode (ATM), Fiber Distributed Data Interface (FDDI), or even token ring. Disk, tape, and other peripherals span several brands.

A related aspect is the concept of a software *stack*. A stack typically starts with an operating system. Layered on that are one or more *middleware* products, such as a relational database, a Web application server, or a transaction monitor. On the top are the applications that end users actually interact with.

Perhaps most important for this discussion, all of this software running both within a single server and across all servers in the production infrastructure probably come from many different suppliers. At any one time, a large IT shop may be running hundreds of software products from a dozen or more vendors. Try fitting all that into a test variation matrix and you will have a new appreciation for the word "headache."

Size

A related characteristic of production environments is their sheer size: terabytes of data, thousands of MIPS (Millions of Instructions per Second, a metric for processor capacity—sometimes affectionately known as Meaningless Indicator of Processor Speed), miles of interconnecting cable, acres of floor space, and megawatts of electrical power. You get the idea. This kind of scale is probably impossible for the tester to replicate and difficult to emulate, but it's necessary to try.

Service Level Agreements

Another characteristic of the production environment is the existence of a *service level agreement*, or SLA. An SLA is a contract between the provider of IT services for the business (typically the company's own IT department, or an outsourcing vendor), and the users of those services. Companies take their SLAs seriously, so much so that the jobs of the Chief Information Officer (CIO) and/or his staff may depend on meeting them. As a tester, it's not too much of a stretch to suggest that their jobs are in your hands. SLAs often limit both planned and unplanned down time to minutes per month. That in turn leads to an insistence on tight control over changes and very narrow windows for rebooting systems to pick up software fixes, make configuration updates, or perform other maintenance. Think about that the next time you're asked to recreate a software problem a dozen times to gather enough diagnostic data to debug it.

Continuous Availability

Globalization and the influence of the Internet have put additional pressure on corporate IT departments and their SLAs. For decades, companies have run their interactive applications during the day, then locked down their databases at night to perform consolidation and reconciliation activities, reconfigure the network, or do other disruptive tasks, often by running streams of specialized batch jobs. There is even a term for this down time: the *batch window*. Now, as companies expand operations across several continents and time zones, consolidate data centers, and serve customers who use the Internet to place orders, access accounts, or perform other transactions at any time of day, the concept of a batch window is often little more than a memory.

Instead, companies must keep their systems up for weeks, months, or longer without an outage. System down time or unplanned outages, even of short duration, can cost millions of dollars in lost revenue. Enabling Technologies Group [Bothwell01] reports that surveyed IT users identified down-time costs of up to one million dollars a *minute*.

In such an environment, reboot is not a valid recovery option. Production users don't think about availability in terms of minimizing the length of an outage; they think in terms of minimizing outages—period. The most important element in keeping these systems humming is rock-solid, reliable software that refuses to fail, regardless of how heavily it is pushed or how long it has been running. Proving such levels of reliability is a major challenge for testers, requiring special focus in such areas as recovery and longevity testing.

Backup and Recovery

So what if your software is robust, your testing is perfect, and your product is shipped without a single defect—your customers still cannot rest easy. There's always the risk of an earthquake, flood, hurricane, tornado, power outage, terrorist attack, or other calamity that can put an entire data center out of business. Smaller-scale disasters, down to a damaged disk array, can also strike. All these risks lead IT professionals to create backup and recovery plans for their production systems. These can range from geographically dispersed, redundant data centers to local backup and restore capability intended to ensure that a data center can pass the "roaming elephant" test (i.e., if an elephant wanders into the data center and randomly picks a spot to sit, could it take down any critical applications?). Such plans rely on tools and technology to achieve their desired ends, and so have their share of bugs for testers to target.

Compatibility

Few production environments pop up overnight. They evolve and grow over time, and so do their application suites. It is not unusual for a business to have many millions of dollars invested in critical applications that have been operating and evolving for years. Needless to say, businesses are not anxious to jettison these investments and start over in order to use a new version of anything, no matter how clever its features. They expect each new release of a given software product, be it an application, middleware, or the operating system itself, to be compatible with its own prior release or set of releases.

IT departments must be able to migrate smoothly to a new release in a staged manner, upgrading the software product gradually, one system at a time, until the entire complex is transitioned over. If a product required a "big bang" approach, necessitating all copies across the data center to be upgraded at the same time, a chorus of screams would erupt from IT departments and the new version of the product would end up on a shelf gathering dust. The poor manufacturer who had devised such a "migration plan" would be forced to appease CIOs around the globe by explaining how it intended to solve the problem.

Naturally both compatibility with exploiting or corequisite products and with one's own prior releases, must be verified by the tester.

Virtualization

Imagine a case where dozens, hundreds, or even thousands of programs or users must operate at the same time on a single machine, but each must believe that it is alone on the system, that it controls the entire machine's resources and can do with them as it wishes. To accomplish this, a single server would need to be split into hundreds of images, each running its own instance of an operating system. To each such operating system instance it would need to appear as if it has sole possession of a set of resources (e.g., CPU, memory, disk, networking), so that it in turn could serve up those resources to programs requesting them.

To perform such magic requires something called a *hypervisor*, a piece of software that hosts multiple copies of other operating systems. This hypervisor pools server resources in a way that allows them to be shared efficiently. It then hands out virtualized instances of those shared resources to the operating systems it hosts (making them appear as though they are dedicated to each) and manages those resources to balance their usage effectively, all the while ensuring each virtual host is completely fenced off from the others. Long used in the mainframe world, this technology has begun permeating other server types as well as a way to maximize the use of expensive hardware.

For the tester, virtualization doesn't present a challenge, but rather offers very useful opportunities for creating effective test environments.

All the Elements

Heterogeneity, massive scale, restrictive SLAs, continuous availability, backup and recovery, compatibility, and virtualization are all elements of production environments that the wise tester must keep in mind (or take advantage of) when devising attacks for uncovering weaknesses in order to give software its best chance to survive in the real world.

MISSION-CRITICAL SOFTWARE

We've discussed some of the characteristics of industrial-strength software and the nature of the production environments in which it is deployed. As a final point in this discussion, we will look at that elite subset of industrial-strength software that is more than simply important for running a company's business—it *is* their business. This is what is often referred to by enterprises as *mission-critical* software.

All of the characteristics of industrial-strength software described above are amplified for mission-critical software. That's because it is so vital to an enterprise, that without it, the business simply could not operate. For an online retailer, if its Web site is down, its business is closed. Or if the subset of its site that processes orders fails, that's enough to temporarily stop it dead. For that matter, if the site is up but response time is too slow, customers will quit and go elsewhere. For that retailer, its Web site and its ability to process customer orders are clearly mission-critical.

An overnight delivery service must be able to track packages precisely. The packages must go from courier pick up to regional processing facilities, where they are loaded on planes and flown to a central hub. From the hub, they must be reloaded onto other planes that will deliver them to the correct destination. Before those planes can land at their respective airports, bills of lading describing the plane's exact contents must arrive at the airport. All of this occurs within a 24-hour window. If the software that tracks those packages fails and packages are loaded on planes headed to the wrong destinations, the company's entire business is compromised. Or, if those bills of lading do not arrive as scheduled, the planes could be forced to circle the airports, waiting. For that overnight delivery service, its tracking system is mission-critical.

Some companies must do more than simply satisfy their customers—they must also satisfy governments. For instance, the United States Securities and Exchange Commission (SEC) dictates trade clearing, account balancing, and other daily deadlines that financial services companies must meet, or they will face significant fines. For such companies, any system that is key to their compliance with government regulations is mission-critical.

One Core Element

We can glean another important characteristic from these examples: at its core, mission-critical software usually revolves around mission-critical data. For the on-line retailer, that data is customer order information and available inventory. For the delivery service, it's information about package destination and current location. Furthermore, while the data typically lives in a single, well-protected location, it may be accessed through several different channels. The online retailer's customers access product and order data through a Web-based storefront, while the warehouse fulfillment team accesses it through an inventory management system. The overnight delivery service must record package information at the point of pick up, then track the parcel via handheld scanners as it passes checkpoints along the route to its destination. Once a package is loaded on a plane at the hub for its final destination, a back-office application must be invoked to include it in the appropriate bill of lading. All the while, an eager customer may be tracking the package's progress through a Web application.

So we can see that managing and protecting data is often crucial to mission-critical software. Let's look in detail at another example which will expose the true level of complexity involved in production environments and the software that drives them. It's not a short tale, so if you're already enmeshed in such an environment, feel free to skip ahead. Otherwise, hang on for the ride.

CASE STUDY: A PENSION PLAN MANAGEMENT VENDOR

Most midsized and large companies provide a pension plan for their employees, be it a traditional defined-benefit plan, a defined-contribution plan (such as a 401(k)), a cash-value plan, or some other variation. Many companies don't want to be bothered with managing the plan themselves. Instead, they outsource the plan's management to one of several vendors who specialize in that area. Figure 2.1 illustrates how such a vendor might configure its data center to manage this workload for multiple client companies.

The data lives at the center of their operation. It includes the complete status of pension accounts for each client's employees, as well as detailed information about

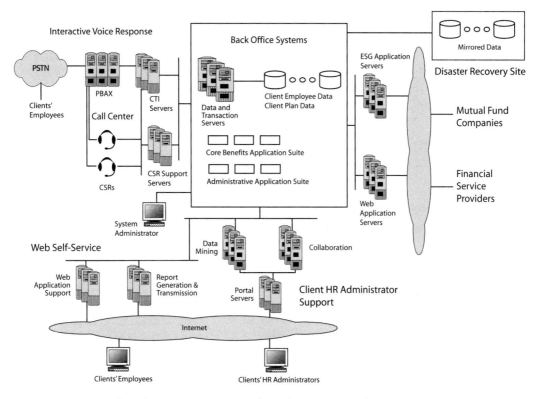

FIGURE 2.1   Pension plan management vendor's data center configuration.

each client's pension plan rules and parameters. Controlling this data is a set of mainframe servers, each running relational-database and transaction-monitor software. Within these servers runs the vendor's core benefits applications, which handle everything from processing employee and retiree inquiries and investment change requests, to processing applications for retirement, to completing death-benefit transactions. These servers also run a set of administrative applications that handle functions such as trade settlement and reconciliation, proxy voting, and governmental regulation compliance and reporting.

Direct Presentation Channels

There are three direct presentation channels available for employees to use to access their benefits packages. The first is Interactive Voice Response (IVR). For IVR, telephone calls from employees arrive from the Public Switched Telephone Network

(PSTN) into the vendor's Private Automatic Branch Exchange (PABX) switch. The switch interfaces with Computer Telephony Integration (CTI) servers running a set of communications applications that interact with callers through either touchtone or voice recognition technology, process the requested transaction, then relay responses to the caller through a text-to-speech application.

If the IVR system cannot satisfy a caller's request (or, if the caller indicates up front that they wish to speak to a person), then the CTI server can transfer the call to the next available Customer Service Representative (CSR) in the Call Center. When the CSR's phone rings, a screen on his desktop computer simultaneously displays detailed information about the caller and the stage reached in the conversation with the IVR system, so the CSR can pick up where the IVR left off. Additional servers provide the CSRs with direct access to client employee data.

The final direct presentation channel is Web Self-service. Here, employees can access their account directly from their Web browser, perform queries, initiate transactions, or request account summary reports to be generated and e-mailed to them.

Client Human Resource Administrator Support

While the channels described earlier serve clients' employees, each client company also has a set of human resource (HR) administrators who need to stay abreast of general trends regarding its employees' involvement in the pension plan. Is participation in the 401(k) plan running high? Are employees optimizing their investments? What's more popular, the Web Self-service channel or the Call Center?

To support these client HR administrators, the vendor has set up Web portal servers. These portals interact with servers running applications that extract data from the back office systems to create data marts from which the HR administrators can perform data mining. In addition, because the HR administrators are interested in exchanging thoughts with their colleagues about best practices, the vendor has also added servers running collaboration software off of their portal as well.

Pipelines to Other Providers

On the other end, the vendor maintains pipelines to financial service providers who can supply the vendor's clients with additional features such as customized financial advisor software that incorporates an employee's account data into its modeling and recommendations. To achieve this, the vendor houses a set of Web application servers running data exchange applications that extract employee data from the back-office systems and package it with XML for exchange with the other providers.

A major aspect of managing pension funds is providing appropriate investment vehicles (e.g., stocks, bonds). Our pension-plan vendor doesn't manage these investment vehicles itself, but rather interfaces with mutual fund companies through a set of servers running Electronic Standards Group (ESG)-compliant applications for trade processing.

Administration

Finally, the vendor's own system administrators access the back-office systems through terminal emulator sessions in order to monitor system status and initiate administrative batch jobs. Also, the vendor mirrors its critical data at a remote disaster-recovery site.

Even More Complexity

If this seems complicated, it is, and that's a grossly oversimplified view. The interactions between applications and the maze of incompatible protocols and standards haven't been mentioned, nor have the extensive security requirements involved in a Web-facing environment such as this. The truth is, each of these applications is so sophisticated that an entire chapter could be written about any one of them, yet they all must coexist and often interoperate in a single context.

Furthermore, all of the components of the vendor's production environment didn't pop up overnight; they were developed and added over time, and so are exploiting different technologies and server platforms from a variety of vendors, depending on what seemed best at the moment each new service was introduced.

What Is Really Mission-critical?

Notice how everything in this vendor's production environment revolves around its clients' data—querying it, updating it, mining it, augmenting it, and managing it. The data is centralized, but accessed through multiple channels. The employee account and plan data are clearly mission-critical, as are the back-office benefits and administrative applications that control and manipulate this data.

Moving out from this back-office core, but still tightly linked to the clients' data, are the IVR, Call Center, and Web Self-service applications. These are also mission-critical. If any of them fail, large numbers of employees will be unable to access the vendor's services. Similarly, the software responsible for data and transaction exchange with various mutual fund companies is mission-critical; if it goes down, so does the vendor's ability to execute trades and other key functions.

On the other hand, the portal-server applications for HR administrator support may not be considered by the vendor to be mission-critical. The same can be said of the systems linking to additional services supplied by other financial service providers. While they provide valuable and important functions, these elements are ancillary to what the vendor offers its clients, rather than core.

Industrial-strength Characteristics

This example environment embodies the characteristics of production systems described earlier. It's certainly large and heterogeneous. Self-service IVR and Web applications require 24 hours a day, 7 days a week availability. Contracts between the vendor and its clients would certainly specify response time and availability requirements, leading to SLAs for the vendor's CIO and support staff. And disaster recovery is integrated into the overall operation.

The environment is rife with what was described earlier as industrial-strength software. The back-office systems alone are running large benefits applications that manipulate huge amounts of critical data, and must interface with a variety of other applications ranging from IVR, Call Center support, and Web Self-service to the systems of mutual fund and other financial-service providers. These back-office systems would likely be stressed constantly by hundreds to thousands of employees from multiple client companies, requiring intricate serialization to keep all the parallel activities from interfering with each other. Robustness and the need to run at high levels of system stress for extended periods of time are a given. Of course, software supporting an environment this complex would need to evolve over time, requiring migration to new releases.

SUMMARY

The complexity of actual production environments is immense, as is the potential for a single software defect to shut one down. The software running in these environments is equally sophisticated and demanding. As a software tester, it is your job to prevent any critical defects from slipping through into this serpentine infrastructure. One measure of your success is what Kidder [Kidder81] described as the rule of pinball—if you win, you get to play again.

Testing such software is not a job for one person, or even a single team. Testing usually flows through several phases, each with its own set of goals. In Chapter 3, "The Development Process," we'll discuss the objectives of various test phases and where they fit in different software development models.

Part II

The Testing Ecosystem

Testers don't work in isolation. All software development organizations have their own ecosystem. The structure of that ecosystem, where testing fits into its food chain, and your ability to influence its stakeholders impacts your success. You need to navigate that maze with clarity and precision. The next two chapters will guide you through it.

In the pages ahead we will look at the series of testing phases that most software projects pass through. Each is well suited to extracting certain types of defects, and inefficient at catching others. Knowing which is which will help you aim your testing at the most suitable targets. Those testing phases are also applicable across a variety of development models, each with its own strengths and weaknesses. The choice of model that your organization follows may not be up for debate. But if you understand the universe of possibilities and how testing fits into each, you may be able to infuse useful aspects from other models into your own work.

We'll also examine the people who populate a software development ecosystem. You'll learn the difference between makers and breakers, and why many software developers don't make ideal testers. You'll also learn techniques for building your technical credibility within the organization, which is critical for testers who want their shouts for quality to be heard and their careers to advance. We'll even take a look at different organizational models, and which are best suited to strengthening the hand of the test team. Now let's get to it.

3 The Development Process

In This Chapter

- The challenging nature of software testing
- Test phases and processes
- Traditional software development models
- Iterative and agile software development models
- The pitfalls of skipping phases

There's a popular phrase among software professionals faced with tight budgets and impossible deadlines: "Cheap, fast, good: pick any two." Most testers instinctively focus on high quality, so if offered a vote they would likely be forced to choose between cost and speed.

Let's consider cost. One determining factor of a defect's price is where in the development cycle it is uncovered. The earlier it is found, the less it costs the project. A big piece of this expense is the number of people who get involved in the discovery and removal of the bug. If a developer finds it through his own private testing prior to delivering the code to others, he's the only one affected. If that same problem slips through to later in the development cycle, it might require a tester to uncover it, a debugger to diagnose it, the developer to provide a fix, a builder to integrate the repaired code into the development stream, and a tester again to validate the fix. And that doesn't even include the time spent by a project manager to track its status.

Johanna Rothman studies these costs and suggests formulas to help clarify the actual costs associated with late-cycle defect discoveries [Rothman02]. You can plug in your own estimate of a defect's price into these formulas and confirm that it is indeed more and more costly to fix problems as the project proceeds. In a perfect world, all bugs would be found and removed by developers before their code sees the light of day—or before those bugs are inserted into the code in the first place. However, that's not realistic, which is why the world needs professional testers.

Then there's speed. Your customers probably want new solutions yesterday, and if you're in the business of selling software, then your management team is probably in a hurry too. Various development models have been built to streamline the code delivery process. They take different approaches to attempt to reconcile speed and cost without sacrificing quality.

In this chapter, we'll examine different test phases, their associated costs and limitations, and the classes of bugs each is best suited to extract. Then we'll take a look at several development models, with an emphasis on how each incorporates testing.

TEST PROCESS DEFINITIONS

Different test phases target different types of software bugs, and no single phase is adept at catching them all. That's why we can't squash every bug during the earliest and cheapest phases of testing—because they aren't all visible yet. Finding bugs during a development cycle is like driving for the first time along a foggy road at night. You can only see ahead a few feet at a time, but the further you go, the more you discover—and if you drive too quickly, you might end up in a ditch.

Each test phase has its own associated limitations and costs. Software that aspires to be customer-ready must cross through several. Let's examine them.

White-box versus Black-box Testing

Terms such as white box, clear box, gray box, glass box, and black box are popular phrases for describing the technical approach taken for verifying software. *White-box* testing, also known as *clear-box*, is a technique where an understanding of the software internals is key to creating the test plan and approach. *Black-box* testing assumes little, if any, understanding of the internals. Instead, it relies on a comprehensive view of the software's inputs and external behaviors for formulating a plan of attack. *Gray-box* and *glass-box* testing combine the use of strict externally-driven tests of black-box and the details and internal processing examined in white-box testing. Regardless of the definitions, it's more important to keep sight of what you do and accomplish, rather than what category of test it falls under.

Unit Test (UT)

Unit test is the first real test phase that a piece of software undergoes. It's "man versus code" at its lowest level.

Scope

During unit test, the developer of an individual module or object tests all new and changed paths in his code. This includes verifying its inputs and outputs, branches, loops, subroutine inputs and function outputs, simple program-level recovery, and diagnostics and traces. That's the technical scope of unit test. A large software project will involve many such programs. So, multiple programmers will be working in parallel to write and unit test different modules that will likely be shipped together.

In addition to single module testing, groups of developers can choose to work together to integrate their unit-tested programs into logical components. This is optional, but in a complex project it can serve as a useful precursor to the next test phase. An integrated UT effort takes aim at uncovering simple module-to-module integration failures. It verifies that when parameters are passed between routines, the pieces communicate correctly and generate appropriate outputs. This allows the development team an overall view of the combination of parts and whether they will provide the promised function to the next test phase.

Targeted Defect Types

Unit testing targets the extraction of obvious coding errors. Those errors may be basic, but if missed during this phase they could become very disruptive to later testing activities. Typical defects found in UT include problems with loop termination, simple internal parameter passing, proper assignment statements, simple recovery routine logic, and errors in functions and subroutines.

Environment

Unit testing is done primarily on a single native system. In some cases, new hardware may not be available to drive the unit test scenarios, or it is in short supply. This often leads to the use of virtualized or emulated environments during unit test. Such environments also have some unique advantages in terms of debugging capabilities that interest unit testers, whether or not they have a shortage of hardware. These environments are discussed in detail in Chapter 16, "Testing with a Virtual Computer."

Limitations

A single major component of a complex software product usually consists of many individual modules or objects, all working together to deliver that component's functions. Before those pieces come together, different developers will work on them independently, and perhaps even on staggered schedules. The testing is also largely isolated to a single module at a time. That isolation enables UT's tight focus on new and changed code paths, but at the same time is a major limitation. It prevents the tester from seeing how the code will behave in a realistic environment. This weakness can be partially relieved through the integrated UT approach, but is nevertheless a reality for most development teams.

This isolation leads to a related limitation of UT. Much of the component may not be in place when the UT for any individual module is done. These holes in the component create the need for *scaffolding*. Like the patchwork of temporary platforms that serve as a supporting framework around a building under construction, scaffolding used during UT is a collection of bits of code that surround the component to prop it up during early testing. These bits of code, or *stub routines,* do little more than receive invocations from programs within the component in question and respond to them according to an expected protocol. In essence, they fool the other program into believing it is actually interfacing with its peer. One real weakness of UT is that developers must rely on such program-to-program scaffolding rather than being able to test their modules alongside their true counterparts within the component.

Costs and Efficiencies

In most organizations, UT is performed by the development team—usually by the coder on his individual code. Having the developers perform the unit test is the most efficient approach at this point in the development life cycle. There are exceptions, but generally the developer has the best understanding of which lines of code were added or changed and their expected behavior.

To remove a defect from software costs money. As we've discussed, the earlier the problem is caught in the development process, the cheaper it is to find and fix. Ideally, all problems would be found during requirements definition, design, and development, when their associated cost is minimal. But in terms of test phases, UT is the most cost-effective place to find them.

Function Verification Test (FVT)

After the development community completes its unit testing, the individual modules are integrated into a package that the next test team can begin to examine. Because such packages are usually oriented around major functions, we call this next phase *Function Verification Test,* or FVT. Some in the industry refer to this as the

Integration Test phase, because it's the first time all of the pieces of a function are integrated. However, that usage suggests product-wide integration, which obscures a simple reality: for large, complex software projects the pieces are usually integrated and tested first on a function-by-function basis, rather than across the entire product. That's why we'll use the more specific term FVT.

Scope

The function verification test team focuses on validating the features of an entire function or component such as a storage manager, work dispatcher, or input/output subsystem. The team looks at the function as a whole and validates its features and services. The testers go after its mainline functions, internal and external interfaces, operational limits, messages, crash codes, and module- and component-level recovery. FVT is focused on a white-box approach.

Targeted Defect Types

FVT searches for defects in the function or component at a higher level than during UT. These defects could be that the component does not enforce its operational limits, application programming interfaces (APIs) or system services do not provide the function advertised, program recovery routines do not retry in cases where they can, panels display incorrect values, diagnostic trace entries contain bad values, messages issued to the system console are wrong, and communication between programs or components fails. Certainly this is not an all-inclusive list, but it gives you an idea of the breadth of responsibility of the FVT team.

You might ask why the UT team members can't find all of these problems. For starters, one of their key limitations is that they look at each module in isolation, rather than at the whole function. The people performing the UT activities are also very close to the code and therefore can't be objective. Beyond that, a common practice is to bring in a new, objective team to pick apart the software. At this stage in the process, FVT testers begin to "question" the software in all regards. They ask, is it performing as it was designed to? More importantly, is it performing as our customers would expect?

Environment

The FVT can be performed on native hardware platforms or virtualized and simulated environments. For very large projects where native environments are either limited or very difficult to use in diagnosing problems, virtualized environments can really shine. In Chapter 16 we will review, in much greater detail, how these virtualized environments provide many benefits to software development teams.

FVT can exploit these virtual environments to allow each tester the capability to have his own virtual machine, without worrying too much about the cost of the real thing. This capability allows the team to wreak havoc on the software without impacting others. Cool concept!

Diagnosis of the kind of defects targeted by FVT can be challenging on native hardware platforms. Not all such platforms have appropriate tracing and break-pointing capabilities to allow for instruction stepping or storage alteration without creating a totally artificial test environment. Some virtualized environments are specifically designed with these capabilities in mind, making it easy for testers to create intricate scenarios and track down those tough problems.

Limitations

FVT's limitations lie in a few areas. First, by definition, its scope is limited to a single function or component of the overall software package, rather than on the package as a whole. This is by design. It enables the team to zoom in on lower-level functions that later test stages can't address, but it also can prevent the testers from seeing the full-product picture.

FVT is also largely a single-user test. It doesn't attempt to emulate hundreds or thousands of simultaneous users, and therefore doesn't find the kind of load-related problems that alternative testing does.

If the team chooses to reap the benefits of virtualized environments, it must also realize that such environments can, on rare occasions, mask certain types of timing-related problems. For example, such environments can alter the order in which hardware interrupts are surfaced to the software. The FVT team would then have to rely on later test phases to catch such problems.

Costs and Efficiencies

FVT can require lots of testers. There can be many functions in a single software product, and each one might need its own test subteam. The sheer number of people involved represents a major cost of this phase. In fact, there may not be enough people to cover everything, which would create a serious limitation for the FVT team.

Strong software test and automation tools can help. Finding a tool that improves your team's effectiveness and productivity can aid in reducing overall project cost. Such tools might be costly to build or learn in the beginning, but in the long run they can really pay off.

System Verification Test (SVT)

Once the FVT team has completed its efforts, *System Verification Test* takes all of the software components and tests them as a single unit for the first time. What was formerly a collection of seemingly unrelated code now is viewed as an entire product. The SVT team verifies that all of the product's elements will work in concert to solve customers' business problems.

Scope

SVT tests the product as a whole, focusing on the software's function, but at a higher level than UT or FVT. It's the first time testing moves beyond single-user mode and into the more realistic realm of multiple, simultaneous users. Heavy load and stress is introduced, with workloads and test drivers simulating thousands of clients and requesters. SVT pushes the software to its limits and ensures that the entire solution hangs together while exercising both old and new functions.

SVT views the software from the perspective of a customer seeing the whole product for the first time. For example, the team validates that businesses will be able to migrate from one version of a product to another smoothly and without disruption. It also determines if multiple versions of the software can coexist and operate across several loosely coupled or clustered systems, if appropriate. And, unfortunately, there are times when a customer's software deployment does not go as planned. The SVT team ensures that customers can fall back to the prior version of the software. The testers also verify that the software can withstand harsh environmental conditions such as memory shortages and I/O saturation—and if a failure does strike, that the software handles it gracefully.

Targeted Defect Types

The SVT effort pursues some of the most complex defects in the software, such as timing and serialization problems that high-system stress is so adept at exposing. Heavy workloads also push open the processing windows where data integrity might be compromised. Data aging or fragmentation problems are sought over the course of extended test runs. Security defects are also pursued. Complex recovery defects are other prime targets—failing systems, subsystems, and components of any software package proving they can restart and continue processing clients' requests.

Environment

On some computing platforms, SVT is where the software meets the real, native hardware for the first time. UT and FVT may have been performed under emulation or virtualization. In that case, SVT will help identify defects such as architectural disconnects that may have occurred. But even if the earlier tests were done on native hardware, the systems used during SVT are generally significantly bigger and faster, as they must accommodate the requirements of load and stress workloads.

In addition to processors, the SVT team will attach lots of peripherals. These might include large numbers of storage devices, networking routers, printers, scanners, and digital recording equipment.

SVT teams can sometimes exploit virtualized environments similar to those used in FVT and UT when enough real hardware is not within the budget, or the goals of the test can be achieved without it. However, the virtualized environment in which SVT is performed needs to be robust enough to achieve its goals and objectives.

Limitations

By design, SVT's aim is limited to a single product. If that product will later partner with others to deliver a complete solution to customers, SVT's focus usually isn't broad enough to catch cross-product defects. At the other end of the scale, because of SVT's full-product view, it is limited in its ability to catch problems with messages, commands, and other low-level interfaces that are the purview of FVT.

Because SVT is normally performed on native hardware, the tools available to diagnose problems may be limited, as tools used on virtualized environments are not available. This can also be considered a strength, however, since the SVT team must then rely on the same debugging tools that their customers do, such as log or trace files and memory dumps. As a result, they may discover defects or weaknesses in the tools themselves.

In cases where SVT is performed in virtualized or simulated environments, the amount of time the software package spends on real hardware before customer use is limited. This is a risk that the project leaders must consider before deploying the software to customer sites.

Costs and Efficiencies

Heavy costs arise when building SVT hardware configurations that support heavy load and stress workloads and mirror some of the most typical customers. Asset management is more important than ever and careful decisions must be made to achieve SVT goals while meeting budget challenges.

Some platforms support *partitioning* (see Chapter 16 for details), which can help alleviate the hardware budget crunch by splitting a single server into multiple, independent sub-servers, each capable of running its own operating system. Another approach the team can use when faced with limited hardware is to spread the testing across multiple shifts per day and share a common pool of servers. Don't cringe—you might find you enjoy lying in the sun during the day and doing your testing at night!

Performance Verification Test (PVT)

Though not the focus of this book, *Performance Verification Test* must be included in a comprehensive list of test phases. The UT, FVT, and SVT test teams can verify that function works and can handle the myriad of clients that use it, but their focus is generally not on how fast something runs. That's the realm of PVT.

Scope

The PVT team's objective is to identify performance strengths and weaknesses. The team designs measurements that target performance-sensitive areas identified during the software's design stage or by customers executing within existing environments. Measurements are performed, results are documented, and a detailed analysis is conducted. Conclusions drawn from the analysis may suggest the need for further measurements, and the cycle repeats.

PVT may also focus on how the software compares to industry benchmarks. This work also tends to iterate between analysis and measurement cycles, until all teams are satisfied.

Targeted Defect Types

The PVT team searches for bottlenecks that limit the software's response time and throughput. These problems usually lie in excessive code path length of key functions. They may also be related to how the software interacts with a specific hardware platform. This is particularly true with some industry benchmarks. For example, the software may run well on a processor with a broad and shared memory cache, and poorly on one where the cache is deep but narrow, or vice versa.

Environment

Real performance studies are measured on native hardware. Any studies performed on virtualized platforms are primarily targeted at studying distinct path lengths.

Limitations

One issue associated with true performance analysis and measurement work is that the software and hardware need to be stable before formal performance studies can be completed. If the slightest error pops up while a measurement is being taken, it can force extra processing and thereby invalidate the results. So a close relationship between the SVT and PVT teams is critical to the success of the performance test. The stress driven by SVT creates the foundation for a successful PVT.

Costs and Efficiencies

A good PVT requires even more hardware than SVT. You want to ensure that all encountered bottlenecks are due to the software, rather than memory shortages, I/O bandwidth limits, or too few CPUs. But that's not all. Performance issues are, in many cases, the most costly defects to resolve. Yes, some performance issues can be addressed quickly and successfully with minimal impact. More significant performance problems often require much more complicated solutions. The development and test activities and resources needed to provide such a solution can be costly and throw a real monkey wrench into what you thought was a project that was winding down.

But one efficiency offered by PVT is the use of simulated or virtualized environments to help review basic path length. Combined with skills in real-time monitoring and workload tweaking, performance measurement specialists can uncover major path-length problems early, giving development ample time to provide fixes.

Testing for Defects versus Performance: The Load/Stress Equation

The testing literature sometimes treats load/stress testing and performance testing as synonymous activities. Furthermore, some software tool vendors of load/stress generation tools aggravate this perception by focusing on performance. But load and stress testing techniques are effective for much more than just performance testing. They are also a key defect-removal tool in test phases such as SVT and Integration test. Let's briefly examine the contrast between using load and stress for performance analysis versus defect removal.

Performance Analysis through Load/Stress

As noted earlier, performance analysis seeks to identify the degradation in software that is caused by functional bottlenecks (defects in their own right) and to measure the speed at which the software can execute. The team uses a scientific approach. This includes carefully controlled conditions and environments, repeatable measurements, and detailed task lists. The stability of the software is critical to the team's success. The performance test team's objective is not to uncover unsightly defects. In fact, those testers would rather not see any functional defects, because they just get in the way of the primary goal: gathering precise measurements. Performance testers might not even touch the keyboard during a measurement for fear any extra processing it causes will invalidate the results.

Removing Bottlenecks

Functional bottlenecks are those unintended behaviors in the software that act as choke points for throughput. For example, all processing might get backed up behind a slow search algorithm. Note that functional bottlenecks are different from physical ones, such as memory or disk exhaustion. Heavy workloads help bring these functional bottlenecks to light. This is the first place where load and stress factors into the performance measurement and analysis portion of the process. The stress workload must be smooth and repeatable since, as with any scientific experiment, it's through repeatability that the performance team gains confidence in the results.

Establishing Performance Rates

Once the bottlenecks are removed, the performance test team sets out to determine the maximum value to place on the software's speedometer. You'll find many industry benchmarks for performance that help measure some widely available classes of computing such as Web serving or transaction processing. A variety of benchmarks are maintained by consortiums such as TPC (Transaction Processing Performance Council) [TPC04] and SPEC (Standard Performance Evaluation Corporation) [SPEC04]. In addition, computer manufacturers often establish their own performance measurement workloads to drive their individualized comparisons. These workloads and benchmarks are used to determine the maximum throughput for a specific hardware and software combination. As stated before, repeatability is important, but so are consistent environments. You have to make sure that you are comparing apples to apples and not apples to kumquats.

Testing for Defects through Load/Stress

System verification test, on the other hand, is in the business of defect removal. It targets defects related to such things as complex serialization and data aging that escaped function verification test. To target these areas, SVT teams apply load/stress to the software through a variety of workloads intended to mirror customer-processing patterns. In this respect, they are similar to performance test teams.

However, there is a critical difference between the PVT and SVT objectives for a load/stress test. As previously noted, the performance team aims for clean, smooth, controlled test runs that allow it to gather precise, repeatable measurements. Performance teams abhor a system that is taking memory dumps or creating other chaos, because the extra processing involved invalidates their measurements. The SVT team, on the other hand, uses load/stress testing as a tool for *creating* chaos. They seek to throw as much conflicting work as possible against the software to tie it into knots and force it to cope. They hate a clean, smoothly running system because it's probably not surfacing bugs. The performance test team demands stable software; the SVT team tries to prove the same software is not stable. Even though the tools they use may be similar, their objectives are diametrically opposed.

Integration Test

So far, the test teams have done a lot of work to stabilize the software. The new code has handled heavy workloads from thousands of users and performs like a streak of lightning. But if a customer can't integrate it with their other software solutions, run it all day, all night, and all year, then the job isn't done. That's when its time for integration test.

Scope

While some software products lead isolated lives, most must work with others to provide a complete solution to customer problems, as we saw in Chapter 2, "Industrial-Strenght Software, It's Not a Science Project." Integration test looks at that entire solution. It moves beyond the single-product domain of SVT and *integrates* the new software into a simulated customer environment. Integration test, also known as Acceptance Test, takes the big picture approach where the new software is merely one of many elements in the environment—just as if it had been thrown into live production.

How necessary this phase is depends on the software and the breadth of its expected interactions, dependencies, and exploiters. It's not a test that every product undergoes, and in practice is rarely used for new, immature products. But experience has shown that the more mature a test organization becomes, the more likely it is to have learned (perhaps the hard way) the value of performing an integration test.

This test is often done in parallel with beta test (early customer testing). It sometimes even continues after general availability of the product. The goal there is to stay one step ahead of your customers in exercising extremely complex environments, improving usability, and exploring other "soft" aspects of the support.

Targeted Defect Types

Integration test targets problems related to how different software products interact. It assesses how successful the software will be when dropped into a complex environment with tremendous interoperability needs. The test also focuses on nontraditional defects, such as systems management issues and operational weaknesses.

The integration test team will also attempt to use the innovative functions provided by the new software. This may require the team to modify existing applications or create new workloads. Integration test is similar to SVT in that it drives out defects of timing, serialization, recovery, and integrity. But the bugs themselves are different. They surface because the software is in a new context—namely, as one element of a bigger solution.

As in SVT, migration and coexistence bugs are hunted, but with a twist. Under the SVT model, testers ensure the new software doesn't create major incompatibilities with prior levels. The integration test team takes a different tack. It checks to see if it's possible to migrate to a new version of the software without disrupting the flow of work in the environment as a whole. It's another excellent way to exercise the software from the customer's point of view.

Environment

Configurations for your integration test efforts are as varied as your customers. They are comprised of banks of servers, networks, and storage devices, all with the goal of driving scenarios and workload in a way similar to that of businesses and organizations.

To illustrate, IBM's mainframe platform supports a nonstop testing environment that provides the first real customer-like configuration into which the newest products are introduced. The testing here operates with many objectives, including achieving service level agreements, maintaining availability targets, migrating to new levels of software in a controlled fashion, and providing a complex configuration on which to execute heavy stress and inject failures against the platform. The software is then exercised with resource managers, networking products, and applications as part of an end-to-end solution to a business problem [Loveland02].

Limitations

Because integration test takes such a broad view, its success relies on earlier test phases extracting lower-level bugs and significant stability problems. If the integration test team spends all of its time fighting mainline functional problems, it will never get to the interoperability defects the team was put in place to find.

Also, while the integration test team attempts to achieve a customer-like environment, it can't possibly be all-inclusive. It must, however, aim to be representative. The team's effectiveness will be limited by the quantity and quality of customer information at its disposal. Talking directly with customers to better understand how their configurations are built and how they choose to use software packages to solve their business problems can help the integration test team build an environment that is an amalgamation of many customers. See Chapter 5, "Where to Start? Snooping for Information," for techniques on how to better understand your customers.

Costs and Efficiencies

You can see that costs could escalate quickly when building this type of environment. Hardware, software, and skilled personnel all are factors.

Since the integration test effort strives to be as much like a customer as possible, the team might choose to increase its efficiency by modeling its staffing as the customers do. Team members can take on roles such as base operations, database administration, networking, application development and deployment, and capacity planning. As a result, team members will encounter the tasks of integrating a new product and the issues that come along with it.

This effort can also drive efficiencies into real customer environments. Some teams choose to share the experiences they gain while integrating these new products. They often go so far as to publish their practical insights in technical papers or hints-and-tips Web sites. By providing a guide to deploy the new product, you can truly delight your customers.

Service Test

Even after you perform a wide variety of tests against the software, inevitably and unfortunately, defects will escape and be discovered by customers. Fixes to software defects need the same attention as a new function. Once the defect is identified, a streamlined process similar to that of the product's original development should be used to design, develop, and test the fix. The same rigor is required because a customer's expectations don't relax. In fact, the customer expects more after something severe has occurred that has disrupted his business.

Scope

While new releases of software are being developed, the primary test activity that keeps watch over existing software is service test. Its fundamental objective is to test software fixes, both individually and bundled together. It should look not only at the fixes themselves, but also ensure those fixes don't have side effects that interfere with other areas of the software. It is required at the UT, FVT, and SVT levels. Some organizations may decide to omit one or more of the primary phases we have discussed here, but such a decision should only be made after careful consideration.

A typical flow goes like this: individual fixes are validated by a UT and/or FVT team. Then they are grouped into a fix pack or bundle of service. The bundle is fed into a comprehensive service test environment, which may or may not be the same physical environment as the product's SVT. Here the SVT team (or a separate service test team) will run all the test scenarios and workloads they can to ensure that no single fix or combination of fixes causes the software to regress. If a particular fix or fix pack requires targeted, system-level testing under heavy load and stress conditions, the development, FVT, and SVT teams will design a special test as the primary plan of attack. Service test is the customer's day-to-day ally in maintaining system stability.

Targeted Defect Types

Service testing mainly targets two kinds of defects. First and foremost, it makes sure a fix correctly resolves the original problem reported by the customer. Secondly, and just as importantly, it ensures that the fix doesn't break something else. A mishap in either area is sure to irk users.

Environment

The environment for service test can vary. It can exist on simulated or virtualized platforms, especially for UT and FVT, so they can more easily ensure a bug has been fixed. However, more comprehensive platform environments are needed to validate maintenance at the SVT or integration test level. As a result, you'll sometimes find service test teams operating with large, complex configurations that mimic those of their largest customers.

Limitations

The amount of testing that the service test team can perform is often limited by time constraints. This comes down to speed versus thoroughness. There's the speed required because your company wants to get a new software product out in the marketplace. There's an entirely different degree of speed needed when a customer's business is stopped dead and they demand a fix. That intense need for speed in turning around fixes often forces compromises in test coverage, particularly if the volume of fixes is high.

Costs and Efficiencies

Bundling fixes into fix packs can be considered efficiency. It limits fix grouping to one combination, so only that specific combination needs to be tested.

Of course it costs money to rigorously test fixes rather than crossing your fingers and blindly sending them out into the world. But service testing protects your customer base, since happy customers tend to be loyal ones.

Beta Test

At some point, usually part way through SVT or integration test, project and test management start to consider passing their software jewel along to real customers. This is referred to as a *beta* test. It's also known as a first customer ship or an early support program. Whatever you call it, it's essentially another test phase from which you can benefit.

Scope

All of the testing discussed so far has had its unique contribution to validating the software. So what is gained by giving a select set of customers the code early?

No matter how realistic you try to make your test environment, ultimately, it is still artificial. Beta customers deploy the software into *real* environments, with all of the associated variability and complexity. Because each customer is different, beta testing broadens the range of environments and experiences to which the software is subjected, leading it down new paths and revealing fresh bugs.

Your beta customers will also become essential, outside critics. Each customer's unique perspective on the software's impact to its business during migration, deployment, and use serves as valuable input to the development team in assessing its readiness for general availability.

Targeted Defect Types

This one's pretty simple. Anything and everything that will affect a customer's business are the target defects for a beta, whether it is installation, migration, regression, or something altogether different. Multiuser environments with extreme software load will be another focus area. Early support-program participants don't want to be bit by a new timing window or failed recovery situation. Beta test will also quickly expose defects related to whether the new software will work with other products your customers use and depend upon.

Environment

Every beta environment will be unique—that's the beauty of this test phase. Each customer will generate different, new defects based on their configuration.

Limitations

An obvious limitation of the beta is that it can't cover every possible environment. An additional limitation may be the amount of time that you allow your beta customers to run with the code before you determine it is ready to ship to everyone. Some early support programs depend on customers installing and running the software in a production environment in addition to their test environments. If the time allotted for beta is too short, it can limit this possibility.

Costs and Efficiencies

An efficiency you can introduce to your beta program is analogous to eating your own cooking. Before going to your outside customers, first provide it to internal accounts within your own primary business unit. These accounts should be introduced to the product as early in the development process as possible. Taking the software for an early spin within your own organization should help smooth the deployment experience of external customers. There is also efficiency from the customer perspective. By participating in early support programs, customers can get a jump on their competition by gaining early experience with the new software. This can be a huge advantage for their business.

Of course, there are also costs generated by beta test. Your goal is that your customers will deploy the product somewhere, experiment with it, run their key applications using it, and ultimately feel comfortable enough to place it into production. All of these activities have an associated cost for the customer. They compete with other, unrelated business goals and initiatives that the customer must also address. How much emphasis is put on the new software as opposed to other pressing business problems will be different for every beta account.

Test Phases and Your Needs

The test phases we've reviewed here have been proven to be effective in the development of many large software products. In different forms and flavors, these test phases can be applied to a variety of development models. They can be your and your customers' ally in the quest for robust, reliable software. Let's examine these development models and discuss their pluses and minuses.

TRADITIONAL SOFTWARE DEVELOPMENT MODELS

If you look across the industry, it seems there is always a new type of software development model arising. Whether it's a sophisticated software product implemented by multibillion dollar corporations or a summer project created by tenth-graders, some type of model will be used. Let's explore the landscape for models used today.

Waterfall Model

One of the classic software development models is the waterfall. It is a linear and sequential approach that depends on the prior phase completing before the next begins. The waterfall software development model offers a very rigorous and strict approach for creating software. Key to the effectiveness of the waterfall model is clear, concise documentation created from one phase to the next. Figure 3.1 gives a basic representation of this model.

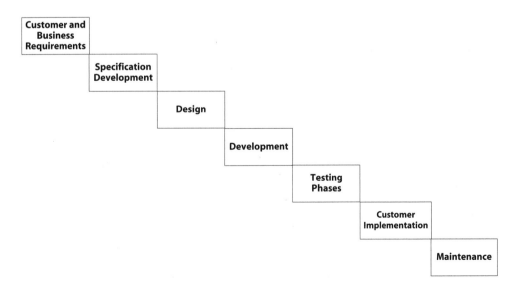

FIGURE 3.1   Fundamental waterfall software development model.

Each phase contributes key deliverables to the next. Checkpoint reviews are conducted throughout to assess progress against entry and exit criteria and determine readiness for the next phase.

If we expand the "testing phases" block of the waterfall model from Figure 3.1, you can see that it looks like a small echo of the waterfall (see Figure 3.2). Unit test, function verification test, system and performance verification test, and integration test flow in a similar fashion to the overall model. Service (or maintenance) test is appropriately tied to the Maintenance block of the larger model.

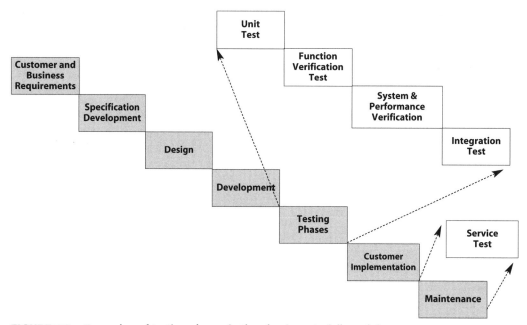

FIGURE 3.2   Expansion of testing phases in the classic waterfall model.

The waterfall model requires that each phase is entirely completed before the next test phase begins. Its strength lies in its thoroughness and rigor, helping to produce extremely robust code. The most significant weakness of this model, however, is its slowness to market because of the dependency between test phases. Since each of the phases of the model likely will not run as expected up front, it is reasonable to expect that problems will arise in finishing a phase and allowing the test to move forward. This is one of the issues that the waterfall model users encounter when implementing it. In fact, it's what makes the task of implementing a pure, classic waterfall model very difficult. What can we do to address this?

Waterwheel Model

Time-to-market pressures demand a different approach to developing software. Within the development stage of the classic waterfall model, the entire pool of code is delivered before the test phases begin. This is usually overkill. It delays the overall development cycle and squelches the opportunity for quick market penetration. Hence, the need for what we dub the *waterwheel model*. This model addresses this weakness of the waterfall model while retaining its strengths. It keeps the upfront activities of gathering requirements, developing a specification, and designing the product. However, the development and testing phases are staged in the waterwheel model. By shipping code in logical groupings, testing can proceed with one chunk of code while the next chunk is being created by development. Another benefit of the model is that it fosters continuous feedback between the development and test teams, enabling ongoing adjustments to the software's design.

Staged Deliveries to FVT

The FVT team can receive the interim code deliveries from development and begin to take the code for a test drive. The earliest code drops will likely include the initial underpinnings of the support creating the necessary control structures and functions. This gives the FVT team the ability to test initialization processing and other basic support. At the same time, the development team is developing, inspecting, and unit testing the next logical chunk of code to be delivered.

The waterwheel approach makes use of structured, continuous code integration. It offers a step-by-step method for verifying first, the infrastructure of the software, followed by more complex support, and finally the bells and whistles. It's like building a house. First you make sure that the foundation is sound, and then you proceed with framing the living space. When building software, you first make sure that the footing of the support is solid. After you are sure that the software can "take the weight," you begin adding additional items that flesh out the ultimate deliverable.

In this model, the high-level structure of the classic waterfall stays fairly intact, but development and FVT overlap one another and operate in an iterative fashion. As Figure 3.3 outlines, the development team provides strategic code drops to the function verification phase. Think of these code drops as water streaming into a waterwheel, which carries them down into a pool of code undergoing test.

As problems are uncovered by the FVT team, both defects and design change requests are sent to development. Many of these problems will be solved and shipped with new code in the next drop to FVT. This is akin to the waterwheel scooping bugs out of the pool of testable code and carrying them back up to the development team for cleansing. As those bugs are addressed, their fixes flow gently into the pool of water below into which the waterwheel trickles the code. Some of the problems will be more complex and require more time to resolve, and so will

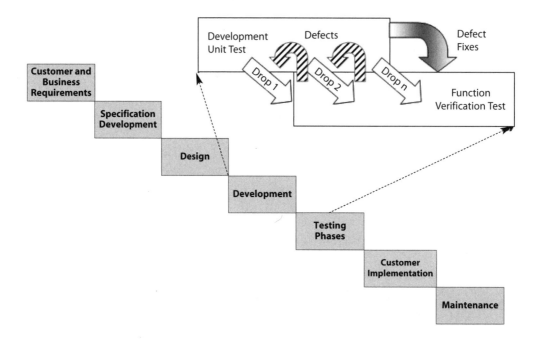

FIGURE 3.3   Waterwheel software development stages.

require more "filtration" up in the development stream before they are ready for the waterwheel to deliver them back into the testing pool. After the final delivery of code has been made to FVT, development will continue to deal with defects arriving from FVT and all the other test teams that will "stir up" the code throughout the product cycle. The waterwheel will spin until all of the defects have been resolved and the pool of code is clean and clear. Figure 3.4 provides a visual representation of the waterwheel model.

Staged Deliveries to SVT

Up to this point, we have discussed the staged deliveries of testable function into FVT. We can expand that concept to the SVT phase. Think of this as members of the SVT team gradually wading into the pool of testable code just as some of the FVT team members are climbing out and toweling off. All the while, the development team continues toiling up top, filtering out bugs carried up by the waterwheel and then delivering the cleansed code back down to the frolicking testers in the pool below.

Staging of the SVT phase will add to the overall project's risk. The SVT team's primary objective is to drive all components and functions together as a single

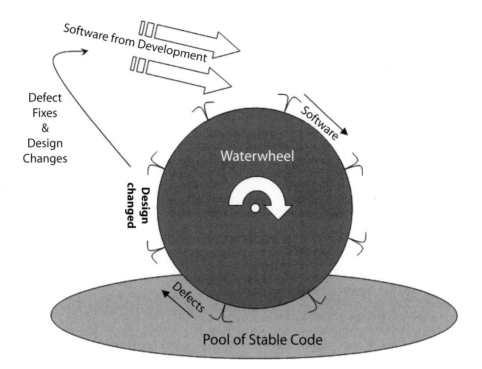

FIGURE 3.4 Waterwheel software development model.

product—and that's hard to accomplish with only pieces of function. Also, with both the FVT and SVT teams playing in the same pool, they're likely to bump into each other frequently—in other words, they will waste time and effort tripping over some of the same bugs. However, in excessively large and complex projects, a staged SVT is usually needed to meet the time-to-market goal.

The initial drop of code into SVT would likely be run through comprehensive regression testing by a few members of SVT entering the pool. Or, this early testing might focus on system or application initialization, exercising parameters and settings. Additional deliverables to SVT would follow this initial one. If the software has several major functions with little or no operational intersection, they can be delivered at different times. Not optimal, but it's been done before and in some cases it can work pretty well. Consider this to be the rest of the SVT team diving into the water. Eventually, the last stragglers from the FVT team will tire of the water and climb out, leaving only SVT in the code pool.

Parallel development streams can also be maintained to avoid disruption to the test environment in the event that a major function is delivered to SVT late. In this case, this late-arriving function can be kept in a separate code stream until it has achieved stability, at which point the two streams can be merged and SVT performed on this final package. This is akin to two different streams of water feeding into two different waterwheels, each with its own set of testers playing in separate pools down below, with a dike between them. When the SVT leader gives the nod, the build team pokes a hole in the dike and the two pools can finally intermingle.

The classic waterfall software development model is a well-known approach. Morphed into the waterwheel method of staging testable entities, it gives the development and test teams more flexibility and can significantly reduce time to market. The waterwheel model is a proven method that has delivered strong results on many industrial-strength projects.

Common Elements

Both the waterfall and waterwheel models require careful project management focus and a strong build process. Let's briefly examine each.

Checkpoints, Criteria, and Overlap

Moving from one development phase to the next requires checkpoint reviews. These reviews will assess whether criteria established during the planning phase have been satisfied, and whether the next phase is set to begin. We will look at entry and exit criteria in more detail later in the book, but understand now that they are critical to ensuring that the upcoming test phase has a reasonable chance of success.

The entry and exit criteria will help control the total amount of phase overlap in these development models. This overlap concept is not limited to development and test phases; it also applies to activities such as requirements definition and design. Can development begin low-level design activities while the design team is still finalizing the overall recoverability plans for the software? Sure, it's possible. But clear, concise criteria will allow development to begin its basic program design and coding activities without having to backtrack and redo work later.

Build and Installation

No software development model will ever be successful without an efficient build and installation process. The technical professionals performing this are critical to the project's success. Without the build and install team, there would be nothing to test.

The effort to consolidate all the different code being developed into drops is not a trivial one. Software is developed by a large number of different teams and the pieces might not all be completed at the same time. However, the FVT team needs cohesive deliveries. The install team must build a plan that details when the development team will integrate its code drops and considers the technical dependencies between the various components and functions. Ultimately, development and test need to agree on a schedule that both can live with.

When the development team delivers all of its planned code, the test teams still need a mechanism to receive fixes to defects. Because of this the overall build plan must include these deliverables in the schedule. Fixes to problems that aren't too severe will generally be included in these drops. For severe bugs, some software development processes also give the teams a way to provide fixes quickly, without waiting for the next planned code deliverable.

The product build schedule is a key driver behind the software development process in the models we have discussed thus far. As the schedule nears completion, the install team will take all of the final deliverables and build an official software product. A final regression test will be performed, and the package will be ready to deliver to customers.

ITERATIVE SOFTWARE DEVELOPMENT MODELS

Industry's need to move in many different directions and meet time-to-market challenges forces the software community to make intelligent shortcuts to meet customer needs. Iterative software development models help that effort. Let's contrast these models with the waterwheel model and examine the role of testing in each.

Agile Processes

Agile software development processes drive for working code with a focus on rapid production [Turk02]. Their base selling point is to address the primary issue many professionals have with the traditional waterfall model—time to market. The objective of agile development processes is to deliver software early and often, making it an iterative development model. Some Agile "test-driven development" techniques consider development as the actual customer of testing. Unit tests are devised and created before the code that will actually implement the desired function is completed. The intent is to cause the program to fail and then fix it.

Waterfall and waterwheel software models depend on crisp technical requirements defined at the beginning of the project and the expectation that new, incoming requirements will be few and far between. That's not necessarily reality. The strength of Agile development processes is their ability to handle changing requirements throughout all development and test phases. Finding a development process that addresses the problem of constant and changing requirements is a treasure for any software team. So can this model work for all projects?

According to Turk and his associates, the Agile model works very well for small teams in close proximity. This belief is supported by Williams and Cockburn, citing

Agile researchers who found that Agile is best suited for collocated teams of 50 people or fewer [Williams03]. This is a significant limitation of Agile models, since many software development teams are larger than this.

The Agile process is also dependent on close collaboration between developers and eventual users of the technology. In fact, it is suggested they physically reside near one another. However, it's not unusual for large development and test teams to span locations, and often they cannot possibly reside within the same location as their users. In such situations, change control is a critical means for ensuring that everyone stays in sync and all the pieces of code mesh smoothly. However, change control appears to be less of a focus in the Agile models.

Since the Agile model is all about time to market, code is delivered with incredible speed. Coders are coding as fast and as efficiently as they can, which is a strength of Agile models. However, there is also a hidden weakness. When coding furiously, there will be times when you don't have time to stop and look around at the solutions your colleagues have come up with. It's likely they have written something that can be reused to help fix your problem. Don't let the speed of coding get in your way of reuse [Turk02]. In large projects where the waterfall or waterwheel model is used, you have more time to plan for reuse. That way, the software routine only has to be coded and tested once and then can be used many times. It also reduces the possibility of the same function being implemented multiple times, which could result in unusual symptoms from the same problem. So when following an Agile development model, be careful not to ignore opportunities for reuse. Now we'll take a look at one of the most popular Agile models.

eXtreme Programming (XP)

Baumeister and Wirsing define Kent Beck's eXtreme Programming (XP) model as a quick and nimble software development process that uses methods to handle requirement changes while keeping a focus on overall quality [Baumeister02]. The fundamental premise of the XP model is that, because traditional development models like the waterfall are slow to market, greater flexibility is needed.

XP, as is the case with other Agile processes, is designed to react to quickly changing requirements through an iterative process. Developers start by working with the users to generate tests and then develop the code that allow the tests to succeed. Once they are working the code is integrated into the product [Reis00]. The process is based on an important characteristic of the XP model: feedback. Without continuous feedback from the customers of the software, there would be no way to steer the ship. And while the proponents of XP tout the importance of this feedback, it's important to note that traditional software models have that same implicit feedback mechanism. The difference is that in the traditional models, feedback is used to correct errors or weaknesses in the design. In XP, it's the tool used to actually *create* the design. Constant communication and cooperation between development and test across all phases fosters the feedback that is crucial to the success of the XP model.

XP also makes extensive use of the test-driven development feature of Agile software development practices. Developers code or build their test cases for unit test before they begin coding the actual software that will be tested. This is intended to prepare the developer to cover all issues in the code up front. This approach certainly has merit, in that the developer will be constantly considering the tests his code will have to pass. The tests are accumulated and then each drop of code (from any programmer) must pass all of these tests. Progress in test-driven development must be carefully monitored. But who identifies the tests that the developer doesn't consider? The XP model seems to address this question through the customer feedback mechanism.

Traditional software models rely on there being completely different people to test and assess the quality of the code in FVT, SVT, and other phases objectively. XP and other Agile models instead depend on the developers of other pieces of the overall software function to become familiar with their colleague's code so that they can point out issues and concerns. This can only be achieved through cooperative code ownership. Certainly, this approach will provide some amount of objectivity in the product cycle. But, does it offer the same amount as an independent FVT team? As a software project is being planned, its leaders need to consider these issues when examining the requirements.

Another difference between XP and waterfall models is the level of reliance on documentation. The traditional models must maintain requirements and design documentation for use in later phases, particularly testing phases. XP doesn't attempt to provide that level of documentation, because the focus is on providing production-ready software as quickly as possible. Unfortunately, the lack of documentation maintained during an XP development process has a potential downstream disadvantage after it has been completed and people have moved on to other work. If there is a problem and someone needs to revisit the original project, the speed at which new or "once familiar" programmers can get back on board is slowed. By maintaining design and implementation documentation, traditional models have an advantage in this kind of situation. In fact, testers can pick up this documentation and use it to help them devise new test scenarios. Part of that effort may include updating existing tools and test cases in order to be able to test the new function. Under the XP model, this would be difficult at best.

XP's continuous integration practice helps address one of the challenges of the classic waterfall model. In fact, the practice is comparable to that used in the waterwheel. In both models, the iterative code and defect fix updates provide a way to address problems quickly so that testing progress is not delayed.

Agile processes such as eXtreme Programming are best suited to straightforward software development projects. It is unclear whether these models address all of the complexities of a large, complicated project where documentation, strict quality control, and objectivity are critical. By the same token, there are several Agile practices from which traditional waterfall models can benefit.

Spiral Model

The spiral development model, another type of iterative model, also attempts to address the shortcomings of the classic waterfall model. Even though this is not technically an Agile model, software engineering guru Barry Boehm's proposed development model has given the industry a different perspective on software development practices. The distinguishing characteristic of this model is the introduction and use of risk assessment and analysis throughout the development process. Figure 3.5 shows Boehm's Spiral Development Model.

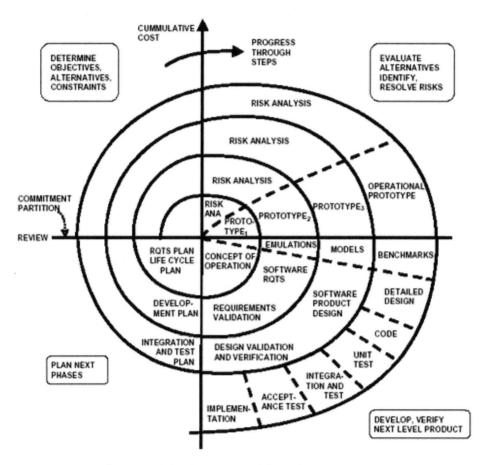

FIGURE 3.5 Boehm's spiral development model [Boehm88].

Boehm's research asserts that the classic waterfall model does not lend itself to some classes of end-user application software solutions. Boehm claims that up-front requirements are extremely difficult to finalize for this type of software because the design is subjective in nature and users are not able to foresee the final product easily.

Four Process Quadrants

The spiral model's four primary processes, represented by quadrants in Figure 3.5, are objective definition, risk analysis, product development and engineering, and next phase planning. These four activities drive the model and are fundamental to its effectiveness. With each revolution of the model, the four processes are performed. Through prototyping, requirements definition, design, and implementation, each revolution independently examines the objectives, risks, implementation, and planning of the phase that follows.

Objectives

Objectives definition and development are an essential part of any software development phase. The spiral concept of regularly reviewing the objectives as the activity type changes provides a continuous focus on ensuring that the project is moving in the desired direction.

All of the activities in the spiral model and all of the phases of the waterfall model look at changing objectives as time moves on. No matter which model you choose, it's important to constantly ask yourself whether you are still in line with the project's objectives.

Risks

Boehm's approach is risk-driven rather than document- or code-driven processes [Boehm88]. This risk-driven analysis is intended to provide a decision point for determining whether the software should proceed to the next phase of work, stay in this phase and continue efforts, or completely terminate the project. The waterfall model lacks this kind of risk review and management, as the only place it can logically occur is between major phases. However, as discussed earlier, the waterwheel model does provide natural risk-assessment checkpoints—through iterative functional code and fix deliverables.

The spiral model supports prototype and risk assessment activities at each phase of the process to address problems such as funding, requirement updates, or hardware issues. The project team will evaluate the risks at each revolution of the spiral so that any improvements can be made to enhance the software or the project itself. The issues identified in the analysis can inspire the team to develop different ways to attack the problems. For example, maybe a prototype approach for development was being used but it was not providing the quality needed to make progress. To help address the quality problem, the team might seriously consider other, scaled-down development models that could be used against this piece of the software.

In addition, the risks identified could indicate a need for a focused testing effort in a particularly soft area. The team will identify the actions and tests (for example, parts of UT, FVT, or SVT) to be targeted against the problematic software. Through iterative analysis, the development and test teams will constantly assess if this focused testing is successful in meeting the quality objectives and the time-to-market challenges. This kind of scenario demonstrates the benefit of the spiral model.

Product Development

The function of the model's product development quadrant is to validate requirements, create deliverables, and verify the next level or iteration of the product. The spiral model is distinct because it assumes a relatively short amount of time within this iteration of product development. On the other end of the spectrum, the waterfall and waterwheel models assume that the engineering or product development phases tend to be quite long. In general, the duration of the phases is a function of the size of the software project itself. This supports Boehm's conclusion that the spiral model best supports the creation of short, end-user software projects. [Boehm88]. The waterwheel model has proven itself to be successful for large and complex software projects.

It is in the product development phase of the spiral model where there is the greatest intersection with test activities. The spiral model's staged test phases are quite similar to those of traditional software development models. They include unit test, integration and test (comparable to FVT), acceptance test (comparable to beta or early-release testing), and implementation or product deployment.

The integration and test phase of the spiral model seems to include the process content of the waterfall model phases of FVT, SVT, and integration test. It appears that the entire concept behind the spiral model, evaluating risks along the way, could be applied specifically in the integration and test phase of the spiral. Boehm's work does not seem to discuss in detail how risk assessment and analysis is performed against only a portion of the revolution (i.e., integration and test).

Planning the Next Phase

The purpose of the final quadrant of the spiral model planning is to look ahead to the next phase or activity that will be undertaken in the subsequent revolution of the model. Regardless of the development model you use, proper planning is always important to the success of the next phase and, indeed, the entire project.

As discussed earlier, the waterfall model has an overall planning stage to create the project's end-to-end schedule and define individual planning tasks for each phase as the prior phase concludes. In this planning phase, the team reviews readiness criteria (both technical and project-oriented) for the upcoming phase. In essence, the spiral model's planning phases are embedded in the traditional phases of the waterfall model.

Evolutionary Model

The Evolutionary Software Development model is a combinational model. It exploits the basics of the waterfall model by flowing from one phase to the next. It also makes use of a feedback loop to ensure that any required improvements to the product or process are made as the project proceeds.

May and Zimmer outline their use of the evolutionary development model (or, as they refer to it, EVO) as a set of smaller iterative development cycles. They point out that breaking the implementation phase of the software development process into smaller pieces allows for better risk analysis and mitigation. [May96].

An often-cited shortcoming of the traditional waterfall model is the lack of a natural feedback loop. As May and Zimmer explain in their research, the waterfall's primary source of feedback is its large test phases—after development has completed. Not so with the evolutionary model, which has imbedded feedback loops within the small waterfall cycles. In the EVO model, the smaller cycles tend to last two to four weeks. Feedback from the prior cycle is evaluated during the execution of the next cycle, and can be critical to the ultimate success of the project. The short cycles include all aspects of design, code, and initial testing of a new version of software.

In large, complex software projects where chunks of code take weeks to develop, cycles as short as these are not as applicable. However, the concept of having miniature "development cycles" within the overall development process is comparable to the waterwheel model discussed earlier because the waterwheel is iteratively delivering functions in code drops, each of which goes through design, development, and test prior to delivery to beta customers, along with additional, post-delivery testing. The difference is that within EVO, interim versions of the product are developed and then provided to real customers as beta code for their feedback. The customers are heavily relied on as testers for the product in the EVO model. The waterwheel model stresses more internal deliveries of code to professional testers who look at the product from both a clear-box and black-box perspective. In other words, the EVO model's minidevelopment cycles are end-to-end in nature (quickly going through development, internal testing, customer delivery and test), whereas the waterwheel is a single development cycle, with an iterative, cumulative code delivery loop between the development and test teams.

Our discussion of feedback so far has mostly focused on defects and product improvements. But don't lose sight of how the development and test processes can improve from these iterations as well. As each code drop is iteratively developed, you should take into account all of the process issues that were encountered in the prior iteration. For example, assume that during the prior iteration, the team did not hold code inspections. As this iteration of software is developed, you can learn from that error and ensure that all appropriate parties are represented in a code review with the development team prior to the code's integration into the software bundle. These kinds of process improvements, made during the smaller development cycles of the EVO model, can help improve the overall quality of the final product.

As we've seen, the evolutionary software development model has many of the same characteristics as the waterwheel model. Its scale is different, but its concepts apply to many types of software development projects.

Test-driven Development: Algorithm Verification Test

When creating intricate computing algorithms to handle very complex tasks, including those where the behavior may not be visible, you need a way to ensure that the algorithm is performing correctly. Development must go under the covers to observe an algorithm's true behavior under controlled conditions. A purely iterative development approach that can fulfill this need is known as algorithm verification testing, or AVT.

Experimentation Points

This method utilizes a white-box testing technique to ensure the system's key algorithms are operating properly. The approach is simple. It starts by defining a set of experimentation points. These points are places where the algorithms make significant decisions that drive the software behaviors. Next, those experiments are performed and data on the results is gathered. The results are analyzed, the algorithms are adjusted, and the experimentation cycle starts all over again. The continuous iterations allow the team to gradually hone the algorithms until they are optimized.

Many times, these algorithms are difficult to drive in the desired manner. Getting the correct mix of characteristics in the workload is part of the challenge, and knowing the software's algorithms is the key. This is the white-box aspect of this model. What is extracted from the white-box analysis helps define the workload. In some cases, this requires brand-new workload development though, in other cases, only adjustments to existing workloads are needed. The workload execution is what provides AVT with an environment upon which to tune the algorithms.

Data Analysis

The development team needs to determine how closely the algorithms are tracking to the desired result. As a result, data analysis must be done in order for adjustments to be made to the code. Of course, in order for there to be data to analyze, the software being evaluated must provide information in a way that can be post-processed. Special tools may need to be purchased or developed in order to massage that data into a form that's useful for analysis. Once the data is analyzed and the development team modifies the code for the next iteration, the team performing the AVT experiments takes the software out for another spin. Chapter 15, "Test Execution," delves further into the process of these iterations.

Test Phase or a Tool for Development?

This particular technique is most effective as an activity overlapping the function verification test phase and the start of a system verification test phase of the development cycle. There are certain functional stability requirements that are assumed as well. Since specific areas of the software are targeted by this approach, functional stability in those areas is critical. FVT and SVT activities can help establish that stability. But is AVT really a testing phase?

Actually, this approach is more of a tool for development than a testing phase. It's like prototyping, except that it is done on what will be the real product code, allowing the development team to refine the algorithms that require special tuning. The test/data analysis/code modification iterations provide feedback to development similar to the type of feedback loops used in the evolutionary model. The activity is focused on finalizing the behavior of algorithms as opposed to verifying functions.

Reactionary Approach

Software development models tend to be very well planned from the start regardless of the technique chosen. Right from the beginning, you know what you want to do and how you want each phase to flow into the next. Unfortunately, in the business world, things don't always go as planned. So when things fall apart and the plan doesn't cut it, a *reactionary* iterative approach can be initiated.

Let's review. The project starts out nicely and is progressing rather normally. Slowly but surely, problems crop up and it is soon clear that the planned development model is starting to collapse. In seemingly no time at all, the impact of the problems with the software becomes so severe that no progress can be made in testing or, worse yet, the product doesn't work at all. The development team provides fixes to no avail. You get a little further, then quickly hit the same wall—test blocked, product broken.

As the project end date rapidly approaches, this continuous state of blocked progress demands that you review what you are doing and how you are doing it. Since extending the deadline isn't an option, how can this problem be resolved?

A One-team Approach

Quickly, the developers and testers need to get together and outline the tasks down to a weekly and, in some instances daily, schedule. The team needs to get a handle on how to get the code back on track and working again. In some cases, it might not be a code issue. Instead, the test team may have fallen behind schedule, and needs help to catch up.

Early daily meetings can help set priorities and goals for the day and help each group to address its current set of issues. When code is ready, the test team needs to install it promptly and run a comprehensive test suite to ensure that it's whole. It's fine for some things to fail, but the base functionality had better hold together. If not, all hands on deck . . . again. This time, developer sitting next to tester is the remedy. Test, identify problems, patch the code, and move on. This iterative approach, even though it's out of necessity, can accelerate your time to market. This means development will start coding immediately and, as code is ready, deliver it to FVT. FVT and SVT can work simultaneously—parallelize. While there are certainly risks with this method, sometimes a team does not have a choice.

This reaction to catastrophe is effective at getting the software back on track. But what happened to the code that the developers should have been writing when they were working so closely with the testers to get stability back? Those functions are still expected to be delivered on time. To handle that, we highly recommend reviewing the work remaining and developing a thorough, proven approach for the development and test and not reverting to a reactionary approach again. The reactionary approach is certainly not recommended as a model to use to kick off your project, but it could be just the thing you need to salvage a disaster.

Iterative Model Summary

The iterative software models discussed here are just a subset of those used today. Each model has its own set of benefits and characteristics that are targeted at solving various issues. The iterative models are quite effective for addressing time-to-market challenges on small- to medium-scale projects. Traditional waterfall models deliver very robust code, but lack an iterative model's flexibility and speed. Combining the flexibility of iterative practices with the rigor of a waterfall model to create a waterwheel approach makes for a very effective software development model—one focused on both time-to-market *and* quality.

THE "LET'S JUST SKIP SVT" FALLACY

As the testing process matures, software teams sometimes become confident that they can take some shortcuts to get the product out the door more quickly. They seem to lose sight of their prize—stable software that satisfies their customers.

They consider skipping portions or entire phases of testing. When they actually follow through with the idea, a subset of the class of defects targeted by the skipped phase will no doubt escape to customers. Those that don't escape will impact the phases that follow, so much so that they may put the software's ship date in jeopardy.

Will Skipping SVT Work?

When organizations create robust integration test environments, those environments may prove very successful at finding both complex and subtle bugs. As a result, the team sometimes concludes that it can save time by eliminating the SVT step and going straight to integration test. This approach tends to fail. Why?

The missions of SVT and integration test may seem somewhat similar on the surface, but if you disassemble the efforts a bit you see a big difference. The SVT teams tend to have many different, distinct tests going on in parallel for different functions, on different shifts, with different workloads. A failure in one area might block progress there, but tests in other areas can still continue. When a fix is available, that previously blocked area can then move forward, even as another area hits a defect that blocks progress there. Testing continues in this fashion, with different functions blocked at different times, but overall progress continues to be made.

Now, if you combine these different functions to create a single, end-to-end, customer-like test as one might in an integration test environment, all of the testing becomes intertwined. A failure in one area might block progress in all others. When a fix for that problem is provided, everything moves forward briefly until a severe bug is hit in another area of the software. This bug again blocks progress on all fronts until a fix is available. Plus, since integration test includes multiple software products working together to create a complete solution, a defect in any one of those products could block progress on all others. Instead of SVT's approach of parallelizing the testing of multiple functions, they've been serialized, which means that a failure in any one area can block testing progress on all of them. By skipping SVT, you actually elongate the total test cycle instead of shortening it.

It Isn't Hopscotch

When you were a kid and played hopscotch, you may have hopped around so much that you ended up with blisters. Well, if you skip test phases, you will end up with something much worse than blisters. You'll have dissatisfied customers who are discovering the problems you missed, or are still waiting for your product to arrive. Therefore, think before you jump!

SUMMARY

Software development certainly isn't as easy as coding or testing a "Hello World" sample program. It must be done with a close eye on both time-to-market and quality. Whether the product is built using traditional waterfall techniques or more recent iterative methods, the tester's goal is the same: to find bugs! Different test phases are best suited to extracting specific kinds of defects, and testers should target their efforts accordingly. The same basic test phases span multiple development models, but each model has its own strengths and weaknesses. Can an individual tester change his organization's choice of development model? Probably not. But by understanding the universe of possibilities, you may be able to apply an aspect of one model to solve a problem your team is having with another. The waterwheel model described here is just one example of combining the strengths of different approaches to improve upon a traditional technique.

Since developers and testers have to work closely to make a product the best it can be, they need to determine how to optimize their working relationship. Chapter 4, "The Test and Development Divide," explains how to build that relationship and how to organize to be the most effective development and test group in town.

4 The Test and Development Divide

In people's daily lives, conflict is usually viewed as undesirable. When dealing with families, friends, or bosses, conflict isn't exactly a goal we strive for. Instead, we are constantly working to overcome conflict by creating strong relationships, both individual and team.

In the world of software development, it is conflict, confrontation, and technical and organizational problem solving that allow us to move forward in developing solutions that work in business-critical environments. Therefore, a successful software development and test organization must include people who take adversarial positions, yet also have the structure to manage conflict constructively. In order to drive objective analysis and evaluation of a piece of software, let's examine the division and what makes for a successful relationship between software developers and software testers.

SHOULD DEVELOPERS TEST THEIR OWN SOFTWARE?

First and foremost, experience suggests it's not a good idea for a person to be solely responsible for testing his own code. This is especially true when developing mission-critical software. The importance of the software demands that it is sanitized by multiple objective and unbiased test engineers, each with a different focus.

It certainly is normal for software developers to perform unit test (UT) of their own code. Verification of code at the unit test level benefits directly from the developer's familiarity with it. The program's design was based on a specific set of input, an expected set of output, and targeted functions. The developer's job is to ensure the program produces the desired results based on the input provided in a given environment. It is safe to assume that developers will attempt to address all of the use cases they envision. There is no other person within the development process who would have a better command of the program than the person who took the design and made it real. The software developer's responsibility is simply to obtain a clean compile of the program and make it work.

As previously discussed, UT is first an individual effort and then an integrated effort with other developers to validate the initial creation or modification of a component or function. Some software developers believe that a clean compile of the program completes UT. This approach falls short from a quality perspective. An explicit, individualized set of UT actions lets the developer confirm that the simplest mistakes are handled.

The integrated UT effort described in Chapter 3, "The Development Process," is targeted at uncovering the basic module-to-module integration failures. The consolidated knowledge of the group of developers performing the integrated test helps bring the first degree of objectivity to the entire assembly of the code. The diverse skills and personalities of the people integrating the code provide an improved level of review of the whole function or component.

Happy Path Testing

If it's logical to allow developers to perform UT on their own code, why shouldn't they continue and execute the function verification test (FVT) and system verification test (SVT)? Experience shows they should not. Despite the best intentions, the developers' objectivity is compromised as they review the code they have crafted. They may be thinking, "How can there be anything wrong with my code? It's bulletproof." From the developers' perspective, their programs do exactly what they were created to do. They have built code based on use cases identified during the design phase, and only those cases. Naturally, they will only test the paths that they know the code is designed to handle—had they thought of other cases, they would have written code to support them. This trap of testing only what you know should work is sometimes termed, "happy path testing." At the conclusion of the happy path test, the developer declares the software ready to ship.

A seasoned tester may innocently (or not so innocently) try things the developer didn't anticipate. That's one reason why there must be a clear line dividing test and development at the beginning of the FVT phase.

Makers versus Breakers

The difference between developers and testers is as simple as "makers versus breakers." Developers are intent on *making* things. Once they've created what they determine to be a successfully functional piece of code, they have little interest in trying to uncover its possible flaws. Developers are responsible for making the code work, and they assume it will. So no matter how good their intentions, developers simply will not be enthusiastic about finding problems with the code they've written.

Testers, on the other hand, get their thrills from *breaking* things. They have a knack for it. They live for bugs, relish them, and treat them like gold nuggets. Professional testers go much further to completely exercise the code. Testers devise their own use cases—some of which will align with what the developer envisioned, others which will not. They enjoy the opportunity to explore a multitude of "what if" questions that may lead to the discovery of more defects. Testers know what is state of the art in the test discipline and also have an understanding of the software. Unlike developers, they believe the code they've been handed *won't* work and yearn to identify the flaws. They might list the bugs they find on their whiteboard so that, at the end of a tough day, they have a concrete reminder of their achievements. Bugs are their passion *and* how they define success, so it follows they will search relentlessly for them.

The World of Open Source Software

The open source software development community follows a different model than that of traditional software development organizations. Even so, it offers an excellent example of leveraging the different skills and perspectives of diverse groups of people to strengthen a final software deliverable.

The open source model starts with code reviews. Once a developer has created code he wishes to contribute to an open source project, he offers it to that project's community. Just as testers have a breaker mentality that drives them to find bugs, each sizable open source project has programmers who are passionate about reviewing new source code and identifying its weaknesses. These advocates dive into the review process with a vengeance, and aren't happy until they've picked the code apart.

After surviving this exhaustive review, the new code may be integrated into an experimental release of the project's software package. It is then made available to beta testers everywhere, potentially thousands of them, each with varying levels of skill and bug-busting passion. In addition, most large open source projects have their share of dedicated beta testers.

It is clear then that the open source community thrives not only on people who enjoy writing software, but also on those who enjoy poking holes in it—and for any particular piece of software, a natural separation is maintained between those groups.

DIPLOMACY: THE TESTER'S RELATIONSHIP WITH DEVELOPMENT

In the waterwheel development model discussed in Chapter 3, there is a wall between the FVT and development teams. Even though this barricade is fictional, the teams must be able to see over it so that they can work together effectively.

As a function verification tester, you must objectively review the developer's specification, design documentation, and code in order to create a test plan. While you need to rely on the developer's expertise and knowledge as well, you must do so with caution. That expertise and knowledge may be correct within the bounds of the requirements the developer received at job start, but the requirements themselves may have been incomplete. In fact, that's often the case. As a result, you must also consider your own expertise on the issues and requirements at hand when defining and executing tests to find flaws in the flow and design of the code. These flaws can show themselves as unexpected results from scenarios that don't match the design specifications, as an abnormal termination of an invoked process or function, or by any number of other symptoms.

You should also define tests based on how you believe customers will use a function. System verification testers can be considered the function's first customer and with their knowledge of real customer environments, they will have a different perspective and different test scenarios.

The First Bug

Since all software has bugs, every tester will eventually get the satisfaction of finding a problem. When the tester identifies what he thinks is a flaw in the design or code, he must then apprise the developer that something doesn't seem quite right. A new tester in particular needs to approach the situation with a thick skin and strong constitution. Challenging a developer for the first time can be a daunting and memorable experience. Picture this scene: Tentatively, the tester approaches a veteran software developer and, with mock confidence, says "the message issued under this condition is not aligned correctly."

"What! Are you kidding? That's not a big deal," snaps the developer, his face pinched into a scowl. "Don't bother me with these types of problems."

After this, the tester picks up his crushed ego, heads back to his office, and opens his first real FVT defect. It may not be an earth-shattering problem with significant customer impact, but the success nonetheless gives the tester the drive to continue finding defects and, more importantly, finding bugs that matter. The insensitive developer described showed little or no diplomacy or compassion, but did help the tester to thicken his skin.

As the tester discovers numerous and more complex defects, he becomes more confident in his ability to uncover the problems with the biggest impact on customers. Over time, testers develop a rapport with developers and, instead of a confrontation, they will engage in a discussion about a flaw and a proposed solution. Even veteran testers get push back from development—as they should. It is this professional tension that fosters the discussion of real issues and comprehensive solutions to a wide range of code and design concerns. In the software development industry, managed conflict results in superior quality.

How do testers and developers build the rapport required to arrive at an amicable and comprehensive solution to problems? Testers can take a variety of steps toward that end. Perhaps the most effective way to build that rapport is by establishing your credibility.

Building Credibility

One of the things that testers must do to build a valuable and respectful relationship with development is to establish technical credibility. In many organizations, the development team is led by experienced designers and programmers who have built complex software solutions and received positive feedback from their customers. This feedback goes a long way toward building the developer's reputation, confidence, and attitude—the same traits the tester will battle. By enhancing their own technical credibility, testers will be on equal footing with developers and can build a mutually beneficial relationship.

The answer to how to grow your technical credibility is twofold. First, get a broad view of how the software you are involved with works, both externally and internally. For massive, mission-critical software packages, this is no small undertaking. Second, dig deeply into one component of the software to understand it thoroughly. Once you've achieved indepth knowledge in one area, you'll find it becomes easier to branch out and extend your low-level knowledge in other areas of the software as well.

The combination of technical breadth and depth is a powerful one. An expansive understanding of the entire software package will give you perspective. It will enable you to draw inferences from system behaviors that a developer who is narrowly focused on a single component might miss. On the other hand, insight into one component will put you on par with its developers. You'll speak their language, understand their issues, and be able to contribute in meaningful ways to problems they are trying to solve. Any developer would consider such a tester to be a valued partner. Together, these two dimensions create a multiplier effect on your technical credibility.

Let's take a look at some ways you can achieve that first step and get a broad technical understanding of complex software. Then, in the next section of the book, we'll look at approaches for diving deeply into one area as a precursor to building your test plan.

Immerse Yourself in Information

In the large-system software arena, one effective way to build credibility is to educate yourself on topics of external interfaces, control structures, internal module-to-module interfaces, functional flow of control, and recovery actions of the component and/or product. At this stage, you're not zooming in on any particular area of the software or new function that you might need to later test. Rather, you're stepping back and studying the complete package. This takes time, so don't expect to become an expert overnight. Also, if your test team is busy (as most are), don't be surprised if your boss won't allot a slot in your schedule for this activity. You'll probably have to be self-motivated enough to tackle it on your own time. Becoming a superstar takes discipline.

Review Customer Documentation

For existing software, the most logical place to begin is to read any publications or other documentation that relate to its external operation and use. Components that have application programming interfaces (APIs), system commands, system messages, and output structures are the easiest components to learn and a good starting point for becoming familiar with the software.

Study Internals

However, many software components are chiefly internal in nature, such that their entire function is provided without any external interfaces to the end user or systems programmer. In an operating system, such components might include storage managers, the input and output subsystem, and the system dispatcher. These components can be much more challenging to learn.

To familiarize yourself with internal components, turn to component notebooks and functional documentation. Mature software products will (hopefully) already have these documents, which provide a lower level of detail on internal interfaces, structures, and flow of control. This information can be your window into gaining a basic understanding of internally-oriented pieces of the software.

Sometimes software components fall into both internal and external categories. In any case, your goal is to become familiar with the full suite of components that comprise the complex software product. By gaining such a wide view of the total package, you are well on the way toward establishing a solid base of technical credibility.

Tap into Your Colleagues' Knowledge

Next, tap into the massive knowledge of other testers. As we noted earlier, testers tend to have wider knowledge of the overall system than do developers. To be successful, developers must focus intensely on a specific aspect of a component or function, or on a set of modules or objects. They need to know all the inputs, outputs, and functions, so their technical skill in that particular area is very deep.

Testers are exposed to behaviors and symptoms from all parts of the software. Through repeated iterations, experienced testers will have developed knowledge in areas other than just their specialty and can help "connect the dots" to show how the pieces fit together. With mentoring and coaching from seasoned testers, new testers can gain insight into components, different perspectives on how components operate, and knowledge of appropriate test approaches, techniques, and tools.

The test organization should be primed with veteran testers whose responsibilities include educating and supporting those with less experience. The organization will be stronger and more productive when all testers continually add to their skills. Building knowledge through technical exchange is also a very effective way to enhance credibility.

Share the Wealth

In addition to seeking guidance from experienced test leaders, a great way to learn about functions and components is to share what you've learned. Teaching teammates what you know will generate insightful questions that will help you see things from a different angle and force further investigation on your part. It's another great way to expand your technical base. We'll look at an organized approach for such teaching in Chapter 6, "Coping with Complexity through Teaming."

A Sweeping View

By mining these sources of information, you can begin to build a wide base of knowledge about the software you're working with. You may have to do much of this leg work on your own time, but if you're serious about testing as a career, it's well worth it.

Later in the book we'll explore ways to acquire an in-depth understanding of one or more components of the software as you build a test plan. But there's one aspect of the "deep dive" we'll look at now: *debugging.*

The Importance of Debugging and Product/Function Skills

In some organizations, a tester is a technician who executes specific scenarios and variations. If anything goes awry, his responsibility is simply to contact the developer and provide him with the test case, symptoms, and any other pertinent data. The developer is then responsible for re-executing the test case, and debugging and fixing the problem. This approach leans upon the developer's in-depth knowledge of the code in question, but also creates a bottleneck as problem reports from multiple testers begin to pile up.

A more effective approach is for testers to perform their own diagnosis of defects as they arise. Requiring testers to debug their own problems can be a "baptism-by-fire" education. At first, this will be difficult and painful not only for the tester and his team leader, but also for development. In the long run, this discipline will pay off when testers develop function and component knowledge comparable to those of the developer.

For very complex software, the process of diagnosing problems they find also allows testers to build diagnostic skills that many developers never attain. These skills include creating elaborate breakpoint scripts in a virtualized environment, reading system memory dumps, devising sophisticated system traps, and employing a variety of tracing techniques. These specialized skills are valuable to the organization and are another means of establishing technical credibility. In addition, by taking on the debugging task, the testers enable developers to spend time *fixing* defects rather than *identifying* them.

Debugging's Influence on the Tester's Relationship with Development

It's quite possible that some testers will develop such in-depth knowledge through repeated debugging activities that they become key to the design and implementation of any change to a particular component or function. For example, in the mainframe world, the relationship between the developer and the tester is sometimes so strong that no fix is made without their mutual agreement. This is a best-case scenario because collaborative solutions are much more likely to deliver a better product for the customer.

Throughout the process of building a strong test-development relationship, testers must be careful to "pick their battles" wisely. Reporting too many problems that end up being "user errors" or unimportant issues can hurt your hard-won credibility. By working to build skill in diagnosing your own problems, you'll catch these errors and your credibility will remain intact. Otherwise, a developer's level of respect for testers will diminish. The point being, push on the issues that matter to customers.

There's very little that's more satisfying to a tester than to walk into a developer's office, point to a line of code, and say, "that's a bug." The technical credibility that comes with such expertise will allow you to pursue even the most difficult and, potentially, controversial code defects and design flaws.

Benefits of a Strong Relationship

We've touched on how a strong relationship between test and development encourages early involvement by testers in the design and development process. One benefit of this early communication is enabling testers to provide critical input on making the product easier to test. *Testability* can be defined as an "ease-of-test" attribute within software and will be fully discussed in Chapter 9, "Planning for Trouble." Injecting this attribute early in the design/development process is much easier than trying to convince development to add it after the product has entered test.

Organizational Challenges

We might need to borrow our favorite contractor's tripod and transit to determine the height of the barricade between development and test. Many ideas and techniques have been implemented to try and determine the correct height of this wall. One way is through organizational alignment. Large software development organizations are always looking for the right balance between the two groups so that neither one is too strong or dominant. So how many bricks should we place on each side of the scale?

Business alignment decisions are often cyclical in nature. The organization works in a certain mode for a few years and then goes back to the way it was before. This may happen because, over time, we see the advantage of change and how it can modify the business environment and employee behavior. In other words, change for change's sake. All organization models have their pros and cons and it's important to thoroughly understand the cons and target them specifically. This phenomenon also applies when determining where to place the FVT team in the organization.

We established that when developing large, mission-critical software systems, a clear separation of development and test is required to provide objectivity and ensure that the important defects get removed. It is a generally accepted practice that SVT, and any other parts of the verification process that follow it, should be in its own organization and midmanagement chain. The real balancing act is between the code development and FVT teams.

Before exploring the various organizational models used to address these issues, let's take a moment to review organizational definitions. We'll define a first-line department as one that contains individuals who perform a specific function for the organization, such as develop a key software component, and who report to a single manager. A second-line department is comprised of a logical grouping of first-line departments led by a manager with broader responsibility and accountability for products. In turn, second-line departments are brought together into a third-line organization. The third-line manager reports to the company's upper-level management. Various organizational structures can be implemented. These include, but are not limited to:

Model 1: Function verification testers work in multiple first-line departments within a second-line FVT organization focused entirely on test.

Model 2: Function verification testers reside in first-line departments within a second-line *development* organization. The FVT departments are charged with performing test primarily against the components and functions developed by its own second-line organization.

Model 3: Function verification testers and code developers work in the same first-line department, but with a clear separation between the two disciplines.

Model 4: Same as Model 3, but with *no* distinct separation between development and test. While developers do not test their own code, they may test the code of fellow departmental developers. Or, the person responsible for testing rotates with every new release.

Models 1 through 3 are pictured in Figure 4.1.

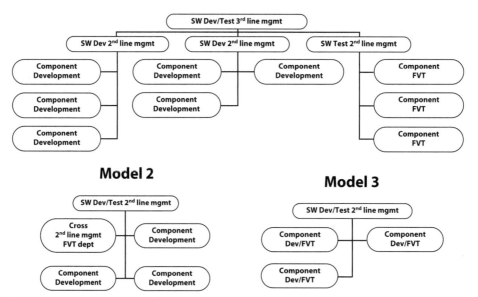

FIGURE 4.1   Development/Function verification test organizational models.

The various organizational models meet at different levels of management. For each, technical disputes that cannot be resolved by the developer and tester rise through model-specific levels of management. Where the models vary is in their ability to foster communication and cooperation, while also carving out a meaningful career path for testers. As you might guess, each organizational model has distinct advantages and disadvantages.

Model 1: Separate Second-line Organizations for FVT and Development

In Model 1, the common point of management is at the third-line level. Depending on the size of the company, a third-line organization might include 100–600 people. In this reporting structure, all FVT activity is grouped under a common second-line manager.

Advantages

This model offers certain advantages:

Improves Objectivity: This organizational model creates the clearest delineation between development and test and by its nature enforces objectivity. The FVT organization can act as the conscience for all of development, with a laser focus on the software's quality, unburdened by issues with which the development side of the shop must cope.

Offers a Higher Point of Escalation: The second-line managers from both disciplines can act as a point of escalation when issues between the testers and developers cannot be resolved. The second-line manager can also be a sounding board for technical and managerial issues related solely to testing.

Fosters Testing Depth: Another benefit of Model 1 is that it encourages testers to come together to create a test community that shares common issues, concerns, and best-of-breed tools and practices.

Supports Test as a Career Path: With the separate test organization found in Model 1, the management team can offer more growth opportunities and develop career paths specifically for testers. In addition, the test second-line manager can act as an FVT advocate, encouraging career growth for testers.

Disadvantages

There are also some significant disadvantages to this approach:

Impedes Communication Flow: One downside of Model 1 is the very high wall between development and test can reduce effective communication between the groups. This may also lead to an "us" versus "them" mentality.

Impacts Early Test Focus: Another potential drawback is how resources and people are allocated within the second-line FVT organization. Since the group provides FVT services to multiple second-line development organizations, there is a possibility that priorities set at the third-line level will inhibit FVT's early involvement in design and development activities. If everyone is testing the current release, no one will be looking ahead to the next one. Priority calls made by the FVT second-line manager are critical in ensuring that the wall is scalable and that the communication pipelines are not disrupted.

Increases Cycle Time: This model does not enable the organization to address time-to-market requirements and challenges with the same aggressiveness as other models do. The extra time spent in resolving cross-organizational issues can cause delays and hamper the ability of test to identify bugs and development to address them with the best technical solutions.

Model 2: Development and FVT in the Same Second-line Organization

Model 2 places FVT teams or departments within a second-line management layer alongside their corresponding development teams. That second-line management layer is responsible for a subset of the entire product development and its associated FVT.

Advantages

This model has its own advantages:

Encourages Issue Resolution: The flattening of the organization provides for a lower point of escalation for both project and technical issues. This expedites problem resolution and helps to reduce the number of issues that are brought forward to the second-line manager.

Improves Communication: Charged with the responsibility for developing code *and* testing it, the second-line manager can work to encourage communication and teamwork between his development and FVT departments.

Supports Early Test Focus: By prioritizing work assignments, the management team can enable testers to get the early involvement needed to lower the mystical test-development wall. In organizations that deploy a Model 2 structure, the relationship between the developer and the tester is less strained than those using Model 1.

Disadvantages

Of course, there are some disadvantages to Model 2 as well:

Weakens Test Community: When there are multiple second-line development organizations, the splintered FVT teams need to make an extra effort to stay in touch in order to share methodologies, tooling technologies, best practices, etc. One of the best ways to ensure communication stays intact is by creating a cross-organizational communication forum. This forum should be led by a technically strong function verification tester who is respected by the test and development communities.

Impedes Test Career Path: Within the second-line organization, the achievements of the test departments may be overshadowed by those of the development departments, since they are the creators and are seen as the ones delivering the product to customers within the second-line organization. Fortunately, the testers still have a dedicated first-line manager as their advocate.

Model 3: Integrated FVT and Development Departments

So how does Model 3 compare to the organizational models discussed already? Model 3 maintains the second-line manager who oversees both the development and FVT departments. However, this model takes the next step to force communication and teamwork into the organization. It integrates developers and testers within the same first-line departments.

Advantages

The following benefits arise from this model:

Increases Communication: Integrating function verification testers and developers within a single department allows for improved communication and provides a higher likelihood of balanced resource allocation and workload scheduling. In Model 3, the first-line manager can promote the teamwork between department members much more effectively than when he must cross department boundaries.

Supports Skill Building and Education: When developers and testers are in the same first-line department, they are more likely to create schedules that enable cross-discipline interaction, resulting in increased opportunities for education and knowledge exchange.

Emphasizes Early Test Involvement: In addition, because the first-line manager controls resource allocation and scheduling, testers can be directly involved in design and provide suggestions for ways to insert testability into the product.

Disadvantages

Naturally, Model 3 also has some disadvantages:

Lowers Escalation Point: This organizational model completely flattens the route for escalating issue resolution to only one level—the first-line manager. However, the leadership structure within the department (created and enabled by the manager), can help reduce the *need* for escalation.

Weakens Test Focus: This model makes it important to have appropriate performance metrics in place for the first-line manager. If the manager is measured primarily by meeting or beating key development dates, he may squeeze the FVT schedule too tightly. In Model 3, it is very easy to treat FVT as an afterthought, which leads to quality issues.

Impacts Test Career Path: Under Model 3, there is the risk that testers (the "breakers") will be overshadowed by developers (the "makers") within the department. In addition, the model does not lend itself to having an organization-wide management advocate for the FVT discipline. Model 3 is only successful if the organization is populated with highly valued testers who are already on an equivalent career path as developers.

Model 4: FVTers and Developers Performing Both Tasks

This model is structurally similar to Model 3. However, having developers and testers perform both tasks violates the "makers versus breakers" definition.

Advantages

Model 4's advantages include:

Enhances Communication: Under this model, testers and developers trade jobs, tasks, and responsibilities like kids trade baseball cards. They tend to reside in the same department, and swap code with each other.

Offers Flexibility: The first-line manager has tremendous flexibility to deploy and redeploy people where they are needed most.

Disadvantages

This model has all of the disadvantages of Model 3, plus:

Uses Strengths Poorly: The people who would prefer to be writing code (because they are "makers") are forced for a time to be testing other developers' code, which they do not enjoy (because they're not "breakers"). Frequently, the job of being a tester is relegated to the newest, least-experienced team members as a means to get educated. Conversely, testers are asked to develop product-level code and may have not experienced the rigors of that process. But more importantly testers have the "breaker" mentality and may be less enthusiastic about "making" code. In this model, each individual's strengths are not fully exploited and code quality can suffer.

Decreases Test Career Opportunity: The situation here is even worse than in Model 3. Because developers and testers are trading jobs and tasks, it is nearly impossible to attain an identity as a tester. Career testers can focus entirely on test activities and, in the process, build test expertise, whereas Model 4 testers do not have that opportunity.

Which Organizational Model to Select?

So after examining the four organizational structures, which model is the most effective in developing large-system, business-critical software? That may depend on the organization and the objectives it strives to achieve. With that said, almost all of these models have some degree of effectiveness.

Isolating the test organization, as in Model 1, promotes testing depth and career growth. This model also provides the greatest objectivity when validating code. Model 2 and Model 3 provide the most effective way for testers to influence the design and implementation of the software through enhanced communication. This early involvement allows them to bring a completely different perspective to the product. The testers bring customer outlook and reliability, availability, and serviceability expertise to design discussions and code reviews. Model 4 gives the manager the most flexibility, but because this organizational model tends to produce subpar results, it is not recommended.

Each organizational model provides its own unique benefits and drawbacks, each of which must be carefully examined. Which model to choose depends on the current set of issues the organization needs to address. It may be appropriate for an evolving organization to change the model it uses over time. For example, it might be appropriate to start with Model 1 or 2 in order to build a strong test community, then transition to Model 3 to benefit from its improved communication channels and earlier test involvement in the design process. In addition, the success of a particular model will be influenced by the current set of organizational metrics and measurement systems used to evaluate management performance.

Is Organization Enough?

Although organizational structures can have a positive effect on maintaining the correct balance between FVT and development, is that the whole story? Models can become irrelevant when the organization has individuals with strong personalities and excellent leadership skills. Planting strong test leaders in departments throughout the organizational model will have a more immediate impact than almost anything else. These leaders and role models provide the technical insight and the interpersonal, negotiation, and communication skills needed to establish the best balance of development and test. These test leaders build respectful relationships with developers across multiple organizations and are able to help other testers build the same kind of connections. They can advise testers on the types of questions to ask, the best approach to inform developers of problems and issues, and recommendations for following up with development throughout the process. Having the right people with the right job responsibilities along with highly skilled test leaders will accentuate the positives and lessen the negatives of these organizational models.

By implementing a model supplemented with an infantry of strong leaders, the end result will likely be an organization that delivers higher-quality software to satisfied customers. Regardless of the organizational model selected or the strength of the leaders of the team, simply altering your test team's construction can have a huge impact. Analyzing the current set of issues with your team and identifying and carrying out specific action plans to address them can be effective as well.

SUMMARY

Employing best practices such as not allowing developers to be the sole testers of their own code, building technical credibility with development, and maximizing the success of organizational models through strong leadership can help foster the most effective relationship between developers and testers and deliver the highest-quality product. Customers of mission-critical software expect this level of commitment.

In Chapter 5, "Where to Start? Snooping for Information," we'll look at how to acquire detailed insight into a specific area you've been assigned to test. Such insight will serve as a basis both for building a strong test plan and for extending your technical prowess.

Part

III

The Best-laid Plans

You have just been assigned to test a major new function in a piece of complex, mission-critical software. Congratulations! Now what?

You need a plan. It's easy to plan a lousy test, but harder to plan a good one. The next five chapters will show you how to do it right. The first order of business is learning everything you can about the new function and what problem it's trying to solve. It's also important to understand as much as possible about the ultimate customers of the software, so that your plan hits the same pressure points that they will. If the complete software package is especially complex, your entire team may need to work together to break that complexity into manageable chunks to ensure that subtle interactions are not missed.

Once you've finished your research, it's time to put something down on paper. Test plans for different test phases will have unique focus areas to tackle. The targets will range from common ones such as interfaces and mainline function, to others that are sometimes overlooked, such as recovery and data integrity. Unfortunately, even the best laid plans can go awry when trouble hits, but there are techniques you can use to anticipate risks and adjust your plan to account for them. You might even find yourself proposing changes to the software itself to make it more testable.

Don't underestimate the value of a test plan. A comprehensive one will chart your course through the turbulent waters of test execution, while a weak one will leave you floundering. The methods described in this section have proven their worth in countless large-scale projects. Apply them to your own situation and reap the benefits.

5 Where to Start?
Snooping for Information

In This Chapter

- The importance of knowing what you test
- Test preparation approaches
- Where and how to find information
- Obtaining knowledge about customers
- Finding your first defects

It's okay to not know something; it is *not* okay to test something you do not know. Proper preparation for a test is as important as the test itself. In fact, many of the steps used to prepare for a test are themselves a form of testing. Defects can be identified through this investigation, making the tester's job easier during the test execution phase.

Good preparation for the test of complex software is well worth the investment. It makes the test more effective and efficient and actually saves time. Also, if done right, the in-depth knowledge you'll gain in the specific area you've been assigned to test will complement your broad product view which we discussed in Chapter 4, "The Test and Development Divide," and cement your technical reputation in the organization. So before you write a test plan, do some "investigative reporting." *Ask questions—lots of them.*

THE IMPORTANCE OF KNOWING WHAT YOU TEST

A test professional needs to be knowledgeable about test techniques, tools, strategies, methodologies, and approaches—it's the additional value you bring to the table. But in terms of importance, that *testing* knowledge is on par with the *product* knowledge of what you must test. The selection of tools to use along with the best approaches and techniques flows from that product understanding—without it, you will miss critical defects. The knowledge of testing and the software under test makes for a powerful combination—it's what makes a professional tester.

Why You Must "Learn the Game"

Assume you have been given the responsibility to test your company's new computer poker game. After you're done celebrating the opportunity to work on a fun project, what are the first thoughts to go through your mind? You need to determine how best to learn about poker strategy and poker players using many different resources.

Subtle Bugs

Understanding poker may not be necessary for you to recognize when the software crashes, but it is needed to recognize a defect that identifies a poker hand of two pair as a winning hand over one with three of a kind. Even if the design document states that a straight beats a flush, tests should not be thoughtlessly developed to show that requirement was met. Externally, there may be no indication of a problem, but if the software doesn't do what it is supposed to do, it's a defect that matters.

A Customer's Advocate

Of course, understanding the requirements of the software is the designer's and developer's responsibility, but it is also an important element of a tester's job. A tester needs to go even further to understand the targeted users of the software, and act as their advocate. The expression "testing to specifications" is common in the testing world and should be heeded. But a good tester goes further and prepares well enough to be able to recognize when something in the specifications might harm customers more than help them. A few examples are presented later in this chapter.

New Technology

More often than not, industrial-strength software will not be as simple as the poker example—it won't be the programmatic implementation of something that is well known. Even if it's entirely new technology, a tester still needs to thoroughly understand it before beginning the test.

Resources to Tap

Information must be gathered before developing the test plan. So, where do you start?

Requirements Document

Most software isn't created or enhanced in a vacuum. Savvy development teams first gather requirements from potential or actual customers to identify what the product should do. Then they fold these requirements into a document, which becomes a key input into the design process. By reviewing this design document, testers gain insight into the software's objectives and can create tests aimed at ensuring the final product achieves its intended goals. It's a great place to start.

Specifications

Once the requirements are understood, they must be incorporated into a design that can be implemented. This design is often documented in what's called a *specification* ("spec"). If the requirements are the *what*, then the spec is the *how*. It is one of the best sources of information testers can use to begin understanding new function. Also known as a design document, you can use the spec to review the same information that the developer followed when creating the software.

Flow and Function

Use the specification to study the overall flow and function of the new support. Start by getting a high-level overview of what is being developed before going back to look at it in more detail.

What's under the Hood?

You'll want to take the opportunity to identify areas of interest specific to your test responsibilities. Pull this information out of the functional internal details. For example, if you are a system tester, look for things that pertain to the focus of system test. Gather detailed information about any locking or serialization areas. Begin making notes on what types of test scenarios you'll need to execute to drive these functions.

Find and make note of *pressure points*. Which areas of the software will have the toughest demands placed upon them? Are there any specific areas that are common to, or invoked by, many other disparate pieces? Are any complex algorithms defined? What are the architectural limits? Continue making notes with what you discover.

Another aspect to investigate is the documented recovery capabilities of the software. The very things the software is designed to recover from are good starting points for the tester's recovery test scenarios. Also, while reviewing the recovery paths explicitly included in the design, begin thinking of additional ways to be harsh with the software. Jot notes, think devilishly, have fun.

If the new function includes enhancements to existing software, look for the most significantly changed areas. Has memory management or the manipulation of storage been changed? Are there any changes to user tasks or other externals? Identify the impacts to installing and migrating to the new software level.

Dependencies

You need to gain a clear understanding of any dependencies of the new software, whether on other software or on hardware. Are they "hard" or "soft" dependencies? Hard dependencies are ones that are absolutely required for the software to work correctly, whereas soft dependencies are required only for the software to work *a certain way*. For example, an application written to monitor the poker game described earlier has a hard dependency on that poker game. But if that monitor program provides the capability to store historical data in a flat file *or* a relational database, it has a soft dependency on a relational database manager.

Exploiters

Does the new software provide services or APIs for use by other software? If so, make note of how those services can be invoked. Are the anticipated exploiters of these services documented? If they are, make a note to find out more about that software and the plans of this "real exploiter." Timing is important here. The exploiters' development plans may not line up with the plans of the software you are assigned to test. If they do line up, you may be able to use the exploiting software to help test the services. If they don't, you may not be able to use that software during your test, but you can still ask its development teams for details on how they plan to apply the new service. This information can be good input for test cases you need to create. If no mention of anticipated exploiters is documented in what you are reviewing, make a note to find out later. Testing of APIs or software services should not be done without an understanding of real or anticipated exploiters.

Just the First Pass

Although considered a great source of information, this is just your first pass through the specifications. Testers must use other resources to enable them to grow their knowledge about the proposed software's function. As mentioned earlier, this is due to the tester's responsibility to validate the correctness of the design and act as a customer advocate. Once more information has been investigated and your knowledge of the function increased, another pass through the spec can be made, this time looking for bugs. We'll look into this in more detail after describing other investigation areas.

Book Drafts

Most software is accompanied by manuals, release notes, help panels, or some other form of external documentation. You can gain a different perspective on the software by reviewing planned external documentation versus internal design documentation.

Know Your Information Developers

It may be unusual for the initial drafts of this information for new software (or a new release of existing software) to be available during the time you are planning your test. If they are, they can be a prime source for building additional knowledge about the new function. In any case, it is a good idea to get to know the people responsible for the external documentation early in the development process. Testers should have a large influence on the documentation. For instance, agreements can be made to supply and/or explicitly test any examples. You can offer advice on documentation content, based on your hands-on experience with the behavior of the software.

Learn from the Past: Post Mortems

As in life, testers learn from past mistakes. Just as importantly, they should repeat things that were successful. In preparing for a new test, seek out and review the lessons learned from previous tests.

Strengths and Weaknesses

Learn about the strengths and weaknesses of prior test efforts. What approaches were most successful? What types of scenarios or test cases proved valuable at uncovering the best bugs? What potholes were hit during other efforts and how can they be avoided in the future?

Teaming

In addition, learn about past teaming issues. What kinds of interactions best helped the team meet its objectives? What hurt? Which communication vehicles were most effective? What was good about the make up and organization of the team? What organizational models should be avoided? Did the team itself identify specific areas of improvement? If so, what were they? Do they apply to your test? Should you implement them?

Tools and Approaches

Understand if new tools or approaches were successful. Were any deemed a failure? Investigate whether you can reuse what was created. It is almost always better to add onto something that already exists than it is to build something from scratch.

What's available to enhance? Were risks mitigated in novel ways? What can be learned from the actions put in place during times of trouble?

Who Has Tested Similar Code?

Post mortems can also be a good way to identify who has already tested the same component or something similar. Make an effort to meet with these testers. Reviewing their input into the post mortem is important, but meeting with them may unearth more things to consider. As in many aspects of testing, leveraging the skills, experience, and knowledge of others when preparing for a test is smart.

Meet with the Experts

Large, commercial software is developed by many people in a variety of disciplines. Meeting with them should be on the to-do list of any tester preparing for a test. All of these individuals will bring their own perspective of the software under development. Getting a grasp of those views can be a huge help to a tester. One of your objectives in meeting with the experts is to find the soft spots you can then exercise through your test plan.

Designers and Architects

In large projects, it is not unusual for the software to be designed at a high level by designers or architects rather than the actual developers of the code. These design professionals will have a unique perspective on what the software is trying to accomplish. They often have intimate knowledge of the requirements the software is attempting to meet, as well as customer needs. Sitting down with the designers or architects will expose a different angle on the intent of the new or changed software and how it fits into the overall picture of a larger strategy. This can help immensely when preparing to define tests in line with this strategy.

Developers

Software developers will not be shy about discussing what they're producing. People generally like to talk about their work—they will be happy you have shown enough interest to go to the trouble of scheduling time with them. Start by describing your view of the functionality—you'll want to show them you have done your homework. Then ask them questions. Some sample questions might be:

- What areas are you most concerned about?
- What areas were the most difficult to code?
- What are you most interested in having the test cover?
- What is the best thing about the function?

You may be surprised where the answers lead you. Many developers will gladly point out weak spots in their code. They will be happy to provide input to your test preparation. However, they will not be happy if you haven't done your homework.

However, if you are on a project for which the developers have not produced any sort of specification to describe what it is they're creating, then your meeting with development will be quite different. In the absence of other information, you'll need education on what it is you're about to test. Schedule time for a "chalk talk." This is a casual sit-down exchange with the developers. Ask them to take you through the externals, then the internals of what they're building. Take lots of notes, and look for interfaces, pressure points, serialization, recovery capabilities, dependencies, and all the other things you would watch for if you were scouring an actual specification.

Once you've obtained this background information, then the meeting can morph into the more test-oriented one described earlier. Discuss the types of test scenarios that should be run against the code. Get the developer's perspective on potential areas of weakness in the new component or function. Ultimately, these sessions can bring all the developers and testers together for an exchange of knowledge that leads to a better product.

Service Professionals

Testers can gain another perspective on the software by meeting with customer support professionals, especially if they are servicing customer calls or problem reports in a similar functional area. They are very familiar with the types of problems customers are reporting, and can share their thoughts on serviceability needs and how hard or easy earlier software was to debug. You'll gain insight into the types of problems that escaped previous test efforts, and you can make note of additional tests to include in your plan. Pay particular attention to any interesting combinations of events that are not self evident but have occurred in production environments and subsequently exposed a defect. For example, support reps may describe a scenario where the software reacted incorrectly when system memory was constrained because of an activity spike of a completely unrelated software application.

Other Testers

Leveraging the skills and knowledge of fellow testers is always a good idea in every part of the test, including the preparation phase. You'll get the most from their expertise by exploring several test concepts in depth. Meet with test team members assigned to the same project as you are. Describe what you have learned so far about the function you'll be testing. Have your team members do the same. Discuss potential areas for cooperation and take notes about them. Then define how the differing test activities can be combined to save time and effort and produce a better test. A format for such discussions is described in Chapter 6, "Coping with Complexity through Teaming."

Large software projects will have several test phases, each focused on specific objectives, each attacking different aspects of the software. Meet individually with testers from the other teams for a high-level discussion about what each of you has learned so far. Go into detail on your thoughts about approach, coverage, and scenarios. If there is a test phase in front of yours, learn where they are seeing the most problems. You may want to emphasize these same soft spots in your own testing. Review each others' notes and look for things that would duplicate effort. Then determine whether it is appropriate for just one test team to address that area or if there is unique value in multiple teams trying a similar plan. Many times, testers are short on time. Ensuring a test activity is not repeating something already attempted or that is part of someone else's test plan will save time and effort. It will also help you stay focused on the very things that provide the most value.

In addition to uncovering duplication of effort, you should also look at the test plans from the opposite angle and identify any holes. Identify specific tests that are needed but are not currently planned by either team. When meeting with other testers, describe your assumptions on what they will cover. They should do the same, and together you can discuss what appears to be missing. You may not find all the holes right then, but at least each team will not rely on assumptions that haven't been validated.

Participate in Code Reviews

Joining a review or walk through of code you are planning to test can be a great way to increase the depth of your understanding. There's nothing like studying a segment of code line by line for expanding your insight into how it operates. Also, hearing the discussion among the developers over issues and concerns regarding the code will give you some additional perspective. However, keep in mind that the purpose of a code review is not to educate, but to eliminate defects. Contribute substantively to the review. Do your homework. Come prepared to point out flaws you've identified. Don't use the review as an opportunity to pepper the developers with questions about how their code works, or you'll probably never be invited back.

Compare Notes

After you have met individually with the designers, developers, and other testers, a formal get-together of all the players at one time can yield additional benefits when preparing for a test. Each tester can describe his view of the most important things to cover. The other meeting participants can provide a sanity check of the proposal and work to reach agreement on the best approaches and focus areas for each planned test effort. The testers should also present the previously identified holes and redundancies, which may help the bigger team uncover additional ones. The test review should satisfy everyone's concerns about the total testing picture. After that objective is met, each tester can feel confident that his test will be properly focused, complete, and effective. It is an excellent way to validate the prior research.

VIEWING ALL SOFTWARE AS A SOLUTION TO A PROBLEM

Customers of commercial software do not implement new technology for technology's sake. They deploy the technology because it solves their business problems. It's no accident that many software advertisements and marketing campaigns use the word "solution." Individual software products are not promoted as raw technology, but as effective solutions to real problems. With this in mind, it is a good idea for the software tester to understand the solution the new function is designed to provide. To do that, you must first fully understand the problem.

Digging into the Problem

Researching the targeted problem in detail is just one task of properly preparing for a test. Once the problem is well understood, you can begin thinking about ways to experience the problem, to demonstrate it. This provides a solid foundation for determining if the solution does indeed solve the problem. Going through this process helps testers identify tests to try and look beyond the specific solution to see whether new problems arise.

For example, when a bottleneck is removed, a new one may appear. Many times when a new solution to an existing problem is implemented, a new, unknown world emerges. Envisioning what is out there can be difficult, even impossible, for designers and developers. Testers will be the first to step into this world, and proper preparation gives them a better chance of finding their way. Then they will return safely from that new world and be able to describe their experiences to others. Testers can do more than demonstrate that the software works; they can also help surface additional issues and solutions in the new function.

CUSTOMER RECONNAISSANCE

There are as many definitions of software test as there are of the role of a tester. Which one you subscribe to is not as important as it is to act as the customer's advocate. Of course, performing this role is difficult without understanding your customers. Gaining their true viewpoint, understanding their issues and expectations, and knowing what is most important to them takes a long time. The task of getting to know customers is not something a tester starts to do after being assigned a test. It is something that is built over time. One benefit of using professional testers to test software is that they spend their careers learning about customers. They also have a view of a much bigger picture than many developers have. Testers get the opportunity to have hands-on experience in large, complex environments—where system test and integration test are performed. They get the chance to act like a customer. Applying knowledge of the customer environment during test preparation helps testers define customer-aligned approaches and focus areas and to develop a plan that will find the defects that matter.

Where to Snoop

Obtaining the mindset of the software's users will not happen by itself. You should take any available opportunity to interact with customers, since having this in-depth understanding of their needs is of utmost importance for an effective test. Let's review a few ways you can obtain it over time.

Get Involved

You will need to seek out opportunities to interact with customers. Sitting by the phone waiting for a call will not help, at least not initially. Start by learning about any activities involving customers and volunteer to assist on those projects. For example, if the customer service organization is nearby, let them know you are available to re-create or help debug any critical problems reported from the field. Afterward, investigate and implement ways to keep that kind of problem from escaping your testing in the future. Offer to present your findings and actions to the customer. The resulting experience is one little nugget you can collect. Each time you add to the collection, you build a little more knowledge of your customers.

Examine Problem Reports

Another way to familiarize yourself with customer operations and issues is to review problem reports. Instead of reviewing problem reports individually, attempt to find a list of problems reported by one customer. Looking at this grouping of problems can help you identify trends and common issues that are exposed in a customer environment. Make notes of the types of trends you find. Then move on to another list from another customer and so on. You will end up with a list of trends. Review that list to find the ones that are most pervasive across the set of customers. This will give you a more global view of customer issues. Focusing too much on any one particular customer is not necessarily bad; it just opens the possibility of viewing one of their unique issues as a pervasive problem when it may not be. Each customer has its own little quirks.

Lend a Hand in Beta Tests

A lot of software goes through a beta test, where the code is introduced to a subset of customers prior to making it generally available to all. You can get involved in these beta tests in a number of ways, from educating beta customers about the new software to helping support some of them. Assisting in beta test efforts offers you the chance to interact with the customers who are most interested in the new functionality, as they are the ones most likely to participate in a beta test. Beta tests also offer the timeliest feedback, since they happen either in parallel with a test effort or immediately following one. Things you learn during the beta test let you add another nugget or two to your customer-knowledge collection.

Build Relationships

You will find that some customers are very open to starting ongoing relationships. These relationships are good for both sides. The testers win by having a sounding board for ideas, and customers benefit by having influence over the types of tests and scenarios executed. Opportunities may arise where an offer can be extended to a customer to make a presentation to the test team. The customer can be asked to speak about their environment, what technology they use and how it helps them, what daily struggles they have, or any other topic. Testers will get the opportunity to ask questions and add to their customer-knowledge base. Sometimes such relationships even evolve to where customers spend a few weeks actually participating in system or integration testing, side-by-side with the test team.

Go to Trade Shows

If you get the opportunity to attend trade shows or user group events, use the occasion to meet with customers. This gives you the opportunity to interact with the product's users in more informal settings. Just by talking to them, you can learn what's on customers' minds. You can ask them questions about the technology and software under discussion or the demonstrations at the show and encourage them to share their thoughts on how they would implement the new technology in their environment. By discussing any concerns they have about the design or functionality of the software, you can gain additional insight into the customer world.

Surf the Web

If you want to truly understand your customers, you need to take the time to learn about their business. A good place to start is their Web site. Find out what they produce, who they think their customers are, and where the business is headed. Your customers may be large corporations, departments in your own company, or somewhere in between, but the approach is most likely the same. If it is an external business, find out what business segment it falls under—financial, manufacturing, insurance, etc. Is it a global enterprise? What kind of competition does it have? What you want to determine is how the company most likely uses the technology you test to give them a competitive advantage.

Apply Knowledge of Customers

By "wearing a customer hat" during test preparation, a tester can provide additional, unique value to the project. The proper environments to set up and scenarios to document can be slanted toward true customer views. With a better understanding of the problems at hand, you'll more easily create the problem, and then create tests to validate the solution.

As with most teams, test teams will likely consist of members with mixed experience levels. As discussed earlier, it takes some time to gain a complete view of your customers. Less-experienced members can leverage the customer insight of the more experienced to validate their thinking on approaches and scenarios to create and document in the test plan.

A SIMPLE TEST PREPARATION TOOL

In the process of preparing for a test, you'll learn about the software's functions from many different sources. Collecting the information is one thing, aggregating it is another. Deep thinking is the next step. Many test tools are available, but none will do this thinking for you. Here is where the simplest of tools can help—create a simple checklist to use as you progress through your investigative process.

Figures 5.1 and 5.2 show some examples of parts of such a checklist for a system test. The questions are just a guide to assist in the investigation phase. There is no magic, there is no high technology. It's merely a way to capture what is found.

The checklist is really a tool for your own use, but it can be used for other purposes as well. For example, the checklist can be used as a consistent agenda when educating other test team members. A test team can review groupings of multiple checklists to find opportunities to merge or perform scenarios together. It can also be used as a training aid for less experienced testers, helping them prepare for their first test. But mostly, it offers a single place to gather all the notes taken during test preparation for use as reference when creating the test plan.

Question	Notes
Function Name	
Lead Designer, Developer, Function Tester, Information Developer	
Brief description of function	
Why are we developing this functionality? Value to our company Value to our customers	
What will we externally advertise?	
Is this function part of a bigger strategy? If so, what is it?	
What is the nature of this function: Support for other functions or components? System constraint relief? Performance enhancements? Enhancements to reliability, availability, or serviceability? Standards compliance? Security enhancements? Other?	

FIGURE 5.1 A sample test planning checklist–general section.

Question	Notes
What are the migration considerations?	
What are the new externals?	
What are the timing or serialization aspects?	
What are the stress points?	
What are the recovery implications?	
How does this new function interact with other components/projects?	
Where does development recommend we focus our testing?	
What are FVT's areas of concern?	
How will this function affect the SVT environments?	
What release coexistence issues are related to this new function?	
What assistance is needed from other component owners?	
Which existing SVT workloads can be enhanced to exploit this new function?	
What SVT procedures need to be updated as a result of this new function?	

FIGURE 5.2 A sample test planning checklist–characteristics section.

DON'T JUST TAKE, GIVE A LITTLE

After you have exhausted your sources of information to learn about the code you will test and you understand its customers, you are now positioned to provide your first feedback on the software. Much of your activity during test preparation is geared toward building your knowledge. But you can also begin giving back.

Injecting Insight into a Review

Review the educational information you've collected. Make another pass through the specification. This time see if the design includes things you now know are required.

Protecting Your Customers

As an example, let's return to the assignment you received earlier—testing a computerized poker game. You did your homework, you independently learned the game of poker and you researched the typical user set. You discovered that the vast majority of users fall into two categories—serious poker players and casual players. You learned that serious players despise wild cards as they alter the percentages and statistical attributes of the game. You also learned that casual users love wild cards because, from their perception, the cards give them more chances to win and they enjoy more high hands.

Return to the design documents and ensure the current design will satisfy both requirements. Look to see that games can be played with wild cards, but that their use can also be disabled. Also, since it is the casual user who most likely wants to play with wild cards, make sure doing so is very easy and intuitive.

Now check if support for the serious player is evident. For instance, the serious player will want "fast path" ways to interact with the game engine—things like special keys or command line interfaces. You previously discovered that serious players will take the time to become intimately knowledgeable about many aspects of the game's functionality. They may even want to make their own modifications—for instance, setting random keys to alter the deck shuffling algorithm. Ensure there are architected ways for sophisticated users to interface with the game.

For casual players, you discovered that their number one concern is to have fun when playing. So, ensure their typical game options are trivial to set or perhaps even the default. Also, look for very easy access to context-sensitive help and an option for a "coach" that guides a player through a hand while explaining strategies.

This example is contrived, but it stresses the point that testers can perform a type of test before any formal test execution begins—even before a test plan is created. Throughout the test preparation phase, testers can already be looking for defects.

Making Your Own Job Easier

While you are in the mood to suggest software design changes for customers, consider suggesting some for yourself. With all of the investigation now under your belt, you may have some ideas about little things that can be added to the software to make testing easier. This notion of adding testability function into the software will be explored in more detail later, but this is the point in the development process where your suggestions should be made.

SUMMARY

Preparing for a test—actually, preparing to write the test plan—is as important as executing it. The time spent is well worth it. Gaining a thorough understanding of the new or changed aspects of the software is imperative and one of the absolute keys to test preparation. You'll want to use a wide variety of resources to obtain that knowledge, including meeting with experts.

Preparing also includes looking back and reviewing the lessons learned by previous testers. Avoid the potholes they identified. Reuse the methods that worked best for them and look for existing things to enhance. Take the customer viewpoint when looking at design details and suggest areas for improvement. Consider using a simple checklist to collect all your thoughts in one place.

For most software projects, zooming in at a detailed level on the new and changed function you've been assigned to test is entirely sufficient for creating a strong test plan. However, for some massive projects, this probably won't be enough. The software's complexity will simply be too overwhelming for any single person to grasp all the subtle implications buried in the maze of interdependencies. In Chapter 6 we'll explore ways teams can work together to produce a topnotch deliverable even when the complexity of the project seems insurmountable.

6 Coping with Complexity through Teaming

In This Chapter

- Complexity of large system software
- Reducing complexity through teamwork
- Leveraging everyone's expertise to solve the complexity issue

Software development is a team sport. Building software solutions for complex business problems requires the diverse skills of people from multiple disciplines, and that's why teaming is so important.

In Chapter 4, "The Test and Development Divide," we looked at ways to get a broad technical view of the software you're working with. In Chapter 5, "Where to Start? Snooping for Information," we examined how you can dig deeper into a specific component of that software by mining various resources in a quest to construct a test plan that thoroughly addresses that area. In most cases, this is enough. If each tester on the team does a great job of focusing on their narrow piece of the product, collectively they can assemble a solid and comprehensive test plan for the overall deliverable.

However, when the software under test is extraordinarily complex, mind-numbing in its array of interfaces, dependencies, and services, then treating each tester like an island may not be sufficient. Another layer of investigation might be needed before a robust test plan can be completed. If you are involved with such software, then this chapter will show you how the entire team can come together to solve the complexity riddle.

COMPLEX SOFTWARE PRODUCTS: YOU CAN'T KNOW IT ALL

Industrial-strength software is complex. A computing platform may consist of an operating system, subsystems, middleware, and many other products. The components of this platform are bound together with years of experience and creativity. The sheer volume of code and interfaces within just an operating system's components is immense and its workings can't possibly be understood by any one person or small group of people. In 1983, IEEE Standard 729-1983 defined software complexity as the "degree of complication of a system or system component, determined by such factors as the number and intricacy of interfaces, the number and intricacy of conditional branches, the degree of nesting, the types of data structures, and other system characteristics" [ANSI/IEEE792]. Seven years later, IEEE Standard 610.12-1990 modified the definition of complexity to be the "degree to which a system or component has a design or implementation that is difficult to understand and verify" [IEEE610.12]. The evolution of these definitions over this short period of time suggests that the concept of complexity itself was becoming too complex.

Complexity is not limited to an individual software component or product. There is also the breadth of the related environment to consider. For example, a given software package may run on multiple operating systems and hardware platforms, each with its own subtle requirements for optimizations and for the operational skills of testers.

With the growing rate of change to requirements and constant innovation in the computing industry, the complexity issue is only getting thornier. Let's examine a specific software platform to understand why.

Case Study: Complexity of an Operating System

The z/OS mainframe operating system is comprised of a myriad of components. Each supports a basic function, such as work scheduling and dispatching, resource serialization and allocation, input/output functions, interrupt and error recovery processing, and diagnostic tools. Together, they make up the "kernel" of the operating system, known as the Base Control Program (BCP). Figure 6.1 shows an exploded diagram of the BCP that by no means is all inclusive. However, this simplistic view does illustrate the vast number of its possible interactions and interfaces.

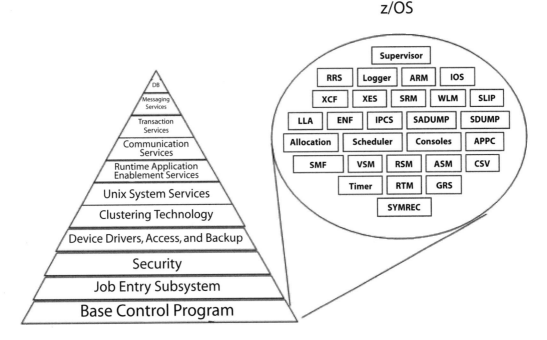

FIGURE 6.1   Composition of the z/OS platform and base control program.

Passed across these intercomponent interfaces are data parameters that have a slew of their own combinations and permutations. Together these imply a high volume of test scenarios that are difficult to fathom, and that's just the beginning.

The Next Level of Complexity

The BCP is merely the foundation of the platform. The pyramid in Figure 6.1 illustrates more software pieces—the service extensions that run on top of the base operating system. They include the subsystems that introduce work into the system and provide security services and protection, as well as software support for multisystem clustering. Others are UNIX-related functions, runtime support for applications, networking communication software, transaction processing subsystems, and databases.

Upping the Ante with Integration

Each of these unique pieces of the environment adds a level of complexity to the BCP, and the integration of all of them into the platform creates an unimaginable complexity. Testers aren't the only ones who must contend with this. The end users of software don't enjoy wading through a maze of knobs and dials to accomplish basic tasks. As a result, the tester's challenge is to ensure all intricacies, including those introduced through integration, are sufficiently masked or managed.

Software can have multiple levels of complexity. There may be core services, mid-level services, and end-user services, with many interfaces glueing them together. As a tester, your challenge is to figure out a way to contend with this complexity.

In order to best approach such an environment, test team members need to build technical skill in multiple components and leverage each individual's expertise so that they can attack the complexity as a group.

REDUCING COMPLEXITY THROUGH COMPONENT SPIES

FVT and SVT teams often struggle to get a handle on the labyrinth of code they're responsible for covering. This is particularly true when an effective software test requires a great deal of interaction between so many components that it's impossible for any single person to study them all, looking for possible ways that one area might influence another. An effective approach to building a comprehensive test plan in such an environment is for individual testers to take ownership of different components of the software, becoming a *component spy*.

What Does a Component Spy Do?

A component spy does more than simply dig deeply into the new or changed aspects of the component they are assigned to test. The spy must explore the *entire* component. Their goal is to become a technical resource within their team for anything having to do with that area. As the test plan is developed, they must be able to see linkages—risks and opportunities for testing that others might miss. Similar to the way testers build technical credibility to enhance their relationship with developers, they must build extensive technical expertise to truly qualify as an ace component spy.

Exactly what form this expertise takes can differ slightly between the disciplines of FVT and SVT. The function verification tester will learn detailed module control flow, data structures, recovery processing, module-to-module communication, and external interfaces. The system verification tester will learn, at a minimum, the operational and external aspects of the component. Familiarity with messages, external interfaces, commands, and configuration options are a given—they must understand these in order to exercise the code within the SVT environment. However, don't be fooled into believing that all system verification testers are aware of only the operational aspects of the component. On the contrary, many also know detailed module control flow, structures, and so on, very much in line with function verification testers.

The Component Assessment

When the test plan is being developed, all of the component spies will complete a component assessment. Key technical leaders within the test organization can use their experience to build an assessment template of key questions that each component spy must answer. The assessment will cover the component in depth, addressing its functionality, history, test coverage, and strengths and weaknesses. The component spies will all come together to present the results of their detailed assessment in a conference of their peers. These presentations provide education for all testers. Each will gain insight into areas in which they are not experts, and will watch for entanglements with their own components. The conference also provides an excellent forum for discussing the best approach to use in testing each component within the context of the overall software package. And the interaction between team members and the key technical leaders of the testing organization helps ensure the team is not heading down a path that it may later regret.

These sessions also help identify weaknesses in test coverage within the component, as well as strengths. The test leaders and management team can then use this information to make skill and personnel adjustments to the team, leading to a more comprehensive test. It is important to keep in mind that the thoroughness of the assessment and its information depends on the experience of the tester performing the work. Naturally, not all will have attained the same degree of expertise. That's okay. The act of performing the assessment and participating in the review boosts everyone's skills, while at the same time exposing all testers to research across a wide array of software components they couldn't possible have time to study independently.

Component Basics

The questions to be answered during the component assessment cover a broad range of the component's characteristics. Initially, the assessment focuses on the basics.

Technical Description

The assessment begins with an overview of the component and what it tries to accomplish.

Functions

All of the functions the component provides are described. This should include both external *and* internal functions. Some components may be so large that they themselves are almost minisystems. In that situation, the discussion can include a description of how the component breaks down into subcomponents, if applicable. In turn, an analysis of these subcomponents and their characteristics and functions should then be included in this phase of the assessment.

Where Does it Fit?

To fully explain a component, the tester needs to discuss where it fits into the overall software package and what role it plays. Some components may be required for operation at initialization time. For example, a Web application server's startup processing proceeds through multiple components to establish a working platform on which applications can then execute. Also, application services provide interfaces to programs and programmers for exploitation and deployment, and diagnostic components lay the foundation for identifying problems when they arise. Describing where their component fits helps the spy better show its importance to the "big picture"—the total solution.

Dependencies

Another key piece to solving the component puzzle is to understand its interdependencies with other components and products. There will be services that a component will rely on to exploit the full capability of the system. These services and functions are provided by other software components and by technologies within the hardware platform or software infrastructure. The component under assessment can also be providing services to others. Explaining the dependencies in both directions gives the other testers more perspective on where the component fits into the picture and what it provides to end users.

Outage-causing Capability

The component spy also needs to clearly describe the component's potential to cause an *outage*. An outage is a slowdown or complete shutdown of the availability of an application, subsystem, full system, or system cluster. The component assessment probes into how the component could potentially cause such outages. With this knowledge, the team can devise focused tests to expose weaknesses in these and any related areas.

Component Size and Language

The size of the component, in terms of volume of code, provides a pertinent view of the broadness of functionality. That, coupled with the source programming language(s) from which the component is comprised, can hint at potential complexities. For example, the presence of low-level assembler language code may point to performance-sensitive areas. On the other hand, if the programs or modules of the component are built using C++, then it is likely that there are abstractions or object-oriented models in use that would indicate a different type of complexity.

Component Age

When existing software is being enhanced, it is helpful to discuss the age of the component in question and/or the version of the software in which it was introduced. This information helps testers see how deep regression testing must be.

Recent Changes

With existing software, the modifications made to the component over the past few releases should be reviewed during the component assessment, including the specific release numbers and nature of the changes. This history lesson provides the whole team with a valuable overview of the component's function and role over time.

Planned Enhancements

The spy is also asked to describe the enhancements planned for the component. By communication with designers and developers, the tester gains comprehensive knowledge about what changes are coming along and the problems they are designed to solve, and shares this insight with the entire test team. This part of the assessment tends to lead to discussions about new testing approaches or modifications to existing approaches.

Competition

When working with a commercial product, testers need to consider the competition. The existence of competitive products is also a key piece of information that the spy should bring to the component assessment. A deeper investigation of a competitor's product and its functions helps everyone see the many ways a technical problem can be solved. This knowledge can result in a better test plan, especially in cases where the testers are attempting to solve the same technical issues.

Test Coverage

As we've seen, the assessment basics provide the team with an excellent overview of the component, how it fits into the system, its primary function within the system, and its key dependencies. But, a spy must offer more than just this basic knowledge of the component. Testing insight is also critical.

Functional Breakdown

Testers assess coverage by breaking down the component into its major pieces. They answer key questions about each function to help identify the type of testing techniques and methodologies that should be used against it, including:

- Does the component get adequately tested by normal system operation and natural exploitation?
- Are there record/playback script workloads to drive various functions of the component?
- Are there batch workloads, containing many test programs, that can be used to exercise the component?
- Are there manual scenario-driven tests that should be executed as part of component coverage?
- Are there any ported test cases that can be obtained from a prior test phase?

Frequency of Workload Execution

How often are the various workloads, scripts, and scenarios planned to be executed against the component? Are they targeted for once per integrated deliverable, once per release cycle? Or, are they to be used as background noise while other test scenarios are performed? Understanding this frequency allows the test team to make appropriate adjustments to workload execution frequency.

Functional Coverage

The tester is asked to describe which structural aspects of the component are covered by the tests, workloads, and scripts that are to be used against each function provided by the component. These might include initialization, mainline processing, recovery, and migration or coexistence.

Strengths and Weaknesses of Test Coverage

In addition to the critical set of questions on coverage *content*, the tester needs to discuss with the team when the test coverage was *last enhanced* for the component. This is done to identify ways to leverage those enhancements. The remaining test team members will provide their opinions on the appropriateness and strength of the coverage.

Defect Analysis

That's a lot of information already. But an overview of the component, its capabilities, and the planned test coverage is not quite enough to complete the component assessment.

For existing software, an extremely important aspect of ensuring that the test team is protecting its customers is through a defect escape analysis of the component under discussion. The scope of the review must focus on several key areas.

Defect Rate

How many defects have been found by customers in comparison to the size of the component? This, or whatever defect metric the product team uses, provides a means by which the component's quality can be tracked and understood. From a tester's perspective, this could become a measuring stick to use over time for understanding test effectiveness. Does the defect rate decline over time? Might it be dropping because of improved test coverage?

The Top Defects

In order to get a grip on the most significant defects within the component in question, testers are asked to describe the top defects external customers have found with the component. They are also asked to elaborate on three properties of the defects. These include whether these problems caused critical situations or outages for customers, an explanation as to why previous testing didn't find the problem, and what could have been done by test to help uncover this problem originally. This type of information can give the testers a target to shoot for to improve component coverage.

Areas of Improvement

Finally, the tester analyzes the results of the assessment to identify potential areas of improvement. By identifying critical escapes, and exploring the test coverage for the component and its new and existing functions, the tester can articulate the current and future work plans needed for improvement, thereby increasing and enhancing the component's test coverage. Finally, the testers are tempted with one last question, "If you had an open checkbook, what would you recommend be done to improve the testing of this component and its functions?" The answer to this final question helps to steer the team's discussion toward what can reasonably be accomplished.

Team Benefits

Think of the component assessment information as a treasure map in the search for the true pirate's hoard—bugs. By using this divide-and-conquer strategy, the overwhelming task of trying to discover all the nuances of interaction between different components suddenly becomes manageable. As we discussed up front, such a process is probably overkill for many software projects. But for the true monsters of complexity, it can be a life saver.

But the value of establishing component spies and engaging in a component assessment review doesn't end with the creation of a great test plan. The component assessment is also an excellent means of building educational and training resources. By gathering and documenting this information, the tester provides for the future of the entire test team. When its time for the tester to move on, results of the prior component assessment offer a great way for a new tester to get his first exposure to what the component is all about.

The Power of Spying

When a tester builds deep technical knowledge of a component, his expertise benefits the test organization in two ways. The first is that it enables him and his team to develop the most comprehensive test plans possible. The second is that, with this component expertise, test team members can call on one another during the execution phase for help in diagnosing complex, system-wide issues. Taken together, these two benefits allow the test team to leverage their expertise to solve the software complexity problem.

SHARING EXPERTISE ACROSS THE TEAM

In addition to gaining expertise in particular software components, system testers are usually knowledgeable about system operation across different platforms. Some testers will have an in-depth understanding of scripting languages and automation techniques. Still others will have debugging skills or specialized platform knowledge. How can the test organization leverage all of this knowledge to complete the attack on complexity? It can use approaches that pull those skills together as a team in meaningful ways to address specific problems. Here are some examples.

Theme-based Testing

A thorough system or integration test plan for industrial-strength software must provide end-to-end coverage that might go beyond one specific product to span functions, subsystems, and platforms. For example, a Web application server test could involve interactions between multiple Web servers, databases, transaction monitors, firewalls, intrusion detection systems, user registries, authorization and authentication mechanisms, workload routers, and operating system platforms (singly and clustered). In addition, each of these could be involved in activities such as daily operation, data backup, and system maintenance. How can the test team create a set of realistic, complex scenarios for an environment like this?

It requires pooling of expertise. Specifically, a strategy team, made up of senior testers and component spies, can be assembled that contains expertise in all the key areas and has the objective of building cross-component and cross-system scenarios that emulates a customer environment.

Building the Strategy

In order to build an effective test strategy for complex problems, each expert must educate the others on the strategy team about the functions that will be provided in the new software release. Additional experts can be brought into the discussion as needed to provide key technical knowledge and information to all involved. On one hand, this review will be broader than the component assessment because it considers dependent and corequisite products beyond the particular software under test. On the other hand, it will also be tighter by focusing more narrowly on how the new or changed software solves specific, discrete problems.

Once the technical review phase is complete, the strategy team then turns to determining how these discrete new solutions can be combined to help resolve a more complex business problem. The purpose of this process is to define *release themes*. Examples of these themes are security, systems management, and constraint relief. These themes then form the basis of the SVT.

Once the themes are defined, component owners and experts work together to fill in the details. They define the flow of test scenarios across the various components within each theme. By using the expertise of component spies and experts, the strategy team can assemble very complex scenarios that are aligned with expected customer usage. This is especially true when software components, products, and even hardware components and systems must come together to create a complete, end-to-end solution. The theme-based scenarios ensure that the critical paths that wind among all these pieces are exercised in realistic ways. This approach is just one example of how a team can leverage different expertise from across a test organization to solve a complex problem.

Cooperative Problem Diagnosis

Given the degree of complexity of many systems, problem diagnosis is, at best, challenging. When problems are encountered during test shifts, they can range from issues isolated to a specific component where the impact is clear, to issues where isolation seems impossible and the failing component cannot be determined at that time. It is against this backdrop that the test team needs to leverage the expertise it has built.

The first step is to identify the symptoms and then interpret those symptoms until they point to an initial component to investigate. Once that component is identified, the system verification tester can call on his colleagues' experience to hypothesize on what may be occurring. This is where all of the knowledge from the component assessment and component expertise comes into play. The testers can then examine the symptoms from the perspective of the component in question to see if anything appears to be awry, or if they can point to another component based on interface data that seems inconsistent. As the collective set of testers (i.e., component spies) begins to build a picture of what occurred during the execution of the failing scenario, the isolation of the component in error becomes more manageable. Complexity is again dissolved by a divide-and-conquer approach.

SUMMARY

For cases where the complexity of software is enormous, testers need to work together and make use of everyone's expertise to build effective and comprehensive test plans. Since one tester cannot possibly know everything about such software, leveraging the technical expertise of component spies and senior test leaders is a great way to generate a result that will delight your customers.

Now that you have finished the investigation stage, you are ready to begin the creation phase. Chapter 7, "Test Plan Focus Area," describes one such creation—the test plan.

7 Test Plan Focus Areas

In This Chapter

- Who test plans are *really* for, and how they're structured
- Unit Test focus areas
- Function Verification Test focus areas
- System Verification Test focus areas
- Integration Test focus areas
- Special considerations for multisystem testing
- Test Cases versus Scenarios
- Why every tester should love test plan reviews

Can you spend just a few minutes reading about new, upcoming software features and then immediately begin creating your formal plan to test them? Perhaps, but the result will likely not be worthy of a professional tester. The initial investigative work discussed in earlier chapters lays the essential groundwork for creating a solid testing strategy. Once you've researched the entity you're about to test, examined reports of past tests of similar function, met with the experts, studied potential customer usage, and compared notes with other test teams, then it's finally time to put together a detailed test plan.

THE TEST PLAN DOCUMENT

A test plan has several different consumers. Product developers use it to satisfy themselves that their code will be properly tested. Other testers on your team, or other test teams (either before or after you in the development cycle), use it to eliminate overlap and ensure that you all share an understanding of hand-offs, entry and exit criteria, and so on. New testers might use a test plan as an educational tool. Product release managers track progress against it. Auditors use it to determine if you know what you're doing. If the ultimate consumer of what you're testing has access to your test plan (for example, if you are all in the same company), then they'll use it to assess if deployment will go smoothly.

Who Is It Really For?

With all of these people wanting to get their hands on your test plan, it's important not to lose sight of the person to whom it is most important: namely you, the tester. A good test plan lets you crystallize your method of attack and scope out the true work effort in front of you. It offers a trail map to follow as you get lost in the daily jungle of tests and bugs, and a yardstick for measuring your progress. Also, by putting something down on paper, others have an opportunity to fill in any holes you might not have realized existed. Finally, documenting all tests allows you to easily reuse and build on them in the future if needed, so your work is repeatable.

However, as useful as it is, a test plan is just that: a plan. It represents a testing strategy based on the best knowledge available at the outset of a project. It's not a carved stone tablet revealing divine knowledge that is immune to change. As the test progresses, more will be learned about the software's strengths, weaknesses, and vulnerabilities. Ignoring that additional insight would be foolish; rather, it should be anticipated and exploited. Adaptive development models take advantage of this premise, but its usefulness is applicable to more traditional models as well. The key is simply to build flexibility into the test plan up front, so that adjustments can be made in real time as experiences are gained.

One technique for dealing with this flexibility is to reserve time in the plan for a set of *artistic* test scenarios. Artistic testing is guided by the intuition and investigative instincts of the tester, based on experiences with the software acquired during initial, more structured testing. In Chapter 15, "Test Execution," we'll examine artistic scenarios in more detail. Their inclusion in a test plan is essentially a place holder against which time and resources can be allocated. Their content will be devised dynamically as they are executed, once the actual test is well underway.

Structure

What does a test plan consist of? Figure 7.1 shows a sample SVT template. There's nothing magical about this template, and you may choose to delete sections or add others. *IEEE Standard 829-1998 for Software Test Documentation* [IEEE829] defines a more complex template. Some FVT plans are little more than lists of test scenarios or variations (unit test rarely has even that much). Ultimately, the test plan is merely a document. It takes the output of the real work of test planning and packages it. What's important is for that package to be sufficiently complete and digestible enough to be useful to its primary consumers—yourself, other testers, and

- Document Control
  - Distribution
  - Approvers/Reviewers
  - Change History
- Overview
  - Project Summary
  - Overall Test Goals and Objectives
- Test Environment
  - Hardware Configuration
  - Software Configuration
- Tools and Workloads
  - Test Tools
  - Base Workloads
- Administration
  - Test Assumptions and Dependencies
  - Entrance and Exit Criteria
  - Status Tracking Approach
  - Problem Reporting and Tracking Approach
  - Maintenance Strategy
  - Deliverables
- Schedule
- Test Matrices and Scenarios

FIGURE 7.1   Sample test plan template.

those reviewers with the skill, knowledge, and experience to suggest improvements that will help you find more bugs or add other value. Anything more than that is a waste of paper.

Front Matter

Everything in our example template except for the very last line is what we call *front matter*. Most of it will be boilerplate information that can be reused from test to test with only minor modifications. Some of it (such as information on configurations and workloads) is useful to reviewers to give them some context for your plans. Other parts help ensure different teams are in sync. Good entrance criteria are important for ensuring the team doesn't waste time by starting with software that isn't yet ready, and good exit criteria tell you when you're done. Identifying dependencies on specific hardware assets or software products and dates when they are needed will help line things up. The schedule section is certainly optional, since in any commercial project there will be detailed schedules that are tracked by project managers using their own charts and tools. But some folks like to include a few high-level schedule milestones in their test plan as a reference point for themselves and reviewers.

Other sources describe variations on this front matter in great detail, but we won't do so here. It typically covers the entire test team, and so is usually developed and maintained by the test team leader. Other team members don't spend much time contemplating front matter. Their focus is entirely on that innocent looking last line, for that is where the true core of the test plan lies: the test matrices and scenarios.

Test Matrices and Scenarios

This section of the plan lists the actual scenarios each tester plans to execute. While typically the detailed scenario descriptions will be stored in an online test management tool, it's often a good idea to summarize them in the test plan document in order to expedite reviews. We'll discuss reviews a little later, but for now, just realize that the very experts you will want to comment on your plan are almost invariably overwhelmed with work. Asking them to weed through an arcane database they aren't familiar with in order to find each of your scenarios is an approach destined to get your plan ignored.

The truth is, if you want people to review your work, you must make doing so as easy as possible—not for you, but for them. For that reason, summarizing your scenarios in the test plan document is a very effective approach. Try creating a brief description for each scenario—often a single line is sufficient to convey a scenario's essence. By listing these one-liners together in your document, you'll provide a concise view of your proposed test coverage that will help reviewers quickly identify trends and spot weaknesses.

Matrices that summarize coverage of key tests across different hardware or software environments can further condense and highlight important information. If you use these techniques, always provide a pointer to the test management tool (or wherever your detailed scenarios descriptions live) as well, so ambitious reviewers can study the specifics. A cleverly designed test management tool would even allow you to extract scenario summary descriptions so you could drop them directly into the test plan document without having to retype them. In fact, some such tools allow you to package your detailed scenario descriptions as simple HTML documents, further easing reviewer access.

How Much Detail?

You may wonder how much information should go into the detailed scenario descriptions, wherever they live. There are two schools of thought. The first is to document each scenario in explicit detail. This *cookbook scenario* approach has the virtue of completely capturing all relevant knowledge. It has the disadvantage of demanding huge amounts of time—in some cases, the time spent generating the documentation could be longer than what's required to actually execute the test. This approach is sometimes used by teams where there are a small number of highly skilled testers (who become the plan writers) and a large number of inexperienced testers (who become the plan executors).

The second approach is to jot down only enough high-level information to remind the tester of everything he wants to cover within that scenario. This *framework scenario* technique captures the activity's essence, but trusts the tester to work through the specific steps required. It is frequently used when there is a broad level of skill across the team, so that every tester writes his own scenario descriptions. It saves a great deal of time that can then be applied to researching and executing the test, rather than sitting at a keyboard. Figure 7.2 shows an example of a framework scenario.

We recommend the latter approach, even in cases where there are many inexperienced testers on the team. Certainly the team leader and other experienced testers will need to review what the newer folks come up with, but what better way for the newbies to take ownership of their work and build skills than to do this test planning themselves?

Test Considerations and Variations

A related technique is to start by creating a test *considerations list*. These considerations are one-liners that identify key areas of concern that should be the test's focus. No results or specific test procedure steps should be included. The intent is simply to create a quick outline of the work to be done. This list can then help the team estimate at a gross level the number of tests that need to be performed prior to spending a lot of time creating the formal test plan.

Title:	**RDBR0051: Relational Database Software Server Failure**
Objective:	Explore the failure and automated recovery of database server software while a heavy transactional workload is running.
Test Scenario:	Set up an automation policy to restart the database server software in the event of a failure. Start a workload that executes transactions which read from and write to the database. Cancel the database server.
Expected Results:	Database server shuts down. Associated transactions are backed out. Shared locks are registered. Automation restarts the server. Transaction manager reconnects to the database and locks are cleared. Normal transaction processing resumes.

FIGURE 7.2   Example framework scenario.

A first pass at creating the considerations list is done by looking at the software from the outside, noting all of its inputs, outputs and actions, and adding them to the list. Then the team pulls back the covers and examines the actual modules that make up the software component. They look for key internals such as serialization points, resource access, and recovery support, and add them as appropriate to the considerations list. An example test considerations list is shown in Figure 7.3. This list covers a particular product's ability to process configuration parameters that would be read during its initialization. A subset of those parameters could also be dynamically reloaded later to change the product's behavior on the fly.

Once the test considerations list has been outlined, a list of *variations* for each test consideration will be developed. These variations represent the actual technical plan of attack on the function and form the core of the test plan. They describe in more detail the conditions that need to occur to drive a specific code path, as well as the expected results. Figure 7.4 shows a sample variations list that was derived from a portion of the earlier considerations list.

Server Configuration File Test Considerations
<u>Load/Initialization</u>
Each keyword:
–keyword not specified
–value not specified
–minimum value
–maximum value
–less than minimum
–greater than maximum
–other invalid
–special

<u>Reload</u>
Each reloadable keyword:
–not specified
–valid
–invalid
Nonreloadable keywords not reloaded
All keywords changed in one Reload

<u>General (load and reload)</u>
–comments
–duplicate keywords
–config file not found
–only keywords without defaults specified
–all keywords with defaults have errors (multiple errors)
–unknown keywords
–empty config file

FIGURE 7.3 Example test considerations list.

Once completed, the team would send the variations list out for review. Many FVT teams in particular have had success using this considerations/variations technique for creating their test plan.

Content

What should test scenarios or variations focus on? It depends. Different test phases are most efficient and effective at finding different types of defects, so they should focus their testing in those areas. This is true regardless of how a given development model may have arranged those test phases. Let's take a look at the key test plan focus areas for four different test phases: unit test, function verification test, system verification test, and integration test.

Configuration File Reload

Keyword Name	Old Value	New Value	Expected Result
THREADS_NUMBER			
–keyword not specified	30	–	old value used (Message 11)
–valid	16 (min)	47	new value used (Message 11)
–valid	75 (max)	16 (min)	new value used (Message 11)
–invalid	31	0	old value used, Message issued (Message 8, 11)
MT.TIMEOUT			
–keyword not specified	15	–	old value used (Message 11)
–valid	10 (min)	300	new value used (Message 11)
–valid	720 (max)	10 (min)	new value used (Message 11)
–invalid	120	721	old value used, Message issued (Message 8, 11)
–invalid	51	A	old value used, Message issued (Message 9, 11)
TRACE_LEVEL			
–keyword not specified	2	–	old value used, (Message 11)
–valid	0 (min)	2	new value used (Message 11)
–valid	4 (max)	0 (min)	new value used (Message 11)
–invalid	3	5	old value used, Message issued (Message 8, 11)
TRACE_BUFFERSIZE			
–keyword not specified	128	–	old value used, (Message 11)
–valid	64 (min)	1024	new value used (Message 11)
–valid	16384 (max)	64 (min)	new value used (Message 11)
–valid (special)	136	75	new rounded up value used (Message 11)
–invalid	1028	6K	old value used, Message issued (Message 9, 11)

FIGURE 7.4   Example test variations list.

UNIT TEST FOCUS AREAS

The unit test of a module is performed by the developer who wrote it prior to merging that module into the overall development stream. The goal of unit test is simply to ensure that all the obvious bugs are removed before anyone but the developer sees the code. It is achieved by forcing the execution of every new and changed line of code, taking all branches, driving all loops to conclusion, exercising all object behaviors, and so forth. Typically, this is accomplished by the developer stepping through the code, setting breakpoints, and forcing the necessary conditions. A documented plan isn't necessary in order to achieve this goal, and frankly adds little value.

That's not to imply that unit test isn't important—quite the contrary. Unit test clears out the underbrush of obvious defects and thereby allows for a smooth integration of the module into the development stream. It also enables the function verification test team to focus on the next level of defects. Naturally, it's in the developer's best interest to do as thorough a job of unit test as possible; after all, the more defects he can extract during unit test, the less he will be bothered later by testers who are proud to find another bug.

FUNCTION VERIFICATION TEST FOCUS AREAS

Once the developers of various modules have merged them into a common build stream, it's time to move beyond the single-module domain of unit test and into the more complex area of Function Verification Test (FVT). The scope of the FVT is that of a complete, yet containable functional area or component within the overall software package. There are several focus areas typically targeted in an FVT. Let's examine them.

Mainline Function

A major part of FVT is to see if the program correctly does the big things it's supposed to do. In other words, testing its mainline function. If it's an online bookstore application, you would define scenarios to browse categories, search for books by title or author, put items in your shopping basket, check out, and so on. Conceptually, what you need to cover in mainline testing is fairly obvious; though doing a good job of it requires careful study of the program in question and a solid understanding of likely customer usage patterns and environments in which it must survive. Mainline testing overlaps with some of the other areas listed later, although they are all special areas of focus in their own right.

Security Support

Security support is part of mainline function, but it is so important (and sometimes misunderstood), that it's worth calling out separately. There are multiple security features that may be incorporated into a piece of software:

Authentication: Confirming that a user is who he claims to be, through the use of a user ID and password combination, token, biometric, or similar approach

Authorization: Limiting an authenticated user's access to permitted areas only, through an access control mechanism

Confidentiality: Hiding private information from public view, usually through encryption

Integrity: Ensuring that information was not altered in transit, by using such tools as Message Digest 5 (MD5) sums

Nonrepudiation: Preventing a sender of a message from later claiming he didn't send it, through digital signatures or similar techniques

The use of Secure Sockets Layer (SSL) encryption to protect the confidentiality of data flowing across the wire from a user's browser to a merchant's Web site has become pervasive—so much so that sometimes people believe SSL is all there is to security. But what good is the SSL-protected transmission of a customer's credit card number to an online bookstore if it is stored there on a publicly accessible database? Or, if *any* user can gain access to a customer's account information?

During FVT, it's important to thoroughly exercise all security mechanisms just as you would other mainline functions. Check that users are properly authenticated during sign-on, can only access the account data they are authorized for, that encryption is doing its job, and so forth. It's also important to look at security from the outside in, as an invader might. Any software running in production environments may someday come under attack. This is not only true for external Web-facing applications exposed to hackers or terrorists—surveyed companies continually attribute a big chunk of security breaches to their own authorized users or employees [Hulme03].

System security testing, also called *penetration* or *vulnerability testing* is an art unto itself. To discover a program's vulnerabilities, you'll need to learn to think like an intruder. You must search for any unintended behaviors in the program that allow you to bypass its armor and do things you shouldn't be able to do. Generating buffer overflows, forcing the program to use corrupt files, faking sources of data, sabotaging the flow of a communication protocol, and dozens of other tricks are the name of the game here.

A quick Internet search on "hacking tools" will find a bounty of programs used by (or sometimes against) the bad guys. Some may be useful for your testing, or at least get you thinking in the right direction. Entire books have been written on this topic. For an excellent introduction to the ins and outs of security testing, see Whittaker and Thompson [Whittaker03].

Software Interfaces

There are several different classes of software interfaces to consider.

Private Module-to-Module Interfaces

In order to do their job, all of the various pieces of a given functional area or component must communicate with each other through a set of interfaces. These interfaces often consist of nothing more than passing parameters through call stacks. But they can also include techniques such as the establishment and modification of more complex control structures in some shared storage area. Since FVT is the first place where all of the pieces come together, one of its goals is to test the interfaces. Ideally this is done by studying the module interactions and understanding what conditions are needed to fully exercise them, then creating scenarios to drive those conditions through external stimuli (e.g., executing a command or invoking an API). Unfortunately, for some interfaces this may prove difficult to accomplish, and the function tester will need to resort to artificially rigging conditions to force their execution. But this practice is less realistic and should be minimized.

Private Component-to-Component Interfaces

In addition, a given component will often need to communicate with other components, also through a set of interfaces. These interfaces could be simple programmatic approaches as mentioned earlier, or more complex network-oriented methods such as TCP/IP sockets or Remote Procedure Call (RPC). Regardless, if those other components have already been merged into the common build stream, testing is similar to the single component case.

However, in large software projects, all components may not be ready at once—typically they vary in size and complexity and so might be staged in over time. But if other components are not yet in place when you start your FVT, how do you test your side of the interfaces? You may need to resort to erecting scaffolding around the component, as described in Chapter 3, "The Development Process." This approach is only useful for preliminary testing, and the scenarios being exposed cannot be considered complete until real components sit on both sides of each interface. But the use of scaffolding allows you to execute tests much earlier than you otherwise could.

Application Programming Interfaces (APIs)

Components that are intended to be invoked from other, external programs will provide one or more public APIs. An API could be in the form of an RPC call as mentioned earlier, a macro interface, or another mechanism. But because these APIs are intended to be used by programs outside the software package under test, they can always be invoked entirely via external stimuli (e.g., test programs using the APIs), easing the test requirements.

Simply invoking the API multiple times using all of its options and combinations is certainly one area that a test plan must address. However, with extremely complex APIs, complete coverage of all combinations may not be realistic or cost effective. Some researchers even advocate the use of mathematical algorithms and tools to limit the number of combinations that need to be tried to provide adequate test coverage.

But focusing only on invocations may not be sufficient. To do a complete test, you might need to include scenarios that invoke the API while other environmental conditions are tugging at the component, such as a memory shortage, I/O bottleneck, or an error recovery situation. Also, the test case's state when the API is invoked should be varied. For example, is there a mechanism for authorizing the test case to invoke the API? Are only Kernel-mode programs allowed to use it? The more you understand about the various pressures the component may find itself in, and the more devious you are, the longer your list of API-related FVT scenarios will become.

Human Interfaces

In addition to communicating with other components, some functions will need to communicate with humans as well. This communication can take several forms. Let's briefly look at several.

Graphical User Interface (GUI)

A GUI interface can be a complex beast with a seemingly endless array of screens, pop-ups, and mouse clicks. You must obtain or create a map of all the possible paths through the GUI, then try them all. Use both valid inputs and ones that don't follow the rules. Ensure clicked-on functions are carried out correctly, without unintended side effects.

GUI testing can be time consuming. There are tools available from various vendors to help automate the task, but beware: while tools that record your key strokes and mouse clicks into a script for automated replay offer a lure of quick payback, that promise can be misleading. If every time there are minor changes to the GUI you must rerecord your scripts, you may spend more time doing script maintenance than you save via the automation. A better approach is to create a framework for these scripts that separates the intent of each test case from the screen navigation logic used to implement it. This can represent a significant (and costly) development effort, so it pays to establish up front how likely it is you'll see this cost recouped over the life of the software being tested. But done properly, for the right situation, GUI automation tools can be very effective.

Line-mode Commands

In addition to GUIs, most software products have the capability of being manipulated through line-mode commands. While these commands are often handy for the experienced user who has tired of wading through GUI screens, their primary value is probably for automation. Line-mode commands can be included in automation routines ranging from simple shell scripts to much more sophisticated vendor tools.

As with GUIs, testing line-mode commands is conceptually simple but time consuming. Every option and combination of options must be tested, including those combinations that are invalid. Your goal isn't simply to try all these options, but to ensure you obtain the desired result—and *only* the desired result.

Messages

Most large software packages issue messages to indicate both success and failure. You must define scenarios to force out every possible message. In some cases, this will be easy to do. For others it may be quite tricky, especially for some of the failure messages. Nevertheless, each message represents a path through the code, and must be exercised. For particularly thorny cases, the preferred approach of using external stimuli to create the necessary conditions may not be practical, so conditions may need to be rigged to force out the desired message. But this should be the exception rather than the rule.

Naturally, it's also important to validate the contents of each message. Are its contents accurate? Is it useful in the context in which it's displayed? Does it provide the necessary information to allow the user to take appropriate action? Scrutinize each message from the perspective of an unknowledgeable user to identify areas of potential confusion. Also, if the messages are supposed to follow a predefined standard, check to see if they have done so. Some automation and monitoring tools depend on standard message formats.

Error Codes and Dumps

In addition to messages, a sophisticated software package will issue some error codes and memory dumps in response to nasty situations. In the mainframe world, they are called ABEND (ABnormal END) codes, and each is associated with a dump and a recovery routine that cleans up any mess and allows the component to continue. In other systems, they are called *errno* values or something similar. Just as with error messages, the tester must plan to generate conditions that force the software package to issue every defined error code.

Logs and Traces

Software packages can often write a great deal of information to logs and trace files for use in diagnosing problems. The volume of such data is normally user-selectable, ranging from brief to verbose. As with messages and error codes, you should plan to force out all defined logging and tracing information at each volume level, and ensure it is complete and correct. Unfortunately, this area is often overlooked by inexperienced testers, a fact that anyone who has attempted to weed through the gibberish in many trace files can attest.

One interesting example occurred several years ago in a very popular middleware application. The software included support for exploiting a hardware cryptographic feature. A customer had enabled the hardware feature, and wanted confirmation that the middleware application was in fact using it. The middleware product's support team instructed the customer to turn on a specific trace level, and then restart the product. That action should have forced a message to the trace log indicating whether or not the product was using hardware cryptography.

The customer complied, but was confused to find that not only did the trace log not have an entry indicating that cryptography *was* being used, it had no message saying it *wasn't* being used either! It turned out that the product was indeed using the hardware cryptography correctly, but there was a bug that suppressed its associated trace entry—something which had been overlooked during testing. A simple bug, but its escape led to customer confusion and use of the support team's expensive time. Don't fall victim to a similar omission in your FVT.

Limits

This one is less of a single focus area and more something that permeates many areas. It's not exclusive to FVT either, though it is critical to any good FVT. *Limits* testing (also known as *boundary condition* testing) simply means testing a piece of code to its defined limits, then a little bit more. In the movie *This is Spinal Tap*, a character proudly explains that while normal guitar amplifiers can only be turned up to "10," his can be turned up to "11." Limits testing is something like that. If an input parameter has allowable values ranging from one to ten, test it with a value of one, then with a value of ten, then with eleven (you would want to try it with zero and probably negative values as well). It should accept values in the allowable range, and reject values outside of that range.

It's not practical, or even worthwhile, to test every possible input value. Testing just around the limits is both sufficient and efficient. The same approach applies to many other situations, from loop exit triggers, to storage allocations, to the content of variable output messages. Always test the limits.

Recovery

Recovery testing during FVT explores any support the software has for addressing error situations. Can it restart cleanly after a failure? Does it self-heal? Can it recover successfully from error conditions it anticipates? What about those it doesn't anticipate? Does it provide adequate diagnostic data?

Recovery testing is an area that is often either overlooked completely or given inadequate attention. This is odd, because not only is recovery support usually rich in bugs, it's also fun to test. And given the inevitability of errors, recoverability may be a software package's most vital characteristic for ensuring high availability. The next chapter is devoted entirely to this exciting area.

Internationalization

If the software you are testing is a commercial product, it most likely will undergo translation for sale in multiple countries. The implications go beyond simply translating text. A keyboard's keys vary from country to country. Sorting by ASCII values may not make sense in some languages. Time and date formats differ. Some languages require more space than others to describe the same thing, so menus, dialog boxes, and other user interfaces may need to be adjusted. The list of considerations, and their corresponding scenarios, can grow quite long. Thorough testing of these functional aspects of the internationalization support is usually done during FVT, and frequently can be accomplished without the need for testers to understand the different languages being supported.

In addition to the functional aspects of the internationalization support, there's also the accuracy of the translated text to consider. The first time a product undergoes translation for a new language, thorough testing is usually in order. That requires testers fluent in the language at hand, and it often makes sense to outsource that testing to specialists in the target country. Depending on what has changed, subsequent releases may only require a brief review. See Kaner, et al. [Kaner99] for more detail on testing for internationalization.

Accessibility

Testing for accessibility determines if the software will be usable by people with disabilities. There should be keyboard equivalents for all mouse functions to accommodate blind people or those with limited hand use who cannot accurately position a mouse. Visual cues should be available for all audio alerts to accommodate those who are deaf or hard of hearing. Color should not be the sole means of conveying information or indicating an action, to accommodate blind and colorblind people. Every window, object, and control should be labeled so that screen-reading software can describe it. Documentation should be available in an accessible format.

If software is intended to be accessible, the development team will probably have followed a checklist of accessibility techniques and requirements from either industry or government, such as one available from the United States government [USGOV1]. The same checklist can be useful for generating test scenarios. Testing techniques include using the same tools as disabled users will, such as keyboards and screen readers. Printing GUI screens in black and white is useful for detecting if any information they communicate is not discernible without the use of color. Commercial tools are also available to aid with accessibility testing. IBM has a detailed accessibility checklist available on the Web, along with rationale and testing techniques for each item [IBM03].

SYSTEM VERIFICATION TEST FOCUS AREAS

System Verification Test, or SVT, is the point where the entire package comes together for the first time, with all components working together to deliver the project's intended purpose. It's also the point where we move beyond the lower-level, more granular tests of FVT, and into tests that take a more global view of the product or system. SVT is also the land of load and stress. When the code under test eventually finds itself in a real production environment, heavy loads will be a way of life. That means that with few exceptions, *no SVT scenario should be considered complete until it has been run successfully against a backdrop of load/stress.*

The system tester is also likely the first person to interact with the product as a customer will. Indeed, once the SVT team earns a strong reputation, the development team may begin to view them as their first customer. This broader view influences the focus areas of the SVT plan. Let's take a look at several of those areas.

Installation

Naturally, before you can test new software you must install it. But installation testing goes beyond a single install. You'll need scenarios to experiment with multiple options and flows across a variety of hardware environments and configurations. In fact, this testing could be done during FVT rather than SVT if the FVT team has access to the right mixture of system configurations. Regardless of when the testing is done, after each installation it's important to exercise the software to see if it's truly whole and operable. Uninstall scenarios should be covered as well, as should the ability to upgrade a prior release to the new one, if supported. Your customer's first impression of the software will come at install time—make sure it's a good one.

Regression

The idea behind regression testing is simple: see if things that used to work still do. Production users insist on this kind of continuity. Testing is required because whenever new function is introduced into a product, it almost inevitably intersects and interacts with existing code—and that means it tends to break things. This is what Kenney and Vouk refer to as a new release of software *stimulating* the discovery of defects in old code [Kenney92].

Note that some in the testing field also describe a regression test as the rerunning of a test that previously found a bug in order to see if a supplied fix works. However, we prefer the term *fix test* for that activity.

Regression testing is best accomplished through a collection of test cases whose execution is automated through a tool. These test cases come from past tests, of course. It's hard to imagine something more effective at discovering if an old function still works than the test cases that were used to expose that function in the first place.

Evolving Roles

There are two roles regression testing can play in SVT. First, an automated collection, or *bucket*, of old test cases makes an excellent first workload to run at the beginning of SVT. It can serve as an acceptance test to determine if the code meets a predefined stability baseline. By definition, the regression workload won't *explicitly* exercise any of the new (and probably unstable) code. But, it may *implicitly* test updates to existing function. This is particularly true for functions that provide services or support for the rest of the software package (such as an operating system's lock manager). So, regression testing is a great tool for assessing fundamental stability before you proceed to more complex and stressful testing.

But once this initial testing is complete, should the regression workload go into hibernation until the beginning of the next test cycle? No! It can live a second life as a source of background stress upon which other tests are executed. As test cases for new functions are completed, they can be rolled into this existing regression bucket, or into a new regression bucket that's specific to this release. This ongoing test case integration ensures that code added to the product later in the SVT cycle (for additional features, fixes, etc.) doesn't break those already-tested functions—creating a living, ongoing regression test, at no additional cost to the team.

We strongly advocate integrating the regression bucket into daily SVT runs as one means of driving background load/stress. Such a bucket, built up over several releases, exercises a rich variety of paths, options, and features in the product. However, it will likely be only one of several means available for generating background stress. Indeed, some teams prefer to run the regression bucket on the side, outside of their mainstream tests, to ensure it is run continuously. That approach is often employed by FVT teams as well.

What If It's the First Time?

But what if the software under test is brand new? Obviously, in that case there isn't a regression workload available to run at SVT entry. But the test team should waste no time in constructing one. It can be used as the test progresses to ensure that tests which worked at the beginning of the SVT cycle still work at the end. Chapter 10, "The Magic of Reuse," discusses one way to jump-start this effort.

Migration/Coexistence

The intent of migration testing is to see if a customer will be able to transition smoothly from a prior version of the software to the new one. Which prior release? Ideally, all currently supported prior releases, though sometimes that isn't practical. If we call the new release under test "n", then at a minimum you'll need to test migration from release n-1 to n. It can also be productive to test migration from releases n-2 and n-3 as well. This gets especially interesting if the user will be allowed to migrate from, say, the n-3 release directly to the n release, without first moving through the interim releases, since the potential for trouble in this case is magnified. However, the longer n-1 has been available and the more pervasive its use, the less important it becomes to test older versions.

What exactly does migration testing consist of? It depends on the nature of the software being tested. For a database program, it includes making sure the new code can correctly access and process data created by the prior version. For an operating system, it includes ensuring you can upgrade to the new version without having to reinstall and reconfigure (or rewrite and recompile) existing applications. For a Web application server, it includes checking that the new version can coexist in a cluster with systems running the older version. In all cases, test scenarios should include ensuring that any documented steps for performing the upgrade process are complete and correct.

Load/Stress

As has been mentioned already, load/stress is the foundation upon which virtually all of SVT for multithreaded software is based, either as the primary focus or as a backdrop against which other tests are executed. In this section, we look at load/stress as a primary focus. This testing goes beyond any stress levels achieved during initial regression testing, reaching to the ultimate levels targeted for the project. There are two dimensions involved: *deep* and *wide*.

The Deep Dimension

This dimension primarily aims for throughput-related targets. You seek *timing and serialization* bugs (also called *race conditions*) that only extreme levels of stress will expose. Why does stress have this effect? If you've ever tried running anything on a busy server, you know that saturating the system with work slows everything down. Tasks competing for precious resources must wait in line longer than normal. This widens timing windows around multithreaded code that hasn't been correctly serialized, allowing bugs to reveal themselves.

The throughput targets you choose are up to you. Examples include:

- CPU utilization percentage
- I/O path utilization percentage
- I/O interrupts per second
- Transactions per second
- Number of simultaneously active processes
- Paging or swapping rate

Targets based on percentages of hardware utilization are probably the best, since they can remain constant over time, even as new hardware gets faster. But regardless of the targets chosen, your test plan should also be specific about what measurements will indicate the targets have been met. For example, you can list specific fields from a report produced by a performance monitoring tool.

What Kind of Workload?

Simply achieving throughput targets using a trivial program loop misses the mark. The point is to see how the software holds up under the most extreme real-world conditions, and to do that your workloads must simulate those of actual production environments. You should include an appropriate mix of workload types, running either concurrently, serially, or both.

For example, in the SVT of z/OS, workloads might include:

- A combination of batch jobs processing sorts and simulated time-sharing users editing files
- Simulated transaction-monitor users invoking transactions that read from, write to, and update a group of relational databases
- Simulated Web users generating HTML traffic to access back-end applications
- Test cases that repeatedly thrash through thousands of pages of memory to put pressure on the real storage manager and paging system

The first three cover wide swaths of the operating system support, while the fourth narrowly focuses its stress on one key area. All could be run individually to uncover the effects of a single, focused workload, or simultaneously to find problems arising from the resulting interactions. In the latter case, thought should be given to alternately raising or lowering the intensity (e.g., the number of users or threads) of each workload to further vary the mix.

Coping with Stability Problems

It's possible that you won't be able to reliably achieve your target load/stress levels with all workloads until the SVT is near its completion. This does not mean that you can't use load/stress as a backdrop for other testing in such a case. If the problems are intermittent, then they might not interfere significantly with other testing progress. Or, if the difficulties are confined to a subset of the stress workloads, simply refrain from running those workloads as background stress until the problems are resolved, and increase the intensity of the others. Barring that, you can also dial down the stress levels to achieve sufficient stability so that background stress problems don't interfere with other testing going on in the foreground. However, this is the least desirable option and so should be a last resort. It also suggests the need for a retest of the foreground tests once the stress issues are resolved.

The Wide Dimension

The wide dimension of load/stress testing addresses maximizing volumes and resource allocations. It's really a form of limits testing done on a system-wide scale while the program under test is processing real work. What might this include?

- For an application, the number of files that can be open concurrently or the size of an individual file
- For a database program, the count of distinct database tables that can be joined together, the size of each table, or the number of simultaneous users who can issue queries or updates
- For an online retail store, the ratio of browsers to buyers, the number of shopping carts that can be open at once, or the aggregate contents of individual carts
- For a file system, the sum of individual disks that can back a single instance
- For an operating system, the amount of real memory it can manage, simultaneous users it can handle, CPUs it can exploit, or other systems it can cluster with

Again, the objective in system test is not to push these limits through simplistic, artificial means, but rather by using realistic workloads that might be encountered in production environments. Also note that there's nothing wrong with driving both the deep and wide dimensions of load/stress at once; indeed, it is an effective approach. But it's useful to keep these different dimensions in mind as you build your test plan.

Mainline Function

This is similar to what is done in FVT, in that you are targeting new and changed functionality. But rather than narrowly focusing on function at the component level, your scope is expanded to view it end to end. Whereas in FVT you would exhaustively exercise every aspect of individual component interfaces, in SVT you should devise scenarios to exhaustively exercise the entire software package's supported tasks from an end-user perspective. You wouldn't try every combination of inputs to a system command. Rather, you would use that command to perform an action or, in concert with other commands, enact a chain of actions as a customer would. You'll want to check if complimentary functions work together appropriately. Of critical importance is performing these tests against a backdrop of heavy load/stress, because functions that seem to work fine in a lightly loaded FVT environment often fall apart in a high-stress SVT environment. We'll explore the contrast between FVT and SVT test case development in Chapter 11, "Developing Good Test Programs."

Hardware Interaction

This is really a special case of mainline function testing, but because of its tie-in with an expensive resource (hardware), it's worthwhile to document separately. There are really two aspects to this focus area. First, if the software under test has explicit support for a new piece of hardware, as is often the case for operating systems, emulators, and networking tools, then scenarios must be included to test that support.

Second, if the software has any implicit dependencies or assumptions about hardware that it will run on or interact with, then scenarios must be included to put those factors to the test. What do we mean by implicit dependencies or assumptions? For example:

- Timing loops based on processor clock speed
- Network bandwidth or latency dependencies
- Memory availability
- Multitasking on a uniprocessor versus a multiprocessor
- I/O latency
- Reliance on quirks in the *implementation* of an architecture or protocol

Unfortunately, it's not always apparent that software is making these implicit assumptions until it meets an unexpected hardware environment and causes mayhem. It is often good practice to test software across a range of available hardware environments to see how it reacts.

Recovery

Recovery testing is just as important in SVT as it is in FVT. However, in SVT the scope broadens from a component view to a full product view. The need to restart cleanly after a crash expands to consider system-wide failures. The impact of clustered systems and environmental failures begins to come into play. Recovery testing during SVT will be discussed in detail in Chapter 8, "Testing for Recoverability."

Serviceability

Errors are inevitable. Serviceability support responds to that fact by providing features such as logs, traces, and memory dumps to help debug errors when they arise. Thoroughness counts here. Customers take a dim view of repeated requests to recreate a problem so that it can be debugged, particularly if that problem causes an outage. They've already suffered once from the defect; they want it fixed before they suffer again. In particular, they expect software to have the capability for *first failure data capture* (FFDC). This means that at the time of initial failure, the software's serviceability features are able to capture enough diagnostic data to allow the problem to be debugged. For errors such as wild branches, program interrupts, and unresolved page faults, FFDC is achievable. For others (e.g., memory overlays or data corruption) it is quite difficult to accomplish without continuously running detailed traces and accepting their associated performance penalties. Nonetheless, for production software, FFDC is what most customers seek.

System-level testing should explore serviceability features' ability to achieve FFDC in a heavily loaded environment. Rather than defining specific serviceability scenarios in the test plan for FFDC, the usual approach is "test by use." This means the testers use the serviceability features during the course of their work to debug problems that arise on a loaded system, just as is done in production environments. Any weaknesses or deficiencies in those features should then be reported as defects.

Another aspect to serviceability support is its practicality for use in a production environment. Detailed traces that seem perfectly reasonable in a lightly loaded FVT environment might fill up an entire disk with data in less than a minute in a heavily stressed SVT environment. If these traces are in place to capture diagnostic data for a bug that takes hours to recreate, then they simply are not practical. The test plan should include specific scenarios to explore the practical aspects of using serviceability features on a heavily loaded system.

Security

Probing for security vulnerabilities during SVT is similar to what is done during FVT, but with a system-level focus. For example, this would be the place to see how your software holds up under a broad range of denial-of-service (DOS) attacks. Such attacks don't try to gain unauthorized access to your system, but rather to monopolize its resources so that there is no capacity remaining to service others. Some of these attacks have telltale signatures that enable firewalls and filters to protect against them, but others are indistinguishable from legitimate traffic. At a minimum, your testing should verify the software can withstand these onslaughts without crashing. In effect, you can treat DOS attacks as a specialized form of load and stress. There are quite a variety of well known attacks that exploit different vulnerabilities, and have exotic names such as "mutilate" and "ping of death." Once again, an Internet search will unearth tools you can use to emulate hackers, crackers, and other bad guys.

Data Integrity

Certain types of software, such as operating systems and databases, are responsible for protecting user and system data from corruption. For such software, testing to ensure that data integrity is maintained at all times, regardless of external events, is vital. It's also tricky, since most software assumes that the data it uses is safe, it often won't even notice corruption until long after the damage is done. Chapter 12, "Corruption," is devoted to discussing techniques and tools for this interesting yet challenging area.

Usability

In a perfect world, a program's end user interfaces would be designed by human factors and graphic arts specialists working hand-in-hand with the program's developers. They would go to great pains to ensure that input screens, messages, and task flows are intuitive and easy to follow. In reality, interfaces are often assembled on a tight schedule by a developer with no special training. The results are predictable.

Thus, it may fall upon the test team to assess how good an interface is. There are two approaches for usability testing: explicit and implicit.

Explicit Testing

This method involves observing naive users as they interact with the software, and recording their experiences. Where do they get stuck? How many false paths do they pursue? Can they understand and follow the messages? Such testing can become quite elaborate, even involving a dedicated lab with two-way mirrors. Ironically, that much care would probably only be taken for projects that also had specialists designing the interfaces—or, on the second release of a product whose first release was deemed a usability disaster.

Implicit Testing

Testers of a software package are also its first users. Through the course of your work, you will explore all of a program's interfaces and task flows. You'll probably become frustrated at times—the source of your frustration will likely be a usability bug.

This implicit testing through use is how most usability testing is done. It doesn't require a separate test phase or even any specific scenarios in your test plan. It does require you to pay close attention, notice when the program is frustrating you, and write up a bug report. You must resist the natural urge to assume your struggles are due to your own naivety. By the time you've gone through the trouble to learn about the new software and create a test plan for it, you probably understand it much better than the average new user will. If you're having trouble, so will they.

Reliability

Also known as *longevity* or *long-haul* testing, the focus of this area is to see if the system can continue running significant load/stress for an extended period. Do tiny memory leaks occur over several days which eventually chew up so much memory that the application can no longer operate? Do databases eventually age such that they become fragmented and unusable? Are there any erroneous timing windows that hit so infrequently that only a lengthy run can surface them?

The only way to answer some of these questions is to try it and see. Reliability runs typically last for several days or weeks. Frequently there are multiple reliability scenarios, each based on a different workload or workload mix. Also, because a piece of software must be quite stable to survive such prolonged activity, these scenarios are usually planned for the end of the system testing cycle.

Performance

As noted in Chapter 3, a clear distinction should be made between system testing and performance testing, since the goals and methodologies for each are quite different. Explicit performance measurement is not normally part of SVT. However, some obvious performance issues may arise during system test. If simple actions are taking several minutes to complete, throughput is ridiculously slow, or the system can't attain decent stress levels, no scientific measurements are required to realize there's a problem—a few glances at your watch will do the trick. We refer to this as *wall clock performance measurement*. An SVT plan should at least note that wall clock performance issues will be watched for and addressed.

Artistic Testing

As discussed earlier, artistic testing is a freeform activity in which you use new technical insights gained during the test to devise additional scenarios dynamically (see Chapter 15 for more detail). It's a good idea to define some artistic testing scenarios in your plan. Initially, there won't be any content in these scenarios; it will be added later, as more experience with the software is gained. But documenting the scenarios up front allows time and resources to be scheduled for them. Listed here under system test, artistic testing is applicable to function and integration testing as well.

INTEGRATION TEST FOCUS AREAS

SVT focuses on testing a software package as a single entity. We can move beyond that to broaden the scope yet again, to view that entity as one element of an overall system environment and see how well it works and plays with its neighbors. This is what the mainframe world refers to as an integration test. This test emulates a complete production environment. Many software packages operate together across a complex hardware configuration to accomplish multiple goals in parallel. It targets problems related to the interaction of those different software products. Integration test aims to see if it can provide very high levels of service to applications and simulated end users by establishing a pseudoproduction environment.

The test plan focus areas are similar in name to those of an SVT, but the scope is broader:

- Regression testing ensures the updated product can still interact correctly with other older products. This is also termed *compatibility testing*.
- Migration testing may attempt to migrate the full environment to multiple new or updated products in a recommended sequence.
- New function is exercised against a richer, more complex environment with more intertwined interactions through which to navigate.
- Not just one, but multiple products must compete for system resources under heavy load and stress.

Recovery testing can address the failure of not just a single product under test, but all other products in the software food chain that it depends on. It can also look at mean time to recovery—focusing as much on the ability to rapidly restore service as to gather diagnostic data. Because software at this stage in its development life cycle should be fairly stable, reliability testing is extended to provide a final proving ground before it is sent into the unforgiving world of an actual production environment.

SINGLE-SYSTEM VERSUS MULTISYSTEM TESTING

Most software is intended to operate as a single instance running on an individual server. That single instance is a lone warrior fighting a harsh battle against abusive users, down time, and restrictive SLAs. It may interact with other products on its own server or across the network, but for the actions that it is required to take, it must face them alone.

Other software is designed to work in a clustered environment as a member of a team. Multiple copies of that software, each running on its own server, will work together to accomplish their tasks. They could be operating systems forming a loosely coupled, single-system image with no single point of failure; a distributed file system that appears to end users as one entity; a group of Web application servers that share the processing of incoming work and back each other up in the event of a failure; a collection of federated databases that work together to provide a complete picture of data; or a grid that processes bits of a single problem across a multitude of systems, then collates the responses and presents them to the user as a cohesive answer.

Multisystem testing can span the FVT, SVT, and IT disciplines. In many ways, multisystem testing is similar to single-system testing. But a multisystem tester must devise scenarios to address special considerations.

Sympathy Sickness

If one system in your cluster or grid gets "sick," it should either shut down or limp along as best it can, without causing a chain reaction in which other systems in turn get sick in "sympathy." The sickness might take on many forms, such as locking hangs, memory leaks, or endless loops. The remaining systems must remain immune to side effects from their interaction with the sick system (e.g., deadlocks, message passing hangs, database conflicts). The tester should define scenarios to generate or emulate various forms of sickness, and explore how the remaining systems react.

Resource Contention

In this case, no system is sick, but all are competing vigorously for common resources. These resources could be external, such as shared databases or LAN switches, or internal. By internal resources, we mean programming constructs used to serialize and control the flow between systems, such as locks and synchronous messages. Is it possible for one system to be a resource hog, effectively locking all others out? Can dynamic upgrade or system service actions create a spike in resource contention that spirals out of control? Will resource deadlocks arise under heavy load and stress? The tester with a highly evolved "breaker" mentality will create scenarios to find out.

Storm Drains

Clustered systems usually have a workload router or sprayer in front of them that attempts to spread work evenly among all members. That router needs to follow an algorithm to decide where to send the next piece of incoming work. Some products will use a simple round-robin approach, in which the sprayer runs through its list of systems and sends work to each in turn. This approach is easy to implement, but doesn't take into account the varying capacities of each system to accept new work. If one system is overloaded while another is underutilized, it would be better to send new work to the one with available cycles. So more sophisticated sprayers use a workload management algorithm in which agents on each system periodically inform the sprayer of their available capacity, and the sprayer in turn uses this information to make its routing decisions.

But what happens if one system in the cluster stumbles into an error condition that causes it to flush work rather than complete it? If the system is flushing all new work sent its way, to the outside world it might appear to simply be executing very quickly. Whenever the workload router checks, it finds that system to have available capacity. The router sends more work to the troubled system, which is immediately flushed, so the router sends it more, and so on. Eventually, almost all new work coming into the cluster gets channeled to and flushed down the failing system, like water down a storm drain.

Well-designed software will include trip wires to prevent such an effect from materializing. The clever tester will attempt to create a scenario along these lines to see how the system reacts.

TEST CASES VERSUS SCENARIOS

The terms *test case* and *scenario* are sometimes used interchangeably, but they mean different things. IEEE 610.12 defines a test case as: "A set of test inputs, execution conditions, and expected results developed for a particular objective, such as to exercise a particular program path or to verify compliance with a specific requirement." IEEE 610.12 doesn't mention scenarios, but does define a test procedure as: "Documentation specifying a sequence of actions for the execution of a test.[1]"

This definition of a test case actually maps nicely to what was discussed earlier as a test variation. In practice, we find that the term "test case" is often used to describe a test that is embodied within a test program. When the test requires a sequence of actions to be performed, it's usually called a scenario. With that in mind, in this book we'll use the following definitions:

> **Test Case:** A software program that, when executed, will exercise one or more facets of the software under test, and then self-verify its actual results against what is expected.
>
> **Scenario:** A series of discrete events, performed in a particular order, designed to generate a specific result.

Test cases are often small in size, though complex ones can become quite large and may encompass multiple test variations. A scenario is often intended to emulate an expected customer activity or situation. It can consist entirely of issuing a series of command-driven operator actions, or can include executing a series of testcases in a particular order. Let's look at an example that includes both concepts.

---

[1]From IEEE Std 610.12-1990. Copyright 1990 IEEE. All rights reserved.

Case Study: Testing a Data-in-Memory Cache

The z/OS operating system includes a feature called Hiperbatch that speeds sequential reads against a specific type of file by a collection of applications accessing it in parallel. The multithreaded support works by caching data read by the first reader as it works its way through the file, then satisfying subsequent readers of the same data by pulling it from the in-memory cache [Loveland02].

Multithreaded software is capable of running work for many users at the same time, which often requires serialization techniques to coordinate events. Bugs in such serialization will typically be exposed only when multiple events are being processed.

Initial Testing

System testing this function involved creating a group of cloned test cases that would read the same file, then enabling the caching feature for that file and running the cloned test cases in parallel.

Here we see both the use of test cases designed to exercise the software under test, and a scenario that includes multiple copies of those test cases running against a particular file in parallel.

This simple technique was indeed effective in flushing out bugs in the code, but eventually a point was reached where the group of applications could run without error. The next step was to expand the scenario to run multiple groups such as this in parallel, each against a different file. This also found problems, but again eventually completed without error.

Start with the simplest scenarios to quickly flush out glaring bugs, but don't stop there.

Changing the Sequence

At this point, the support could have been declared working and testing stopped, but it was not. The test team recognized that most users of this support would not be running applications that were exact clones of one another against a particular cached file, nor would they necessarily run them in a tight group that all began and finished at the same time. In particular, they realized the applications would likely perform differing amounts of processing against each record before proceeding to the next—meaning that the applications would make their way through the file at different speeds. Also, the applications would normally begin their processing at staggered time intervals.

Design more robust scenarios based on your understanding of how the software will be used. For more information on how to gain that understanding, see Chapter 5, "Where to Start? Snooping for Information."

Combining these two observations, the team defined another scenario in which two groups of test cases were run against a file. The first group was altered to include a small, artificial delay after each read. This "slow" group was started first. Once it was partially through the file, the next group was started. This second group had no such artificial delay and read through the file as fast as possible. Before long, the "fast" group caught up to and overtook the slow group. At that moment the "lead reader," the actual test case instance whose reads were being cached for the benefit of the others, changed.

Simple test cases can be viewed as building blocks. They can be combined in different ways to create fresh scenarios.

The team found that precisely when this "changing of the leader" occurred, a data integrity bug hit. In fact, multiple such bugs hit, all caused by very narrow timing windows. Such windows will normally elude single-user tests or code coverage tools, as they depend not on a single errant path through the code, but on multiple things occurring at the same instant across multiple processors on a tightly coupled multiprocessor system. That is why it is so important to execute such scenarios under heavy load/stress.

Here a scenario was defined to attack data integrity in an environment of high concurrency by *rearranging* the execution sequence of existing test cases. The approach worked, and led to the discovery of new and critical bugs. Importantly, the sequence was not picked at random, but was based on the expected customer usage of the function.

TEST PLAN REVIEWS

Earlier we mentioned that one of the key reasons for putting a test plan down on paper is so it can be reviewed by others. Inexperienced testers often view a test plan review with trepidation, almost as though they're handing in a paper to be graded by a teacher. They fear that others will find flaws in what they've come up with; and of course flaws will be found.

The point of a test plan review is not to provide a venue for others to pat you on the back for a job well done. The point is to improve your plan. That's why you should *love* test plan reviews. Because of their varied experiences, backgrounds, and insights, reviewers will think of things you did not—things that will help you find more bugs or avoid wasting your effort. A good review is one in which people suggest intriguing new scenarios or identify those which you can combine or avoid altogether.

Good programmers are critical by nature. They are detail-oriented people who, if they think hard enough, can find a flaw in just about anything. If you send your test plan out for review and never hear anything back, it doesn't mean people were impressed by your thoroughness or stunned by your cleverness. It probably means they never read it.

Reviews can be conducted by either sending the plan out and asking reviewers to send you comments by a particular date, or by calling a meeting with key reviewers and crawling through the plan one page at a time. The latter approach will almost always deliver a better review, both because it forces everyone to actually look at the plan, and also because the verbal interchange often triggers additional ideas. However, in a busy organization, getting all participants together in the same room may not be feasible, and you'll have to resort to the "send it out and hope" method. In this case, a few phone calls to your most important reviewers to let them know how much you value their comments can go a long way toward achieving decent results.

Regardless of the approach used, reviews usually proceed in two phases, internal and external. Let's take a brief look at each.

Internal Reviews

An internal review is the first opportunity you have for others to comment on your plan. By internal, we mean the review is confined to the tester's own team. This is the chance for the entire team to help each other out and synchronize their efforts. Experienced testers are able to suggest improvements to the plans of their peers, as well as offer guidance to those with less experience. New testers are able to study the approaches used by others—and their fresh perspective may generate naive questions which can in fact lead to interesting new scenarios. Finally, testers working on related functions are able to identify and eliminate gaps or overlaps with each other's plans and discover areas ripe for collaboration.

External Reviews

Once the internal review is complete, the plan is made available to other groups for the external review. The software's designers and developers should be included, as should any other test teams before or after yours in the process. If practical, the software's ultimate end users should be given a chance to offer their insights as well.

Information developers who will be writing the software's documentation will certainly have a different perspective on the software than testers or developers, and so may generate additional scenario ideas. Simply put, your goal is to get your plan in front of anyone who might be able to make it better.

Depending on your organization's process, you may also need to send your plan to one or more approvers to gain final sign off. However, once internal and external reviews have occurred and you have incorporated the resulting comments into your plan, this approval cycle is normally a mere formality.

SUMMARY

Test plans serve several important functions for testers. The simple act of creating one forces the tester to step back, evaluate the project at hand, and develop a set of strategies spread across a range of focus areas. Once created, the plan becomes a road map for the tester to follow and a yardstick to measure progress against. It also provides a vehicle for others to review the tester's ideas and offer additional suggestions. But always keep in mind that a test plan is simply a tool to help you find bugs, not the finish line in a race to see how much paper you can generate.

In Chapter 8 we'll take a closer look at one of the most interesting, yet often overlooked approaches for unearthing bugs in complex software: recoverability testing.

8 Testing for Recoverability

In This Chapter

- Attacking a program's recovery capabilities during FVT
- Focusing on the entire product view in SVT
- Expanding the scope in Integration Test
- An example of clustered server recovery testing

One of the authors once found himself working closely with a highly respected developer on an accelerated project. The developer sat in on the testing effort so as to be ready to turn around fixes to any defects found on a moment's notice. For several weeks, he watched as tests broke his code and forced it to generate one system dump after another. Finally, one day he sat back, and with a sheepish grin commented that next time he would write a program's recovery code first, because that seemed to be the first thing to get executed.

Software's ability to gracefully handle or recover from failure is an important contributor to its robustness. If you accept the premise that all software has bugs, and that testing will never remove them all, then only by creating self-healing software that anticipates and recovers from errors can any program achieve maximum reliability.

Recovery can also be one of the most interesting test focus areas. How much recovery testing is needed largely depends upon the nature of the target program, as well as the operating system environment it will operate within.

In the z/OS operating system, virtually every "kernel," or base control program (BCP), module is protected by one or more unique, customized recovery routines. These routines are automatically given control, in hierarchical sequence, if an unexpected failure occurs. They then capture program status at the time of failure, generate system dumps, restore initial state data prior to a retry attempt, and perform other cleanup activities to allow the module to resume operating normally. As a result, testing any portion of the operating system involves a great deal of error generation to see if this rich recovery environment is doing its job correctly. The same is true of testing any supervisor-state application that runs on z/OS and, to a lesser extent, any problem-state (i.e., user-mode) application.

At the other end of the spectrum are environments in which an application that fails is simply expected to crash and the entire operating system will need to be rebooted before the application can be restarted cleanly. Most software lies somewhere in between.

Various forms of recovery testing span the FVT, SVT, and integration test disciplines. Let's explore each.

FUNCTION VERIFICATION TEST

Depending on the situation, there are several different ways in which you can attack a program's recovery capabilities during FVT. We'll look at each of them. But before you can check how well a program recovers from an error, you need a way to generate that error in the first place. Let's review some options.

Special Tools and Techniques

In some cases, an error can be easily created through external means, such as filling up a log file or killing a process. But many times such techniques aren't enough during FVT. You may need to simulate a bad parameter being passed from one module to another, or force an error interrupt to occur just as the module reaches a critical point in its processing. It may not be obvious to you how to go about injecting such errors, but there are several techniques at your disposal.

Stub Routines

One approach is to borrow a page from the unit tester's handbook. If you need to force another module or component to pass bad input into your target software, replace that module with a small stub routine. The stub routine will do little more than accept incoming requests, then turn around and reply to them in a reasonable way. However, it will purposely corrupt the one parameter you're interested in. Alternatively, rather than replacing a module with a stub you can tamper with the module itself, altering it to pass back bad data when called by your target software.

These approaches will only work if the module you intend to "stub out" is called infrequently under conditions which you can externally generate. Ideally, it would only be called by the module under test. You don't want to insert a bogus stub routine that will be invoked millions of times per second for routine tasks by many other modules in the component. If you do, its identity as an impostor will quickly be revealed and the software will surely stumble. This stubbing approach obviously creates an artificial environment, so it's probably the least desirable method listed here. But under the right circumstances, it can be useful.

Zapping Tools

Some systems have tools that allow you to find exactly where a particular module is loaded in memory on a running system, display its memory, and change bytes of that memory on the fly. This dynamic alteration of memory is called a *zap*. If you can't find such a tool for the system you're testing on, consider writing your own. You'll probably find that creating a crude zapping tool is not a major undertaking.

A zapping tool gives you an easy means to selectively corrupt data. You can also use it to overlay an instruction within a module with carefully constructed garbage, so when that instruction is executed it will fail. As with the stub routine case, care must be used not to meddle in an area that is frequently executed on the running system, or the volume of errors you'll generate will be overwhelming. However, zapping is not nearly as artificial a technique as stub routines. In the right situations it can be very effective.

Error Injection Programs

Another approach is to create a small seek-and-destroy program to inject the desired errors into the system. To create such a program you must first determine exactly what error you wish to inject by studying the target software. Let's say the module in question maintains a queue of pending requests, and a counter which indicates the current length of the queue. When the module scans the queue, it relies on this counter to determine if it has reached the end. You decide to corrupt that counter so that the queue scanning code will fall off the end of the queue and throw an error.

To implement this plan you write a small program that operates with full system privileges. It follows a chain of system control structures until it locates your target module in memory. Your program establishes addressability to this module's dynamic area (i.e., access to its variables), examines the current contents of the counter variable, doubles it, and then exits. The next time the target module tries to traverse the full queue, it's in for a surprise.

This is a simple example, but you can imagine other cases where your error injection program corrupts the contents of a control structure shared by multiple modules within a component, or performs other nasty deeds. In essence, this is nothing more than automating the function of a manual zapping tool. But because the seek-and-destroy program is operating at computer speeds, it can be much more nimble and precise in its attacks.

Emulators and Hypervisors

Through things called *emulators* and *hypervisors*, it's possible to create what's known as *virtualized environments*. These environments are discussed in detail in Chapter 16, "Testing with a Virtual Computer," but for this discussion all you need to realize is that they create another layer of software between an operating system and the hardware it runs on. In some implementations, this extra layer has special debugging capabilities that can be used to set *breakpoints*. These breakpoints can freeze the entire system when triggered. This gives the tester an opportunity to stop the system at a specific point, corrupt memory or register contents, then restart it and watch the recovery support take action.

This is quite different from the sort of breakpoint function available in interactive debuggers, which can create a very artificial environment. In virtualized environments, the operating system and all of the middleware and applications running on top of it are unaware of the existence of this extra layer. When a breakpoint is hit, the entire system stops, not just one module. At that point, the virtualization layer hands control over to the tester.

Such technology is not universally available. But if you have access to a virtualized environment that supports breakpointing capabilities, it probably offers the most powerful mechanism for injecting errors during FVT.

Restartability

The most basic recovery option is enabling a program to restart cleanly after a crash. In FVT, the focus is placed on failures within individual components of the overall product. You'll often need to trick a component into crashing. You can do this in a virtualized environment by setting a breakpoint at some specific location in its code. When the breakpoint hits you can insert carefully corrupted data, set the system's next instruction pointer to the address of an invalid instruction, or zap the component's code itself to overlay a valid instruction with some sort of garbage that's not executable. You then resume the program after the breakpoint, watch it fail, and ensure it generates the appropriate failure messages, log entries, dump codes, etc. If it has robust recovery support, it may be able to resume processing as if nothing had happened. If not, it may force the entire product to terminate.

If the program terminates, you can then restart it and determine if it restarts successfully and is able to process new work (or resume old work, depending on its nature). If you resorted to zapping the component's code with garbage to force it to crash, and that code remains resident in memory, then you'll need to repair the overlay prior to restarting the program (or it will just fail again).

Component-level Recovery from Anticipated Errors

Most commercial software has some sort of component-level (or object-level) recovery, whether it's operating system-managed as described earlier for z/OS, or more basic signal try-and-catch mechanisms employed by some programming languages. At a high level, the idea is to establish a recovery environment around a chunk of code, such that if an error interrupt (e.g., program check, I/O error) occurs, the recovery routine will be given control to take some sort of action. That action could be as simple as issuing an error message. Or, it could be as complex as generating a memory dump, logging or tracing the error, releasing program-owned resources and serialization, and freeing held memory. It might even restore overlaid data in key control structures and retry the failed operation.

There may be a long list of anticipated error types for which the recovery routines take unique actions. At a minimum, your FVT plan should include scenarios for forcing each of those errors. After each error, you should ensure the recovery code processes them correctly. It should issue the correct error messages, trace entries, log records, generate a valid memory dump, or perform whatever action the code is designed for. When choosing locations within a component to inject errors, prime consideration should be given to points where memory is obtained, shared resources are in use, or serialization mechanisms (e.g., locks, mutexes) are held. These areas are complicated to handle properly during recovery processing, and so are fertile ground for test exploration.

Sufficient Diagnostic Data

Your test plan should also include an attempt to verify that any error information generated is sufficient for its intended purpose. If a message is presented to the end user, is there enough information so the user can make an intelligent decision about what to do next? Or, if there's no reasonable action the user can take, is the message necessary at all or will it just lead to needless confusion? If diagnostic data is generated, will it be sufficient to determine the root cause of the problem? This is where you go beyond simply testing to the specifications, and instead determine in a broader sense if the function is "fit for purpose." As a tester, you bring a different perspective to the table than does the developer. Be sure to leverage that perspective to ensure the program's actions are useful and helpful.

Component-level Recovery from Unanticipated Errors

A thorough test plan will go beyond errors that the program's recovery support was coded to handle. It will also investigate how the program responds to unanticipated errors. At a minimum, the code should have some sort of catchall processing for handling unknown errors (if it doesn't, you may have found your first bug). Be a little devious here. Poke and prod a bit. Use the instruction zapping approach mentioned earlier if you must, but find a way to force the code to react to errors it hasn't attempted to address, and then ensure it reacts reasonably. Again, use your own end-user view to determine what "reasonably" means for this program.

Also included in this category are errors that occur at the system level but also impact the individual component. These errors can include memory shortages, hardware element failures, network problems, and system restarts. Force or simulate as many of these types of errors as seem relevant, and discover if the component handles them gracefully—or if it takes a nose dive into oblivion.

SYSTEM VERIFICATION TEST

The objective here is similar to FVT, namely to wreak controlled havoc and see how the software responds. But in SVT, the focus shifts from a narrow, component-level view to an entire product view. It also folds load/stress into the picture. This is critical, because it's common for recovery processing to work perfectly on an unloaded system, only to collapse when the system is under heavy stress.

Restartability

In SVT, there are two aspects to restartability: program crash and system crash. For program crash, because you're operating at an end-user level in which techniques such as setting breakpoints are not applicable, there must be an external way to cause the program to fail. Such external means could include bad input, memory shortages, or a system operator command designed to force the program to terminate fast and hard. Alternatively, input from testers during the software's design might have led to the inclusion of special testability features that can aid with error injection. The next chapter explores this idea in more detail.

An advantage to using external means to crash the program is that you are able to send normal work to the program so it is busy doing something at the time you force the crash. Programs that die with many active, in-flight tasks tend to have more problems cleanly restarting than idle ones do, so you're more likely to find a bug this way.

The system crash case is similar, except that any recovery code intended to clean up files or other resources before the program terminates won't have a chance to execute. The approach here should be to get the program busy processing some work, and then kill the entire system. The simplest way to kill the system is simply to power it off. Some operating systems, such as z/OS, provide a debugging aid that allows a user to request that a particular action be taken when some event occurs on a live system. That event could be the crash of a given program, the invocation of a particular module, or even the execution of a specific line of code. The action could be to force a memory dump, write a record to a log, or even freeze the entire system. In z/OS, this is called setting a *trap* for the software. If such support is available, then another way to kill the system is to set a trap for the invocation of a common operating system function (such as the dispatcher), which when sprung will take the action of stopping the system immediately so you can reboot it from there.

After the system reboot, restart the application and check for anomalies that may indicate a recovery problem by watching for messages it issues, log entries it creates, or any other information it generates as it comes back up. Then send some work to the program and ensure it executes it properly and any data it manipulates is still intact. Restartability is the most basic of recovery tests but, if carefully done, will often unearth a surprising number of defects.

Clustered System Failures

Some software is designed to operate in a clustered environment to improve its scalability or reliability characteristics. Devise scenarios to probe these capabilities.

For example, consider a group of Web application servers clustered together, all capable of running the same banking application. An additional system sits in front of this cluster and sprays incoming user requests across the various systems. If one server in the cluster fails, the sprayer should detect the loss and send new work elsewhere. You could try crashing a server and restarting it, all the while watching how the remaining systems react. Another scenario might be to crash several members of the cluster serially before restarting any of them, or crashing multiple members in parallel. What if the sprayer system crashes? Does it have a hot standby that will take over to keep work flowing? Should it? Does any data appear corrupted after completion of the recovery process? All such possibilities are fair game for the wily tester.

Environmental Failures

Depending on the nature of the software under test, it may need to cope with failures in the underlying environment. In the case of operating systems, this usually means failure of hardware components (e.g., disk drives, network adapters, peripherals). For middleware and applications, it usually means the failure of services that the operating system provides based on those hardware components. What happens if a file system the application is using fills up, or the disk fails? What if a path to a required Storage Area Network (SAN) device fails or is unplugged by a careless maintenance worker (i.e., a sneaky tester)? What if a single CPU in a multiprocessing system fails? Are there any cases in which the operating system will alert the application of environmental failures? How does the application respond to such information?

Even if the application has no specific support for such events, it may still be worthwhile to see how badly it is compromised when the unexpected happens. In the mainframe world, tools are used to inject error information into specific control structures in memory on a running system, and then force a branch to the operating system's interrupt handler to simulate the occurrence of various hardware failures. Similar tools can be created for Linux or other operating systems. This sort of testing is very disruptive, so unless you have your own isolated system, you'll need to schedule a window to execute these scenarios to avoid impacting everyone else's work.

Natural Failures

During the course of normal load/stress or longevity runs, the software being tested will almost surely fail on its own, with no help from the tester. Rather than cursing these spontaneous, natural errors, take advantage of them. Don't look only at the failure itself; also examine how the program dealt with it. Monitor recovery processing to see how the software responds to noncontrived failures.

INTEGRATION TEST

Because integration test introduces the new software into a fully populated environment, it expands the scope of possible recovery testing to include interactions with other software.

Dependent Product Failure

Is the software under test dependent upon other products to process a request, supply it with input, or perform some other action on its behalf? If so, then a set of recovery scenarios should revolve around crashing those dependent products and seeing how the target software reacts.

For example, if a Web-based banking application invokes transactions on a remote system over a TCP/IP connection, what happens if the transaction monitor (TM) on the remote system crashes? How quickly does the banking application realize it's no longer getting responses back to its queries? Does it queue up incoming requests while it waits for the TM to restart, or reject them? What does it do with the requests that were in transit at the time of the failure—are any updates to customer accounts left hanging, only half completed? What does the end user see while this is happening? What happens when the TM restarts? Is the banking application able to pick up where it left off, or must it be restarted as well in order to reconnect with the TM? Now, what if the TM stays up, but the database that it is updating crashes? Or what if the TCP/IP link between the application and the TM goes down?

Integration testers should examine the entire software food chain within which their application operates, and create scenarios to crash, hang, or otherwise disrupt every single element in that chain. This kind of testing presents a number of interesting opportunities—it also happens to be a lot of fun. But most importantly, when done well it yields the kind of robust and reliable solution that software users in real-world production environments demand.

Environmental Failure

This is similar to what was described for SVT, but broader. In the SVT case, the impact of environmental failures is narrowly focused on the specific software under test. But during integration test, the focus broadens to include an entire software ecosystem operating and sharing resources. A failure in any one of those resources will force multiple programs to deal with that loss simultaneously. Think of the chaos on the floor of the New York Stock Exchange moments after a company has announced it is under investigation for fraud; traders shout to be heard as they all clamber to unload shares. It's the same sort of chaos when multiple programs scramble to recover at once—so controlled chaos is the tester's friend.

CASE STUDY: CLUSTERED SYSTEM RECOVERY

Multiple IBM mainframes can be clustered together into a loosely coupled Parallel Sysplex® that employs a shared storage medium known as a *coupling facility* (CF). In addition to one or more CFs, a Parallel Sysplex employs a common time source, software support from the z/OS operating system, and exploiting subsystems and middleware. Unique technology enables all server nodes to concurrently read and write directly to shared disks with complete data integrity, without the need for data mirroring or similar techniques—and to do so with near linear scalability [Nick97]. It also enables the configuration of an environment that eliminates all single points of failure. A view of these elements is depicted in Figure 8.1.

You can think of a CF as being similar to a shared disk, but one that can be accessed at near memory speeds, i.e., much faster than at I/O speeds.

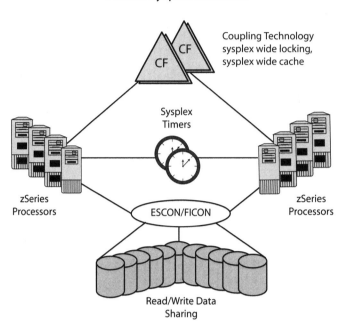

FIGURE 8.1   Parallel Sysplex elements.

The initial release of Parallel Sysplex included the convergence of new function in many elements at once, including hardware, the operating system, a data base manager, a distributed lock manager, a transaction monitor, a telecommunications access manager, a security manager, and more. It was a classic example of the need for an integration test, and so one was arranged. Let's take a look at one aspect of that test, namely recovery testing involving coupling facility structure rebuild.

What Is Structure Rebuild?

Many software elements exploit the CF's hardware assists to enable their multi-system data-sharing support. These assists support global locking, caching features, and a set of queuing constructs. Logically, the CF memory is allocated into lock, cache, and list *structures* in support of these functions, with unique structures created for different software exploiters. In the event of a hardware failure in the CF, the exploiter, working together with the operating system, can *rebuild* its structures on the fly to a backup CF, repopulating their contents based on the collective state information available from each server's local cache.

You can think of a CF structure as a file on a shared disk. Rebuilding it is similar to reconstructing that file on a different shared disk solely through file fragments supplied by all the users of that file.

Testing Structure Rebuild

To test this recovery capability, a series of scenarios was devised. A Parallel Sysplex was configured with several servers and two CFs. The structures for one of the middleware products were allocated on one CF, with the other CF acting as a backup. A heavy workload was then started across the cluster and allowed to run for a short time. When utilization of that CF structure reached a significant level, a failure was simulated by halting the entire CF. Each instance of that middleware product running in the cluster should then have detected the loss, and together initiated rebuild processing to recreate their structures in the surviving CF using services provided by the operating system.

Execute recovery testing on busy systems to challenge the software's survival capabilities under production-like conditions.

Failures can often be simulated by simply powering off or disconnecting hardware. By understanding how a hardware failure is surfaced to the software, you can often find a simple, nondestructive way to simulate it.

As you might imagine, this recovery processing was complex, and trying to perform it amid a flood of new incoming work challenged all components involved. Several bugs were found in both the operating system services and the middleware that used them, along with an occasional bug in the underlying hardware. Once these bugs were fixed and that first exploiter could complete the rebuild process successfully, the scenario was repeated for the next one. That scenario unearthed new bugs, they were fixed, the next exploiter was tried, and so on. Finally, a point was reached where each exploiter could consistently recover from the loss of a CF on a fully loaded cluster.

When testing software recovery in complex systems, it helps to start simply by first isolating failures to individual components or functions.

Combined Recovery

It wasn't time to celebrate yet. Having tried each end-to-end scenario individually, they were now smashed together. The structures for all previously tested software products were allocated *together* on the same CF. A workload was again started up and allowed to stabilize. Then, that CF was killed. This forced all products to undergo their rebuild processing simultaneously.

Even though individually each of these products could reliably rebuild under load/stress, the controlled chaos of this big smash scenario unearthed a whole new set of timing and serialization bugs. This environmental failure scenario is a great example of the value of an integration test that hits a combination of relevant software elements, rather than just looking at each in a vacuum.

When multiple pieces of software can be affected by a hardware failure, be sure to design scenarios that force their collective, simultaneous response to it.

TIP

SUMMARY

Recovery testing is a fun, important, and often-overlooked technique. Instead of ignoring the inevitably of bugs, it faces them head-on by investigating how software will react in the face of trouble. It's applicable across all test phases, and is often particularly productive at exposing bugs on systems under heavy load and stress. Make sure you consider recovery implications when developing a test plan.

But even a tester armed with a thorough and well-reviewed test plan containing a great set of recovery scenarios can run into trouble once the actual testing gets underway. If the software's stability is below expectations, sufficient time has not been allotted for diagnosing failures, or the software itself is simply untestable, you could find yourself in a quagmire. In Chapter 9, "Planning for Trouble," we'll look at approaches for anticipating and overcoming these challenges.

9 Planning for Trouble

In This Chapter

- How much can we squeeze the schedule?
- Leveraging entry and exit criteria
- Using testability to make validating software easier
- A Case Study: overcoming a seemingly impossible testing situation

As German Field Marshal Helmuth von Moltke once said, no plan survives first contact with the enemy. When the initial test plans are developed, everyone has the best intentions to identify all issues, problems, risks, actions, dependencies, and assumptions. But, somehow "Murphy" usually shows up to toss in the proverbial monkey wrench.

Significant software development projects will not progress from beginning to end without issues. In fact, some won't even have started before something goes wrong. By their very nature, testers also cause trouble. That's their job. The combination of the inevitable problems that will occur over time and trouble caused by testers, *must* be considered during planning. Following are suggestions to help the test team plan for all of these unknowns.

SCHEDULING

Software development teams often miss their deadlines, and their code rolls into test later than expected. Unfortunately, testers face an immovable end date, General Availability (GA), when the product becomes generally available to the buying public. Sometimes there is even pressure to pull in the GA date to address competitive "time-to-market" needs. Testers get squeezed on both ends.

Fighting these real pressures to get the product to market while still ensuring high quality is the goal of the test team. A tester's responsibility is to be the customer's advocate. Will a customer want a product if it doesn't work, no matter how early they can get their hands on it? A balanced approach is needed. Yet, the squeeze on the schedule *is* reality. Your test plan must address this accordingly.

Contingency

The dictionary defines contingency as "a possible or chance event." With all of the potential for trouble, the likelihood of such events occurring during the test phase is extremely high. The components of a testing schedule include building the test approach and strategy, defining the scenarios that will form the foundation of the test, setting up and preparing, executing the test scenarios, identifying problems, and resolving those problems. So, how can you construct a timeline that accounts for the many contingencies inherent in these schedule components?

The Contingency Factor

Each phase of the test cycle has its own risks, which must somehow be accounted for in the schedule. One approach might be to study every setup task and test scenario and speculate about all the things that could go wrong with each one; then guess which of them really will go wrong and estimate the associated delays. Finally, sum up the delays, add them to the schedule, and create a perfect timeline. Well, sort of. If you think can you do that with any degree of precision, congratulations. But even if all your speculating and guessing turn out to be correct, by the time you finish this elaborate process the test will probably be over.

A better way is to establish a *contingency factor* as a percentage of the total amount of time or resource required for the test. This factor represents the estimated time required for reacting to problems, waiting for fixes, handling test machine failures, and so on. The contingency factor can then be added to the overall projected schedule as a safety cushion.

So what's the magic number? It depends. For existing software that is being upgraded, let history be your guide. For new software, you'll have to make an educated guess with a more generous contingency factor. A contingency factor of about 50%

is often acceptable for simple and well-understood projects. This means that after sizing the effort, add one-half of the schedule length to that to arrive at the total schedule length. In complex projects, a contingency factor of 100% is common. Determine your effort and schedule, and *double* it. That's likely to tell you when the test will complete and what time it will require.

Techniques

Sizing a large test as a single entity can be overwhelming. It's both easier and more precise to use a divide-and-conquer strategy. Let's look at a couple of different techniques.

Sizing by Individualized Test Tasks

Task contingency can be defined as a cushion of time or resource added to each set of activities performed during a test schedule. By tasks we mean such areas as test strategy and approach, test scenario development, test preparation and setup, and test plan execution. Each task is sized individually under the assumption that things will go smoothly. An appropriate task contingency is added to each date and the result is a realistic schedule. Let's look at factors to consider when choosing appropriate task contingency values.

Test Strategy and Approach

The test strategy and approach stage is a time-intensive aspect of the SVT cycle, where key test technical leaders and component owners evaluate the new software. One input to the process is the availability of a final version of the technical requirements that explain what problem the software is designed to solve. Marketing, design, and development should supply these, but sometimes they don't, or what they do document is incomplete. The lack of crisp requirements will complicate the task of devising a good testing strategy. A contingency factor must be included in this task to cover any potential, missing, or unclear technical requirements yet to be finalized by the marketing and design teams.

Another common challenge during the strategy development phase is the availability of the key test leaders. These are busy people. Many times, the key test leaders and experts are directing the execution of other tests as well. A sufficient contingency factor must be used to account for the frequent unavailability of the very people essential to the development of the test strategy. If this contingency is not considered when allocating a window for this activity, time may run out and the resulting road map will probably be rushed and incomplete.

Test Scenario Development

Once a testing road map is in place, you will begin the task of developing test scenarios. On the surface, this sounds trivial. The strategy certainly gives the team a fine start for scenario definition. All that's left is to hold discussions with teammates and devise test scenarios to execute. What could possibly go wrong?

Things are never as simple as they seem. To start, there may be other testing still in progress during new test scenario development. Scenario development might be impacted by the lack of a final, approved design (or no documented design at all). As an example, assume FVT is underway while SVT is developing its test plan scenarios. The FVT team might uncover new issues which result in a design change.

The scenario development task can also be delayed by its formal inspection. There is *never* a convenient time for everyone to participate. Required reviewers may be called upon to address many other issues and will need more time to complete a thorough review. The test scenario development contingency factor should take into account such speed bumps that are common during this effort.

Setup and Preparation

We are getting closer to test start time but we can't forget a critical portion of the test: setup and preparation. This is the time when workloads and test programs are developed or purchased. If you choose to develop them in house, they will have the same set of challenges that the new product code does, and must themselves be tested. Defects in these workloads and test programs must be found and resolved before they can be put to use. There are also many questions to consider when purchasing prerequisite software products or test programs for your test effort. For example, what if they don't arrive on time? How will the test be impacted? In-house test programs that are expected from prior test phases can also be late or may not arrive at all. In this case, the test team needs to react creatively and will need time in the schedule to do so.

One of the critical components of any test is the hardware it runs on. When it breaks or doesn't show up, what will you do? Is there "react time" in the schedule for unforeseen circumstances like this?

Test Plan Execution

The one task of the test that seems to uncover the most unforeseen issues is its actual execution. If you lay out all of the scenarios required to execute the test plan and assume that all will go well, it shouldn't take too long to run the tests. But things rarely go well.

You shouldn't plan to run a test shift every day. Instead, your schedule should include time between test shifts to debug problems, perform follow-up on issues previously encountered, and enhance tests based on newfound information.

Also remember, testers are *breakers*. Your test will identify problems and concerns. Not all of the problems will necessarily result in actual code defects. Some may turn into enhancements to the software's serviceability, availability, or usability—in other words, design changes. You must allow time for problem discovery, problem recreation, and fix verification. How much time depends on the problem history of the changed areas. When testing new software, its size and complexity are clues to the likely problem volume. Combine this appraisal with a realistic assessment of development's turnaround time for fixing defects, and you can estimate the expected delays and an appropriate contingency factor.

Incidentally, the reality of such delays is as true for "quick" tests as for major ones. When challenged on a test schedule or sizing, you may be asked how long it would take to do if you found no problems. The answer is easy, zero days—because if your schedule is only valid if you find no problems, then why even bother doing the test? A good test execution contingency factor anticipates these and other unforeseen problems and folds them into your schedule.

Total Test Task Contingency

The summation of the contingency from the test scenario development task, the setup and preparation task, and the test execution task yields the total contingency for the test. Remember, a schedule is just a guideline for the completion of a project and without contingency, that schedule will fail.

Sizing by Methodology

Methodology contingency can be defined as a cushion of time or resource added to the schedule based on the test phase or the execution environment. We can further subdivide the sizing of the test phase by breaking down the effort into self-defined, manageable chunks based on their focus area or methodology. For example, the test can be classified by looking at regression, migration, mainline, and recovery testing. In addition, the test team might choose to classify the effort based on environmental requirements such as complex software and special hardware with which the software must interoperate. In either case, the formula is simple. Size each of the chunks, add contingency to each one, and sum them up. The initial sizing of the chunks assumes things go fairly smoothly, and the contingency factor accounts for reality.

Picking appropriate contingency values relies on the same factors mentioned earlier for the test execution stage. Problem history, complexity, and any existing quality issues also apply.

Scheduling Snafus

Ultimately, contingency factors are an educated guess. They are a simple but effective way of factoring time into your schedule for the snafus that typically occur. Resist the urge to reduce or ignore contingency values when putting together a schedule for a project with tight deadlines. Later, no one will remember that you were a hero for coming up with an aggressive schedule; they'll only remember if you met it or not.

Contingency factors alone are not enough to completely protect your ability to deliver high-quality code on time to the marketplace. You also need to know when it is time to start and when your test is complete.

ENTRY AND EXIT CRITERIA

On the surface, establishing entry and exit criteria is both an easy concept to grasp and a very well-known practice in software engineering. However, without proper attention to the creation, measurement, and response to these criteria, they can slip from being a powerful tool for testers into a weak set of paragraphs in a test plan.

There are good ways to use entry and exit criteria and there are less-effective ways. Let's take a look at strong approaches and also identify some common mistakes.

Does the Development Model Matter?

Some argue that using entry and exit criteria is an antiquated software development practice, one that is only applicable to a waterfall development model where direct hand-offs occur from one process step to the next. This argument is flawed because it ignores the rationale behind the practice. Entry and exit criteria are nothing more than a tool that a test team can use to help meet its goals and objectives.

Some reasons to use entry and exit criteria:

- Ensure the test can execute with efficiency and effectiveness, and proceed with a manageable amount of risk
- Properly focus attention on the most important activities at the correct time
- Guide decisions on the next set of actions
- Influence what actions others should take
- Determine when a test effort is complete

It is a good idea to consider all these things regardless of the development process in use. Serial test phases are not required for effectiveness. In fact, it can be argued that the establishment of criteria is more important with parallel or overlapped efforts, since its use can help the teams avoid running into duplicate problems.

Attributes of Good Entry and Exit Criteria

There are a few key attributes common to both entry and exit criteria that improve their effectiveness. Criteria that do not contain these attributes can potentially cause more harm than good.

Meaningful

Every criterion documented in a plan should be placed there for a specific reason. The effect of not meeting each one should be obvious. Such criteria will help make doing a risk assessment easier for both a technical team leader and a project or product manager.

Measurable

A criterion that can not easily be measured is not useful. Neither an entry nor an exit criterion should be subjective; it should be calculable using empirical data. Any discussion surrounding the status of a missed criterion should be based on risks and action plans, rather than mired in debates over whether or not it has been met. The current status of a good criterion is indisputable by its definition.

Achievable

Exit and entry criteria are useful only if they are actually achievable. This may seem obvious, but documenting a criterion that is never met in test is a fairly common mistake, and only dilutes the effectiveness of the entire set of criteria.

Discrete

Each criterion should be defined at a level that will encourage appropriate actions by the people or teams that can respond if the criterion is not met. Combining too many items into one criterion makes it more difficult to determine what is best to do and by whom.

Mutual Agreement

Entry criterion should be the result of discussions among the teams involved in meeting it, measuring it, and depending on it. When a criterion is in jeopardy of not being met on time, it should not be a surprise to the responsible teams. It is a good practice for a supplier to include meeting their customer's criterion in their own list of milestones. Exit criteria should be reviewed by the managers of the entire project and they must be in agreement that they signal the completion of the test.

Example: An Entry Criterion under the Microscope

Let's assume a software product's development plan dictates that the start of SVT will overlap with the final stages of the FVT of widget1, widget2, and widget3. The FVT of those three line items are planned to be 75% complete at the start of the SVT.

Avoid Ambiguity

So would a good entry criterion for SVT be "the FVT of widget1, widget2, and widget3 is 75% complete"? This criterion does have the attributes of being measurable and achievable (though whether it is discrete or meaningful to the SVT team can be debated). However, it's ambiguous. Does each of the individual function tests need to be 75% complete or does the aggregate of all three need to be 75% complete?

Since the criterion is ambiguous, assumptions will be made. Each of the FVT teams might assume that they can rely on the other FVT teams to be more than 75% complete—each assuming their unfinished work can be the bulk of the other 25%. Finding this out at the start of the SVT is too late and can seriously jeopardize the successful beginnings of the SVT.

Document Specifics

Also, what is included in the 75% complete? What is acceptable if it is not finished? The criterion can be measured and met, yet still not satisfy the real requirement. There is no correlation between the specific plans of the SVT team at their start and the appropriate completed FVT items. What are the initial activities of the SVT and how do they map to the FVT plans? These are the criteria that should be investigated, agreed upon, and documented by the SVT team. Good criteria cannot be developed by staring at a product development timeline; they are created through detailed discussions among all involved teams. In this example, the SVT team should sit down with the three FVT teams and agree on which items are most important to be completed prior to the start of system test.

In this example, a good approach to defining SVT entry criteria would be to identify exactly which pieces of the FVT test plans address items whose stability is critical to enabling SVT to begin. Then state that the requirement is for those pieces to be 100% complete. It is also important to state these criteria in terms that are understood and tracked by the FVT teams. For example, "Mainline variations numbered widget1.100 to widget1.399, inclusive; and widget1.422 for line item widget1 must be 100% exposed and successful." The FVT team for line item widget1 is now specifically aware of what is being asked of them. The ambiguity is gone, it is measurable, achievable, and, assuming the SVT plan is really dependent on this criterion being met, meaningful.

Assessing Risk: One Technique

Entry criteria can be used as one tool to help determine an acceptable amount of risk in beginning a test. In large tests that have many different entry criteria, it is reasonable to assume that not all of them will be equally important. In fact, it is conceivable that each criterion by itself has a small influence on the total work effort. So the test can proceed with some risk even if a criterion or two are not met. However, understanding the impacts of multiple, disparate criteria on large work efforts can be difficult.

One approach to addressing this difficulty is to assign a risk assessment value to each entry criterion. Write down everything you would require to be ready at the beginning of your test that would allow you to proceed with no risk. Then assign a value, from one to five, to each criterion based on your understanding of the risk it would add to your test if not met. The value "1" is assigned to criteria that would add minimal risk to test progress if not achieved on time. An example would be a small new function that you could easily avoid early in your test but could reasonably finish on time even if test exposure was delayed. A value of "5" is assigned to criteria that add very significant risk, such as a critical, mainline, initialization function that is required to perform all or almost all of your tests. Assign the other values to criteria somewhere in the middle based on the level of risk deemed appropriate. The total risk is the sum of all assessment values. Figure 9.1 shows a sample table.

Criterion	Risk Assessment Value
Criterion A	1
Criterion B	1
Criterion C	1
Criterion D	1
Criterion E	2
Criterion F	2
Criterion G	3
Criterion H	3
Criterion I	3
Criterion J	4
Criterion K	5
Total	26

FIGURE 9.1   Risk assessment table.

In the sample table, the total risk assessment is 26. If criteria A–K are all satisfied, your risk is 0 and you can certainly start your testing. But this will rarely happen in the real world, so you'll want to be more aggressive than that. You may wish to begin your test even if the risk assessment value is not 0, but not if it is 26, meaning completely blocked from making any progress. In this example, assume you are willing to start as long as the risk assessment is under 18. Prior to your start date, add up the risk assessment values of the criteria not yet met. If the sum is 18 or above, hold off on starting the test and instead use your time, effort, and resources to help meet the criteria with the highest risk assessments first. This helps ensure the team is working on the most important activities.

For successful products that have multiple releases, the values can be honed over time so the total risk assessment is based on historical data rather than guesswork. This simple approach can easily show the cumulative impact of multiple criterion not being met, and is especially helpful to an SVT team responsible for testing a large product made up of many components and functions. Each developer or FVT team may not understand why their "little piece left to do" can have such a negative impact or cause risk to be added to the SVT plan. By using risk assessment values, it becomes clear where the little piece fits into the big picture. It can also greatly aid in determining which recovery actions would have the biggest impact on reducing risk.

Knowing When You Are Done

The aggregate of all exit criteria should be the measure of when the celebration can occur, that is, when the test is complete. Answering the question "how do you know when you're done?" is a common problem in the software test world. A good set of exit criteria eliminates this question. It may not be the only input to the answer, but it sure eases the burden. When a team's exit criteria are met, everyone involved should feel comfortable that the team accomplished its goals and completed its piece of the project.

Another important aspect of an exit criterion is what it's tied to. It is not enough that the individual test team cares about meeting its exit criteria; it is much more effective when others outside that team care as well. This is especially true when meeting a criterion is dependent upon the actions of others.

The Real Uses of Entry and Exit Criteria

This brings us to the most important reason to use entry and exit criteria. Time to market can be one of the biggest contributors to a product's success or failure. Many times software products and releases are driven to very aggressive schedules. This can cause test teams to be challenged to either start before all entry criteria are met or end prior to achieving their exit criteria. This, in and of itself, is neither good nor bad—it is how the situation is managed that matters most.

Proper Focus

In the real world, entry and exit criteria can be used as guides for deciding where valuable resources, human and otherwise, should be placed. Good criteria are a tool to ensure proper focus and attention is applied to the most important activities at the correct time. Criteria and their measured status are not a line in the sand that halts the project's progress when they are not met. Rather, they become a starting point for discussions on what is best to do, by whom, and when.

Getting Attention

Meeting the objectives of a test can be partly dependent on the actions of others. An example is the turnaround of fixes to problems opened by the test team. Even though the business may dictate that a product must ship on schedule even if the test is not complete, a good set of exit criteria can assist in getting development to address, with a sense of urgency, key open problems. This is why it is a good idea to tie exit criteria to something that many people care about. For an SVT, it may be helpful to associate meeting exit criteria with the product ship decision. Having such an association will ease the task of obtaining outside help on the most important items.

An Often Overlooked Practice

Entry and exit criteria are valuable and useful tools for software test teams regardless of the development process in use. For best results, the criteria should be meaningful, easily measurable, realistically achievable, discrete, and commonly agreed upon. Using entry and exit criteria aids in preparing risk assessments and influences where focus, attention, and resources should be placed at the right time. In today's business climate, where many test teams are squeezed for time, proper criteria can provide an easy way to get outside help and inspire other teams to act quickly. This often overlooked, simple practice should be seriously considered by any test team.

INJECTING TESTABILITY INTO DEVELOPMENT PLANS

We have reviewed areas that derail the test team's success; now let's look at a technique that can keep it on track. Testability can be injected into the software to assist test in validating the product. Gupta and Sinha define this type of testability as *controllability measures*. These techniques are used to enable the software to attain states required for execution of tests that are difficult to achieve through its normal user interface [Gupta94].

In environments where creating errors and complex conditions is difficult, these testability measures should be explored. "How easy will it be for our testers to verify and validate this software solution?" is a question that developers and designers should be asking themselves [Loveland02]. This question should be part of any software development checklist.

Testability hooks can be defined as those functions integrated in the software that can be invoked through primarily undocumented interfaces to drive specific processing which would otherwise be difficult to exercise.

Example: Looped Queues and Overlaid Data

Let's look at an example. A component of a large software product is enhancing its recovery processing for a specific, critical resource. The intent of the proposed, new recovery processing is to protect the resource from data overlay and to detect and fix looped queues. A looped queue is a linked list data structure containing an element that points back to a prior element of the queue that has already been traversed through. See Figure 9.2 for an example.

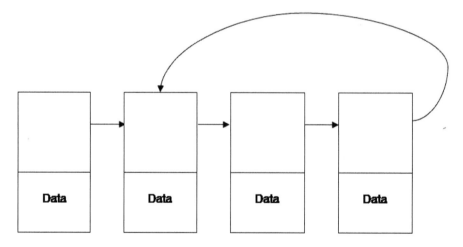

FIGURE 9.2   A looped queue.

The FVT team can drive these recovery scenarios by setting breakpoints and manipulating data, but with minimum amounts of system stress. Within the SVT environment, there is no external means for forcing the error condition that would trigger this recovery action. In fact, the SVT team could only hope these recovery situations occur through normal execution. This combination is certainly not providing sufficient test coverage.

We can use a testability hook to create the looped queue condition. The targeted component also has a set of external commands. The test team suggests the introduction of undocumented keywords in the syntax of a command to invoke a new testability hook's processing. To drive a looped queue condition, the tester specifies the undocumented keyword on the command, telling the software to create a looped queue. When the component processes the command, the component injects the failure condition. "BOOM"—recovery in control!

Test's early involvement in the design and implementation phases of a project can foster the integration and use of testability function. This technique can be a key risk-mitigation action for the test team. Most testability hooks are not documented to external customers. However, at least one software testability hook was so successful it was made available to IBM customers so that they could also benefit from its exceptional capability. Let's see how.

CASE STUDY: THE TESTABILITY OF ERRORS

We've noted earlier that multiple IBM mainframes can be clustered together into a loosely coupled Parallel Sysplex that employs a shared storage medium known as a coupling facility (CF). In the event of a hardware failure in the CF, software components using it can work together with the operating system to rebuild its structures on the fly to an alternate CF. In Chapter 8, "Testing for Recoverability," we looked at an approach for simulating the failure of an entire CF by powering it down. That's a good scenario, but let's take it one step further. The software provides support for reacting to the failure of any individual CF structure by rebuilding it while other structures on that CF continue operating normally. Shutting off the CF would not generate this failure scenario. The question the test team faced was how could they simulate the failure of just one structure within a CF?

Linking Testability Hooks with a Tool

During initial testing, the hardware and software testers could find *no* way to force a coupling facility structure failure on real hardware. Tester discussions with the architecture, design, and development teams (for both software and hardware) led to the idea of a testability hook. A piece of prototype code was embedded in the coupling facility support code, the test team wrote a tool to invoke it, and they took it for a spin. The combination performed exactly as designed. The CF error injection tool was born [IBMZOS03]. This tool allowed failures to be injected within the mainframe's coupling facility structures without interfering with mainline processing (i.e., without setting trace stops, modifying actual object code, etc.). The CF error injection tool is the epitome of a software testability hook.

TIP

If faced with a seemingly impossible testing situation, adding a testability hook to the software itself could save the day. If included in the final product, the hook could be used for future tests as well. By getting involved early in the development cycle you can suggest possible testability approaches.

Building an Error-injection Tool

Special support was added to the coupling facility that could trick the software into perceiving a structure failure had just occurred. All coupling facility structures were owned by a specific operating system component or related product. So a tester could easily introduce a structure failure condition to force the recovery processing of its owner.

NOTE

A failed structure can be thought of as a corrupted file that exists but cannot be accessed.

For example, a system tester could start a heavy transactional load/stress run that pounded on a relational database product across multiple discrete systems, all sharing a database on the same physical disk. The database software used coupling facility structures to coordinate this multisystem activity. Once the load had stabilized and the coupling facility was quite busy, the tester struck. He invoked the test hook, targeting the specific relational database's structure, and requested that a failure be injected against that structure. On receipt of the request, the coupling facility support code stored this request aside to handle on the next logical operation to the targeted coupling facility structure. When the next operation against the structure arrived, the coupling facility noticed the pending failure injection from the prior request and returned a structure failure indication [Loveland02]. The relational database software was notified of the failure and invoked its recovery processing, which rebuilt the "failed" structure on another CF. Refer to Figure 9.3 for a flow of this processing.

The tester could create a script to initiate the error-injection tool. The main parameter of the tool is the specification of the target CF structure name. In addition, and if required, another optional parameter was available that specified whether an old or new instance of the structure was to be targeted for the failure. This parameter was used in CF structure recovery cases.

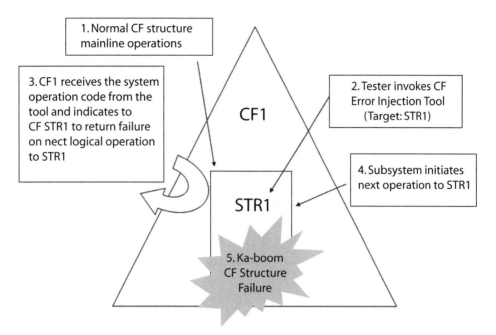

FIGURE 9.3 Coupling Facility error-injection control flow.

With built-in testability functions, using a simple script can often be enough to easily force complex situations that would otherwise be difficult to generate.

Extending the Benefits

The capability to inject targeted errors allowed the test team to validate all of the recovery actions of the operating system and all of its subsystems and other products that use the CF. This use of software testability hooks would not have been realized without extensive teamwork among architects, developers, and testers.

Identifying and implementing testability hooks early in the design is a team effort. Be sure to exploit everyone's expertise.

This program has become an important part of the testing of the z/OS platform, and has even been released for use by customers and other vendors to help create recovery scenarios to test their applications and product solutions. Each time new software that makes use of the coupling technology enters test, the use of the CF error-injection tool is considered. Feedback received from customers and users has been very positive and they have found it critical to the verification and validation of their data sharing environments on IBM zSeries® mainframes [Loveland02].

The CF error-injection tool's simplicity and effectiveness have allowed the z/OS test team to ensure the continuous availability and recoverability of the zSeries coupling technology. With its externalization to customers and other vendors, IBM has provided not only itself, but also its user community with a crafty tool for validating critical components of the operating system and critical applications.

SUMMARY

In business-critical software development, trouble lurks around every corner. Some of it can be averted, but inevitably there will be difficulties to be addressed. The trick is in planning for trouble up front. Building realistic schedules with contingency factors along with crisp, meaningful, achievable, and measurable test entry and exit criteria will provide the test team with the ability to meet schedules without repeated slips. Software testability hooks provide an additional technique and methodology for reducing overall project risk and easing the creation of complex test scenarios.

Planning for trouble is important, but so is maximizing your testing efficiency. Chapter 10, "The Magic of Reuse," describes the importance of reuse and approaches for implementing it in your organization.

Part

IV

Preparing for the Test

You now understand the testing phases, where each fits into your organization's development model, and what sort of defects they should be targeting. You have researched the software you have been asked to test, broken its complexity down into manageable chunks, and perhaps even recommended modifications to make its testing more efficient. You have in hand a thorough, well-reviewed plan, a schedule with adequate contingency, and crisp entry/exit criteria. Are you ready to dive into the test? Not so fast.

A chef can't assemble a culinary masterpiece until the meat is trimmed, the vegetables chopped, and the seasonings measured. A biologist can't make a life-extending discovery unless his specimen slides are ready and the microscope is working. An army commando can't leap into a gunfight without weapons that fire. There's a common principle that underlies most professions, and it's certainly true for software testing: preparation is key.

Before you can begin testing, you'll need to prepare your implements of destruction: test cases and test tools. The next four chapters will show you how it's done. You will see how to use old testing tools and programs to find new bugs, and how a change in context can open the door for taking test cases from one test phase and reusing them in another. You will learn techniques for developing new test programs, and how the rules for such programs vary from FVT to SVT. You will discover why normal testing will often miss data corruption problems, and how to create specialized data integrity monitors to fill the gap. A broad range of tools available to software testers will be surveyed, along with pointers on when it's better to buy a tool or build one yourself. Finally, the pros and cons of porting real customer applications and environments into the test lab will be discussed, including tips on how to do it right.

So sharpen your knives, focus your microscope, and oil your weapons. Let's get ready to test.

10 The Magic of Reuse

In This Chapter

- The reuse of test cases between test phases
- Test case reuse opportunities and techniques
- A Case Study: testing real memory management

The tester stands beside a whirring projector. A field of eyes studies him from around the stuffy conference room. He scratches his forearm, and then clears his throat. "But, uh, we have hundreds of test cases to code. It takes time. We need—"

"I don't have more people to give you. But meeting that accelerated delivery date is critical to our business. You'll have to find another way."

Testers never feel they have enough time to do all they would like. At the same time, project managers under pressure to pull in their delivery dates are always eyeing that big chunk of time allocated to test and dreaming of trimming it some more. Unfortunately, if the developers' schedule for delivering code slides out, the end date usually doesn't; it's the testers who get squeezed. But testers themselves have a lot of code to write.

WHO WRITES MORE CODE: DEVELOPMENT OR TEST?

Sure, your buddies in development might like to brag about how much code they pounded out over the weekend. But who really writes more code, developers or testers? In some organizations, testers write up to three times more. For example, if a developer writes one module that can be invoked through a macro with a dozen options, the tester might write several dozen test cases against it—all macro options must be tried individually and in multiple combinations, erroneous invocations and failure situations must be attempted, and devious manipulations of the macro aimed at bypassing its security must be hacked up.

That's a lot of test cases. They won't be trivial in size, either, since to use the macro in a realistic way, each test case must go to the trouble of establishing a valid environment for invoking and using the macro's services. "Environment" in this context might include running in a specially authorized mode, obtaining required serialization (e.g., locks, mutexes), establishing an appropriate recovery context, or even gaining addressability to other processes or address spaces. Test cases probably won't be written with the same rigor as a developer's module (no one will be trying to hack the test cases for security holes, after all), and many will be near duplicates of one another, perhaps taking advantage of object-oriented techniques to minimize redundant coding. But the point isn't to debate whether developers or testers are more productive; it's rather to highlight the often overlooked reality that testers have a lot of coding to do. That reality cannot be eliminated, but its impact can be reduced through the magic of reuse.

REUSE OPPORTUNITIES AND TECHNIQUES

Both function testers and system testers write test cases, although function testers probably write a great deal more due to the detailed nature of their testing. Both write test tools as well. All are candidates for reuse, though the approach for each may vary.

Test Case Reuse

In Chapter 7, "Test Plan Focus Areas," we discussed the idea of saving test cases from prior tests in a giant test case bucket, then reusing them for regression testing the software's next release to ensure the old functions still work. The same approach was mentioned as valid within the scope of a current test: completed test cases could be folded into a regression bucket that runs continuously to confirm that subsequent changes to the software don't break anything that had been working. Both FVT and SVT teams can take advantage of these methods.

Other important roles were mentioned for such a regression bucket in the realm of SVT. It could be used as the basis for an acceptance test at the beginning of SVT, or as a source of background stress against which other tests are executed. But what if the software under test is brand new?

For new software, the SVT team won't have any old SVT test cases to use for acceptance testing, and they'll be challenged to write new ones fast enough to create a meaningful load/stress bucket in time to meet the team's needs. But there is a way the SVT team can jump start the creation of a good regression bucket.

Reusing FVT Test Cases in SVT

Well before the SVT gets under way, the FVT team will have been toiling away, creating lots and lots of test cases for the new software. If properly constructed, those test cases can easily be reused within SVT to build an excellent regression test bucket. Not only that, FVT test cases can be reused in SVT for more than just regression testing. They can actually become the basis for system testing of brand-new function. Yet, these test cases have already run successfully during FVT. How can using them again to test the same functions during SVT have any value? The answer lies in their context.

The Importance of Context

Bassett defines reuse as the process of adapting generalized components to various contexts of use [Bassett97], and context is the key here. When a test case is executed during FVT, it's normally run in isolation, as the only piece of work running on the system. It may also be executed in a virtualized environment. Virtualized environments are discussed in Chapter 16, "Testing with a Virtual Computer," and can be extremely useful for the tester. But, they also introduce another layer between the software under test and the real hardware which, on occasion, can mask certain timing windows or change the order in which interrupts arrive, and let bugs escape.

When run during SVT, each test case can, in effect, be viewed as an exploiter of the new software, a miniapplication or user that is taking advantage of new services. The stress of running perhaps hundreds of those miniapplications together will generate tremendous pressure against the software under test, potentially exposing erroneous timing windows. So while the test case itself has not changed, its context has. That changed context will stretch the software in different directions, and may lead to the discovery of fresh bugs.

The test case's execution environment may also have changed. Before it may have run in a virtualized environment, now it can run on native hardware. It once had all of the system's memory at its disposal, now it might compete for it. Previously it received instant responses to its I/O requests, now it must wait in line. These kinds of environmental influences also alter context, and so are likely to challenge the software in new ways and expose previously unseen flaws. No one is suggesting that simply reusing FVT test cases is sufficient for a thorough SVT. But doing so is an excellent starting point and, if done properly, is almost free.

Creating Streamable Test Cases

While there is a place for regression tests that are manually executed, you'll usually want them to be automatable. Only through automation can tests be run continuously without sapping huge amounts of time from the test team. This is true for all the various roles mentioned earlier that a regression test bucket can play, either in FVT or SVT.

Tools can be used to automate the execution of test cases, as we'll see in Chapter 13, "Tools: You Can't Build a House without Them." But first, the test cases themselves must be able to run together as part of a large group. We describe such test cases as being *streamable*. In order to be streamable, a test case must meet certain standards [Loveland02].

Self-checking: It must programmatically verify that all functions it exercises have performed correctly. If they have not, an error return code must be set or a memory dump triggered.

Debuggable: When a failure is detected, the test case must externalize as many details as possible about its current status, so when viewed hours later by a human, the source of the failure can be easily diagnosed.

Well-behaved: It must not alter control structures or other resources owned by system components. The test case must also be able to coexist with other completely unrelated test cases (i.e., it can not require the entire system by itself).

Autonomous: It should not need manual intervention, such as requiring an operator to respond to periodic messages before proceeding.

Restartable: During testing, the system can fail at any moment, terminating the execution of many test cases prematurely. Therefore, when a test case begins it must assume it is running in a "dirty" environment, where files or other resources it plans to create have been left around from a previous, aborted execution. So its first step must be to attempt to delete any such resources to ensure its environment is clean before proceeding.

Self-cleaning: This is related to, but distinct from, restartable. In SVT, and particularly in integration test, test workloads can often run continuously for days, weeks, or months at a time. If the test cases in those workloads update system resources, such as databases, they must do so in a way that prevents those resources from "aging" ungracefully, or becoming invalid and in need of re-initialization. For example, a transaction-based workload may consist of many test cases that read, update, add, or delete database records. For an individual test case that updates a record to be self-cleaning, before it completes it must reset that record to its value prior to the update—and do so within the same unit of recovery context. If the test case deletes a record, it must re-add it before ending. In this way, the data does not age; all records of a particular type do not eventually get deleted, nor does the number of records within the database grow. Yet, the required functions of the database system have been exercised.

Creating test cases along these lines is not difficult, as long as you're aware of the rules when you begin. So if the SVT team wishes to reuse test cases from FVT, it's important that they share these guidelines with the FVT team before FVT starts. Not all test cases will be able to conform to these standards, but a big chunk of them will. The ones that do can potentially live forever in automated regression buckets, earning their keep through reuse day after day.

Tool Reuse

Don't forget about test tools when you're searching for reuse opportunities. By their nature, tools are intended to be used over and over again, so you may not view simply running them as a form of reuse. However, using an old tool to meet a new need certainly qualifies.

Homegrown Tools

As noted in Chapter 13, testers often build many of their own tools. Some of these can be quite elaborate. Due to the perennially tight schedules that testers face, there is often pressure to develop such tools as quickly as possible, following a design that only addresses the current function being tested. Such an approach is shortsighted. By focusing on modular design techniques from the start, large tools can easily be extended in the future to meet new needs. Such reuse will not only increase the return on investment for the tool over time, but will shorten the time required for future test preparation.

In addition to elaborate tools, testers also create tiny, niche tools to meet very specific needs. These are often created by a single tester for his immediate task, and others on the team may not even be aware of it. They are often written as "throwaway" code, with no thought toward future extension, which is fine for this sort of tool. But it's surprising how often such tools can actually be extended, rewritten, or used as a base for a future tool. The memory thrasher described in Chapter 12, "Data Corruption," is an example of just such a tool.

Niche tool reuse can have a tremendous impact on the test team's efficiency and effectiveness, but there's one trick: everyone has to know that such tools exist before they can consider reusing them. If all testers are in a single department, this might be easy to do. If they are spread out across a development organization, it can be more difficult. Maintaining an informal, online list of little tools people have written is one way to share knowledge, although the challenge with such lists is keeping them current. Linking the upkeep of a tools list to some regularly occurring activity, such as a test postmortem (see Chapter 20, "The Testing End Game"), can help. But whatever you do, don't create an environment in which tracking the development of niche tools is so onerous that it discourages people from writing them in the first place.

CASE STUDY: TESTING REAL MEMORY MANAGEMENT

One of the major tasks of an operating system is to manage memory. Most handle this by viewing memory from two different perspectives: real and virtual. A computer's addressing range may be larger than the amount of physical memory it has installed. For example, a 32-bit system can address four gigabytes of memory, although it may only have one gigabyte installed. Yet the operating system, working in conjunction with the processor, can make it appear to all applications as though they really have four gigabytes available. This is done by creating a four-gigabyte *virtual memory* space, and mapping the portions of that space that are actually in use to the computer's installed, or *real*, memory. When real memory becomes scarce, chunks of it are freed up by moving them out to a page or swap file on a hard disk. The next time a program tries to access one of those chunks, they are copied back into real memory from disk. All of this is managed by the operating system, making it transparent to the application program.

The z/OS operating system has a component called the Real Storage Manager (RSM) that keeps track of all of these chunks of real storage, known as *pages*. The RSM uses an extensive system of queues to track pages that are in various states of usage, and a sophisticated locking hierarchy to serialize the movement of pages between those queues across multiple CPUs without getting confused. It's a complex component at the very core of the operating system.

At one point, IBM mainframe architecture evolved to, among other things, provide additional virtual storage addressing. It enabled programs to access multiple virtual memory spaces all at once with a full range of processor instructions under hardware-enforced access control [Scalzi89]. The RSM underwent significant changes to support these enhancements.

TIP

Whenever an existing component is updated, you have the opportunity to use both old and new test cases to broaden your testing coverage efficiently.

The FVT for this support included creating a huge number of test cases, which inevitably uncovered some bugs. Since a large percentage of those test cases met the standards for being streamable, the SVT team was able to reuse them. They did so in multiple ways.

Acceptance Testing

First, the SVT team performed an acceptance test using its existing regression test case bucket, without the new RSM test cases included. This bucket included hundreds of test cases from past tests, covering virtually every component of the operating system. Given the core nature of the RSM to overall system operation, changes there had the potential to impact base system stability, so it was important to establish a stability baseline. This testing actually went remarkably smoothly, so the focus quickly shifted to testing the new functions.

When testing enhancements to existing software, start by reusing old test cases to see if prior function has been broken.

TIP

Reusing Test Cases from a Prior Phase

The new FVT test cases were added to the SVT regression bucket, and additional runs were done. The idea was to exercise the new functions while the system was also busy performing more routine work. The speed of test case submission and the number of simultaneous processes (or *address spaces* in mainframe terminology) were ratcheted up until the target stress levels could be sustained without error. Some bugs were found through this approach, but the code's overall stability remained quite good—frustrating for an eager tester.

Reuse existing test cases in different contexts to uncover new bugs.

TIP

Folding In Test Tools

In addition to FVT test cases, the SVT team also had preexisting niche tools designed to put pressure on the RSM by reading and writing their way through huge amounts of storage over and over again. While the updated regression bucket provided stress in the background, multiple copies of these tools were run unchanged as another form of regression testing against the RSM. Again, it survived this attack quite well.

Next, some of these niche test tools were updated to exploit the new RSM support, and then they were included in the mix. The combination of old test cases and tools, new FVT test cases, and updated test tools that pressured the new RSM support proved to be an effective attack. Several bugs were uncovered and fixed. Eventually things stabilized again, and the team moved to the next level.

Take advantage of existing test cases and tools to exercise new functions. Updating old test cases can be quicker and easier than generating new ones.

TIP

Narrowing the Focus

This time, the regression test bucket was stripped down to include only the new FVT test cases that went after the RSM. The intent of this bucket was to intensely focus system activity on exercising the new RSM support. New stress tests were performed using only this trimmed bucket, and it worked. A new group of defects were uncovered.

Once those bugs were fixed, the team moved on to a final round of tests. In addition to the RSM-only FVT test case bucket, the old and new flavors of the RSM niche test tools were also run. The idea was to create extreme levels of stress against the RSM component and the other system services it relied upon. This approach succeeded, and a new set of bugs involving very narrow timing windows were discovered. In normal customer operation, these bugs might not have surfaced for months or longer; but if they did, their impact would have been severe. By focusing the stress like a laser beam on this one area, the team was able to accelerate their discovery from months to days.

Another way to reuse test cases for multithreaded software is to selectively combine them into a high load/stress workload that is intensely focused on the new functions under test.

TIP

Epilogue

This SVT team reused old test cases, reused new test cases from a prior phase, reused existing test tools against a new function, and extended those tools to tackle the updated software. Plus, the team mixed things in different combinations. Taken together, these approaches exposed multiple bugs that would have eluded detection had only a single technique been used, and the extensive reuse kept preparation costs to a minimum.

SUMMARY

Testers write a great deal of code, sometimes significantly more than the code they're testing. Finding ways to reuse that code makes a lot of sense. Test cases written to be streamable can be reused within and between test phases. Old test tools can be used to address new problems, or adapted to changing needs. When starting a new test, the savvy test team always looks for opportunities to reuse the output of prior tests to save themselves time and effort—and help them find more bugs in the process.

But while reuse can jump start a test team's efforts, it's rarely enough by itself. New test cases usually need to be developed. In Chapter 11, "Developing Good Test Programs," we'll look at the characteristics of a good test case.

11 Developing Good Test Programs

In This Chapter

■ Characteristics of good FVT test programs
■ Characteristics of good SVT test programs
■ A Case Study: task termination processing

When it comes to fulfilling your test program needs, reuse is great but it will only take you so far. Eventually, you'll have to write some code. Unfortunately, testers are often given more guidance on how to track status for test programs than on how to create them in the first place.

In Chapter 7, "Test Plan Focus Areas," we noted that for large, complex projects, we equate a test case with a test program, so we'll use the two terms interchangeably. Why is it that while testers sometimes write far more code than developers, they are rarely trained to write effective test cases? Perhaps it's assumed that standard software engineering practices for good code development are applicable to writing test software as well. To some extent that's true. But effective test programs also have unique requirements which must be addressed, and those requirements vary somewhat across test phases. Let's examine the characteristics of good FVT and SVT test cases.

FUNCTION VERIFICATION TEST PROGRAMS

In the previous chapter, we saw six criteria that FVT test cases must meet in order to be folded into an automated test stream: self-checking, debuggable, well-behaved, autonomous, restartable, and self-cleaning. Regardless of whether a test case will ever be a candidate for streaming, there are more fundamental things to consider. Coding good FVT test cases requires that you adhere to practices that are recommended for writing any software, but with test-specific twists. There are also coding practices specific to the test world. Let's look at both types.

Standard Practices

Testers sometimes treat the test cases they write as throwaway code that's more important to do quickly than well. When a test case will only be used a single time, this might be appropriate. But for those that can be reused or adapted for current or future tests, taking a quick-and-dirty approach is shortsighted. Spending a little more time up front to create robust, well-written test programs converts each one from a necessary evil into an asset for the entire test team. All that is needed is to follow some common programming guidelines.

Document through Comments

For all but the most elaborate test cases, it's usually unnecessary to create stand-alone documentation describing how each one works. But if the test cases are going to be included in a regression suite, they may live a very long life. Several releases down the road, someone else may be trying to figure out why the test case suddenly failed. They'll need some basic documentation.

The easiest thing to do is simply comment the code. Establish team standards for documenting test cases, and follow them. For example, define a standard template for a large, block comment that must be inserted at the beginning of each program. The template might include a description of the program's objectives and operation, any required setup or environmental dependencies, a list of inputs and outputs, and all possible success or failure codes it might return. Pay particular attention to information that someone debugging a failure with the test case could find useful.

As with any well-written program, comments should also be included throughout the code to clarify its operation. Make sure the comments are meaningful (e.g. "Mark buffer as ready for error injection," rather than "set bit on."). None of this is complicated. Thoughtful comments can make the difference between a test case that reveals bugs several years later, and one that is discarded because no one can spend the time required to figure out why it's failing.

Avoid Hard Coding Physical Resource Names

Test environments tend to be very dynamic. A test case with a hard-coded dependency on a specific file name, Storage Area Network (SAN) volume identifier, network interface port number, or other physical resource will quickly become obsolete. Such test cases will either be discarded (opening the door for a defect to escape), or will impose an ongoing maintenance cost to the team. A better approach would be to pass such resource names as parameters. Or, you may be able to avoid the physical dependency altogether by dynamically allocating and deallocating (or discovering) each resource as needed, rather than demanding that the environment already contain them. Ensure that any dynamically chosen names are unique, perhaps by incorporating the name of the test case, to avoid collisions with similar test cases that might be running concurrently.

If environmental dependencies are unavoidable, then at least take steps to minimize the potential impact. Establish a small pool of the necessary physical resources that all test cases can use. Then ensure that as the test environment changes, that pool of physical resources is preserved. For example, if you need to hard-code shared Storage Area Network (SAN) disk names, reserve a half dozen or so such devices to be used and reused by different test cases and agree on a naming convention for them. If all test cases are using this same small set of predefined devices, then it becomes easier to manage them as a group and ensure they aren't reused or renamed for other purposes.

Serialize Use of Shared Resources

If you do create a pool of shared resources, then you'll need to protect against multiple test cases trying to use any one resource simultaneously (unless simultaneous usage is the goal). In other words, you'll need to serialize their use. Take advantage of whatever serialization services are available in your operating environment (e.g., locks, mutexes, and system queues) and devise a coordination scheme around them.

Another use of serialization is to control the flow of a group of related test cases. Here you are serializing the execution of the test cases themselves, rather than their use of a resource. This kind of dependent program control is useful if one test case will leave the system in a state that's perfect for the execution of another test case. For example, if you are testing services for creating and manipulating a new kind of data table, one test case could create the table, another could then attempt to store data in it, and a third could delete the table. Each one tests a different service (create, store, delete), but each also either sets up or relies on another to establish the table's state. In this situation, serialization can be assured by coding one test case to spawn another before it ends. The test cases help each other out, though they are still viewed, monitored, and tracked as individual entities.

The first time you execute a new test case in FVT it will likely be the only thing running on the system. It might be tempting to take advantage of that fact and not bother with all of this coordination. However, that would be a mistake. Later when you want to include the test case in a regression suite alongside hundreds of others, you'll regret it.

Test-oriented Practices

Most programs are written to accomplish a task, such as producing useful output or manipulating data. Test cases, on the other hand, are intended to determine if *another* program's task can be successfully accomplished. Kaner describes this as a test case being the question you ask of a program [Kaner03]. The most straightforward question to ask is whether the target program correctly does what it's supposed to do. It can also be interesting to ask the opposite question: are there ways the program can fail? Brainstorm a list of areas at risk for possible failure and then write test cases that generate circumstances aimed at forcing those failures. This approach falls into a category known as *risk-based testing*. Bach suggests framing the risk question around vulnerabilities the program might have, threats (inputs or other triggers) that might exploit those weaknesses, and potential victims of the resulting failures [Bach99].

Another way to interrogate the target component is to consider its possible states and then write test cases that force different changes to those states. In practice, however, for even moderately complex software, the number of states will quickly explode. Simplifications or abstractions will be needed. Weyuker offers a real-world example of this phenomenon, in which the number of distinct states for a telephone call processing application swiftly grew to over 167 million [Weyuker98].

No matter what approach you use for devising test cases, there are specific practices to follow in coding them effectively. While there may be some overlap with other types of programs, these techniques are fairly specific to the realm of test. Let's review them.

Target Your Attack

The test case should target specific functions of the software. It should correctly test those target areas with a crisp definition of what constitutes success or failure. The test program should not be a vaguely defined tour through the target software's functions with no specific purpose or objective. If it has a clear purpose, then success or failure will be easier to determine.

Ensure Correctness

This seems obvious. Of course a test case should be correct, as should any program. This is sometimes trickier than it seems. In the wake of an escaped defect, testers have been known to insist that they had a test case that exercised that code. But after further review, they unfortunately discover that their test case didn't do what they thought. Some minor parameter they hadn't explicitly set defaulted to an unexpected value. That default value in turn caused a slight deviation in the path taken through the new code, bypassing the defect. The test case executed cleanly, but its implementation was incorrect.

Protecting your test cases from such mistakes is a twofold process. First, ensure your coding isn't making any implicit assumptions about default actions or code paths that will be exercised. Be explicit about everything. Second, make a thorough list of all possible indicators of the test case's success or failure, and then programmatically check them all. For example, in our earlier example about testing a service that creates a data table, don't declare its success just by checking a return code. Also verify that the data table was actually created, and that it was created with the correct attributes (e.g., size, format, extendibility). In this example, it would be better to go even further by attempting to use the new table. Store data in the table, modify the data, verify it, and remove it. As noted earlier, this could be done through a self-serializing sequence of dependent test programs, each a test case in its own right. Sometimes you won't discover a creation service has gone awry until you take some actions against what it created.

Stay Unique

You have limited time to test any given function. Don't waste it by creating redundant test cases. This is not to say there won't be overlap. For example, if you are testing a callable service with many possible parameters, you might create multiple test cases to invoke the service in slightly different ways. Some could test limits, others would force error cases, and still others might probe for security holes. These test cases are not redundant. However, much of the code that's related to establishing the proper environment to invoke the service and subsequently report results could be the same.

Include Self-reporting

Test programs can become quite intricate, setting up complex environments and then checking for subtle conditions. Good ones don't stop there. They strip away that complexity to make it obvious whether the test was successful or not. The best test cases are programmatically self-checking, as described in Chapter 10, "The Magic of Reuse." These test cases summarize success or failure through a mechanism another program can easily check, such as a return code.

Decision Points

Self-checking isn't always practical, however. For example, you might want to build a test case that forks at several key points, with each path examining a different aspect of the software. To maximize the number of nonredundant tests in each pass, you could decide you need to control those forking decisions dynamically as the test case is running. Your choices will depend on the state of the system at each decision point. In this case, you might have the test program report critical state data back to you via messages, and then prompt you for a decision on how to proceed. Each such message is a form of self-reporting as to the success or failure of those interim steps.

Null Reporting

Another type of test program might pressure the target software while watching for the occurrence of intermittent or unpredictable errors. In this situation, when the program detects a failure it would report it to the tester, perhaps by deliberately crashing to force a memory dump. If it never detects an error, it could run forever. Here, the *absence* of a reported error indicates success. The data integrity monitors described in Chapter 12, "Data Corruption," are examples of this kind of program.

Self-tracing

What about a test case that "reports" its status by feeding huge amounts of data into a log or trace file? This is indeed a form of reporting, but not a good one. Rather than making success or failure obvious, it forces you to spend considerable time poring over a trace file to determine the outcome. Too many tests like this and you'll miss your end date, your total test coverage will be thin due to lack of time, or, in haste, you won't notice bugs that the test case actually surfaced.

On the other hand, for debugging you may find it valuable to create test cases that can optionally trace their own internal flow: branches taken, return codes received from system services, passes through a loop, etc. If you trace inside loops, you'll probably also want to include the option to dynamically and programmatically limit what's captured to avoid consuming too much memory (i.e., only trace the first two passes through the loop, then suppress the rest). This kind of internal tracing can often prove quite valuable for debugging a complex problem. But it isn't the most efficient way to report initial success or failure.

Avoid the Big Bang

Developers love creating elegant software, in which a few lines of code accomplish a great deal. Testers are often tempted to do the same, creating a single "big-bang" test program that, if successful, will complete many test variations in one fell swoop. A very simple example would be a limits test in which a single invocation of a callable service is made with every input parameter set to its upper limit.

Unfortunately, when multiple variations are intertwined and one fails, the others will be blocked until a fix is available. During FVT, the software is still fairly immature, so such failures are quite likely. Remember, your goal is to find bugs, which means that unlike developers, you *want* your programs to "fail." By creating a big-bang test program, you are in effect devising a test that, if it meets its objective, will by definition put other tests behind schedule. By trying to save time through an elegant test case, you've actually cost yourself time by unnecessarily blocking progress.

That's not to say you shouldn't include several related variations into a single test program. For instance, you might repeatedly invoke a targeted service in sequence, with different inputs set to their limits each time. Often that's a sensible way to minimize redundant coding while still establishing the right programming environment around the tests. Just keep each variation in the program independent of those that precede and follow it. That way, if a bug in one variation is found, it won't prevent the others from being attempted.

Aim for Efficiency

Developers write one instance of a program and they are done. Or, they write services for other programs to use repeatedly. Testers frequently do both at once.

There are many things a test program might have to do that aren't directly related to exposing a test variation. It can allocate a file, obtain serialization or other system resources, establish a recovery environment, issue messages, or perform other tasks to prepare for, or clean up after, the actual test. In order to keep test cases unique and discrete, you may have many programs which perform these same housekeeping tasks. Clearly, you'd like to avoid rewriting those same functions for each test program.

Sometimes testers handle this by carefully crafting one "master" test case that has all of these housekeeping functions included. Then they replicate that test case, making changes only to the code actually involved in each unique test while keeping the other functions constant. The problem with this approach is maintainability. If, halfway through the test, you find a subtle error in one of the housekeeping functions or decide you need to enhance it, you may have to go back and make the same change everywhere. And, if multiple testers on the team are writing similar test cases, they will probably each create their own master test case, wasting even more time.

Callable Services

A better approach is to identify these common functions at the start of the test and then spend a little time up front encapsulating them into callable services (e.g., macros or objects). Some categories of such test case functions include:

- Communication (e.g., putting out a message in a particular format)
- Investigation (e.g., gathering information about the test case's execution environment)

- Injection (e.g., forcing certain conditions, such as failures)
- Verification (e.g., checking bits in a control structure, matching a service's actual return code against what was expected and choosing an action to take if they don't match, or parsing log files for anticipated error messages)

A single function could support multiple actions such as finding a specific process or address space elsewhere in the system, gaining addressability to it, and injecting an error into one of its control structures. Very often these functions will be test-specific, unlike any service that an ordinary program would provide. By encapsulating such actions, it ensures all testers are performing them correctly, so time isn't wasted on errors in the test programs. Naturally, everyone on the team saves time by reusing the shared code, and if fixes or other changes are needed later they can be made in one place. The Software Testing Automation Framework (STAF) is a freely available, open-source framework that makes heavy use of callable services to facilitate test case reuse and automation [STAF]. Chapter 13, "Tools—You Can't Build a House without Them," describes another detailed example of how callable services can be leveraged for the tester's benefit.

Data-driven

You might also create a single test case that accepts multiple input parameters to control its execution. By providing lots of external knobs to twist, you will be able to reuse a single test program to execute several different test variations. The amount of actual test case code could be quite small, relying on input data to provide the variability that drives different paths.

SYSTEM VERIFICATION TEST PROGRAMS

In the previous chapter we saw how FVT test cases can be reused in a different context during SVT, both as a regression test suite and as a collection of miniapplications exploiting new functions. The merging of such test cases into creative, system-level scenarios can create a powerful base for your SVT. In fact, SVT is often more focused on the use of a broad variety of system attack scenarios than on low-level test cases. But sometimes that isn't enough. SVT is aimed at extracting a different class of bugs than FVT; discovering those bugs may require a different class of test cases.

Some of the prime targets of an SVT aimed at multithreaded software are timing and serialization issues. A key approach for flushing out such problems is to put the software under heavy stress. Sometimes this is as straightforward as cranking up a workload or mix of workloads that push the new software functions to their limits. Other times, you must develop test cases specifically designed to uncover potential serialization problems. The key here is to look for functions in the target software that you either know or suspect are protected by serialization (e.g., locks, mutexes), and then create test cases that put that serialization support on the hot seat. Force the simultaneous execution of the function from many threads at once. Then stand back and watch the sparks fly.

The Contrast with Function Verification Test Programs

Note the contrast between this technique and what we saw earlier for FVT. The characteristics essential for good FVT test cases are equally important for SVT test cases. However, an FVT test case will target the function in isolation—if it works once, the mission is accomplished. An SVT test case will not be satisfied with that. It will force multiple instances of the function to execute concurrently on a heavily loaded system. One of its key goals is to poke at the aspects of the software specifically intended to support and coordinate simultaneous execution.

Gray-box or Black-box Testing?

Determining what areas of the new software to target with these kinds of tests is easier if you understand how the support is actually implemented—so-called *gray-box testing*. While not essential, this lets you go after the areas that have been designed with serialization in mind. However, if you're not aware of the software's underlying structure, you can use a black-box approach. Study every new function in the software. If you can think of a way to force multiple tasks or processes on the system to execute a new function at the same time, then write a test case to do it. When you use this technique, you might even trip over an area whose need for serialization was overlooked by the development team.

CASE STUDY: TASK TERMINATION PROCESSING

Before the advent of computer hardware and operating systems that supported 64-bit addressing, applications were sometimes constrained by limitations on the amount of virtual memory available to them. This was particularly true for data-intensive applications that needed to cache or manipulate large volumes of data within memory. A predecessor to the z/OS operating system tackled this problem by creating the concept of a *data space*.

A data space was intended to augment an address space. A z/OS address space is similar to a UNIX process. It owns the virtual memory into which a program is loaded and executes. A data space was similar to an address space, except it could hold only data; no code could be executed within it. Also, a data space could not exist in isolation; it had to be owned by a task, which is similar to a UNIX thread in that it is the smallest element that can perform work.

The FVT Approach

Performing FVT of the support for data spaces included writing test cases to exercise the macro interface for creating and deleting them. A few defects were discovered by limits testing of the macro's parameters. But the FVT effort didn't end there.

Just as with any type of memory a program obtains, good programming practice suggested that when the program was done with a data space, it should delete the data space to return its resources to the system. However, the operating system didn't rely on the goodwill of application programmers in this regard. It provided additional support for task termination processing. If a task ended while still owning a data space, the system would delete the data space on behalf of the task. FVT test cases were written to explore this function. Figure 11.1 shows a high-level example of one such test case.

- Set up test program's environment

- Invoke macro to create one 1Mb data space

- "Touch" each page in the data space

- Exit the program

 Forces task termination
processing to delete the data space

FIGURE 11.1   Data space termination processing: FVT.

The test program created a data space with a maximum size of one megabyte. There was a bit of gray-box testing going on here—under the covers the operating system grouped data spaces into three size categories, and created slightly different control structures for each group. As a result, different tests were required for each size grouping.

 Learn about software's internal operation to help target a test program at otherwise invisible limits.

TIP

Once the data space was created, the test case cycled through each 4096-byte page and "touched" it by storing a few bytes of data. This forced the system to fully populate the control structures it was using to represent the data space. Once this was finished, the test case simply ended, without having deleted the data space. As the operating system went through termination processing for the task, it should have noticed that the task still owned a data space. The operating system should then have done the task's cleanup work and deleted the data space.

That FVT test case was run, and much to the disappointment of the function tester, it worked fine. The termination processing performed as designed, the data space was successfully deleted, and system control structures were properly cleaned up.

FVT test cases typically target verifying a single execution of a given function.

NOTE

The SVT Approach

When this function entered SVT, the tester assigned to it looked at the support from a different perspective. Because deleting a data space required manipulating shared operating system control structures, serialization was required. The system tester wanted to push that serialization hard. One approach he tried was to run lots of copies of the FVT termination-processing test cases at once. Unfortunately, that approach did not reveal any defects; everything worked fine. So the tester got a little more creative. He devised a series of test cases like the one shown in Figure 11.2.

- Set up the test program's environment

- Invoke macro to create 100 1Mb data spaces

- "Touch" each page in each data space

- Exit the program

Forces task termination
processing to delete 100 data spaces

FIGURE 11.2   Data space termination processing: SVT.

The SVT test program was similar to what was created for FVT in every way but one: instead of creating and populating a single data space, it worked with 100 of them. The idea was that when the operating system went through termination processing for the task, it would be forced to clean up 100 data spaces *simultaneously*. This placed much more intense stress on the delete processing's serialization than did the unsynchronized termination of 100 individual FVT programs.

Create SVT test cases that force multiple invocations of a multithreaded function. Execute them concurrently on a heavily loaded system in order to explore aspects of the software specifically intended to support and coordinate simultaneous execution.

The test case was run on a system that was already busy processing other work. It immediately uncovered a serious defect in the termination support. In fact, by running various combinations of such test cases under differing load conditions, a whole series of such defects were found and fixed.

Interestingly, prior to running the test case on a fully loaded system, the tester had tried it out on an unloaded, single-user, virtualized environment under z/VM (see Chapter 16, "Testing with a Virtual Computer," for more on z/VM and virtualization). In that environment, the test case ran cleanly without revealing any bugs. It wasn't until it was tried on native hardware on a busy system that the fireworks began.

Epilogue

This is a classic example of the difference between the kinds of bugs targeted by FVT and SVT. It also demonstrates how seemingly similar test cases can be adjusted to seek out and find very different defects.

SUMMARY

Writing test programs is a lot like writing other kinds of software. Techniques such as thorough commenting and avoiding hard-coded resource requirements are useful in many contexts. But good test cases also have some unique characteristics you should strive to implement. Test cases that are targeted, correct, unique, self-reporting, discrete, and efficient will be more effective at achieving their desired ends in the least amount of time. Also, if you are involved in system testing, watch for opportunities to devise test cases aimed at discovering the bugs that test phase is best equipped to find.

Chapter 12 delves into another class of defect that is critical and yet so tricky to find that it warrants special treatment. This special type of problem is the data integrity bug.

12 Data Corruption

In This Chapter

- What is data integrity?
- How to protect against data corruption
- Why do special testing?
- Data integrity checkers
- A Case Study: memory and file thrashers

Without the ability to reliably maintain the integrity of data, computers would be useless. No one would rely on a system that scrambles bank accounts, garbles inventory data, or loses order information. We saw in Chapter 2, "Industrial-Strength Software, It's Not a Science Project," that mission-critical software usually revolves around mission-critical data. Crucial to that relationship is absolute trust in data's purity. But such trust doesn't just happen; data must be carefully protected by any software that manages it. Bugs in such software can be devastating, so it's important for your testing to uncover them. First, though, it's helpful to understand exactly what we mean by data integrity, and how corruption can occur.

DATA INTEGRITY: WHAT IS IT?

Data corruption occurs when data is incorrectly modified by some outside source and we are not notified that it happened. This can occur in any of the many places where data is found: in main memory, flowing into and out of main memory, to and from I/O devices, or stored on an I/O device. For example, when a record that has been read from a file on a disk is resident in an I/O buffer in an application program, and this record gets incorrectly modified by some outside source—it is data corruption. This modification or corruption could be caused by software or hardware. Data integrity is ensuring that data does not get changed without notification.

Data Corruption Examples

Let's review some examples of corruption.

Wild Store into Main Memory

A *wild store* occurs when a program modifies memory at an incorrect location, thereby corrupting it. A wild store typically occurs when a program uses what it believes is a valid pointer to a data structure and it updates that data structure—but the pointer *itself* has been corrupted, has not been initialized, or was set to an incorrect value. The modification done by the wild store can be as small as just one bit being turned on or off. Regardless of the size of the modification, it's still data corruption.

Incorrect Virtual to Real Address Translation Tables

On virtual memory systems, there are tables that are built by the operating system which the CPU hardware uses to convert virtual memory addresses to real memory addresses. Because the CPU can only access real memory, when an instruction accesses virtual memory, the CPU hardware uses the tables to convert the virtual memory address to a real memory address. If these tables are incorrectly built or modified, major corruption can result because the addresses of two virtual pages can map to the same real memory. If this happens, it can appear to the program as if a whole page of memory has been corrupted.

Incorrect Page Fetched from External Paging Disk

On virtual memory systems, there are tables that keep track of all the virtual memory that has been moved to disk. When a program tries to access virtual memory that has been moved to disk, it will be suspended while the operating system reads the page into real memory. After the page is read in, the program resumes. If these tables are incorrectly built or modified, they can cause an incorrect and unexpected page to be read into real memory. Should this happen, it will appear to the program as if the whole page of memory has been corrupted. There are several flavors of this problem.

One is the case in which the tables that keep track of the used page slots on the disk get incorrectly modified, allowing the same slot to be used for two different pages at the same time. Another is when the tables that track where a page has been stored on the disk get incorrectly modified after the page has been written out. In either of these cases, when the page is read in it will be the wrong page.

Incorrect Memory Manager Data Structures

If the operating system has a service that keeps track of memory and programs call this service to allocate and/or free blocks of memory, the service tracks what memory is allocated and freed via data structures. If these structures are incorrectly built or modified, it can cause data corruption because the same memory can be allocated to two callers at the same time.

Endless Possibilities

These are just a few examples of the kinds of corruption that can occur. Database software has its own tables and pointers for tracking data, and each has the potential to generate corruption. So can message queuing software that moves data from one system to another. Even user-mode applications that manipulate large volumes of data can fall victim to damaged pointers or wild stores that lead to scrambled data. Testers should be dubious of any program that controls the flow of data. Software that provides data management services to other programs has an even greater potential for harm, and so should be viewed with extreme suspicion.

In cases where one or more pages of memory get corrupted, it often causes enough damage for the program to terminate, but it doesn't always. The wild store kind of corruption is more insidious, because usually a smaller amount of memory gets damaged and, as a result, may not be detected until long after the corruption occurred.

PROTECTING AGAINST DATA CORRUPTION

One of the basic design assumptions of computer systems is that every component of the system will adequately protect the data that either flows through it or is stored in it. This means that hardware components like main memory, I/O channels, disk drives, tape drives, and telecommunication links must each protect the data that it touches. Software has a role to play as well. Let's review some examples.

Hardware Protection

Magnetic storage media is not 100% reliable. As a result, when data is written on a disk drive, extra check bits must be written with each record. That way, when the record is read back, the disk drive can determine if any of the data has been corrupted. In this case, the corruption would be caused by electrical or mechanical problems, such as a defect in the magnetic media. Similarly, each of the other computer system components needs to use check bits to monitor its data for corruption and return an error indication when the corruption is detected (if it can't be corrected).

Check Bits

The ratio of check bits to data bits needed is determined by the number of bits in error that we need to detect, and whether or not we want to be able to correct those bits. The simplest kind of checking is through parity bits. One example is to use a parity bit for each eight-bit data byte. For odd parity checking the ninth bit, the parity bit, is set so that there is an odd number of one bits in the nine bits. When the byte is checked, if there is not an odd number of one bits, then the byte has been corrupted and at least one bit has the wrong value. Using this one parity bit for each eight data bits ratio, we can detect all single-bit corruption and some multibit corruption of a data byte. With more check bits and more complex error detection and correction schemes, a larger number of corrupted bits can be detected and corrected.

Software Protection

The operating system, just like all of the other components of the computer system, has to adequately protect data. Just as we do not expect normal programs to check that the *add* function in the CPU is working correctly when it adds two numbers, we should not expect programs to check for corruption in the data they are relying on the operating system to manage. The same is true of databases and other critical system software components. System software depends on careful serialization and other techniques to try to protect it from *creating* corruption problems. However, unlike hardware components, system software does not usually have real-time mechanisms in place for *detecting* data corruption if it occurs. MD5 sums and other postprocessing techniques can be used to identify corruption long after it has occurred, but are not typically used for real-time detection. They also do nothing to prevent corruption in the first place. That's where testing comes in.

THE NEED FOR SPECIAL TESTING

Customers' businesses are critically dependent on every component of a computer system having a high degree of data integrity. That suggests that data integrity should be a priority focus area when testing any vital, real-world software that is involved with managing data, whether the data is in memory or on disk. In particular, the SVT phase should be particularly adept at catching serialization holes or timing windows that can lead to problems with corruption.

Why is a special focus needed? Isn't normal load/stress testing sufficient? Maybe, but probably not. Data integrity problems are among the most difficult to detect with traditional testing techniques. Since normal test applications (or customer applications) assume data integrity is being maintained, they likely will not immediately notice when something has gone wrong. Instead, they simply continue processing the corrupted data. Eventually, they may be affected in some way (such as dividing by zero) that will crash the application and bring it to the attention of the tester. Or, the program may end normally—with invalid results. In any case, by the time the error is detected, the system has long since covered its tracks, the timing window has closed, and prospects for debugging it are slim [Loveland02].

Validating data integrity requires testers to think differently from other programmers. Specialized attacks are required. Test cases must be written that do *not* assume that when a value is written to memory, that same value will later be retrieved. In fact, the test cases must assume the opposite—and be structured in a way that will facilitate debugging data integrity problems when they strike.

DATA INTEGRITY MONITORS

Because normal programs do not check for data corruption, we need to devise test programs that do. It is better to develop individual, small monitor programs for each kind of data corruption than to create a large, complex monitor program that looks for many kinds. This keeps the processing of the test program to a minimum, so the software under test, rather than the test program, becomes the bottleneck. Let's outline a few monitor programs.

Incorrect Paging Table Monitor

Here is an outline of a monitor program designed to detect errors in the operating system tables that track pages on the paging disk:

- Acquire a large amount of virtual memory.
- Initialize each page of the virtual memory with its own virtual address and an identifier that uniquely relates it to this instance of the monitor program.
- Cause the operating system to move our virtual pages to the paging disk.
- Check each virtual page one by one to ensure that it is still the correct virtual page. By referencing the page, the operating system will read it from disk into

real memory. If an incorrect page is detected, the test program will capture diagnostic data and terminate with an error indication.

- Repeat Steps 3 and 4 until either an error is detected or it is manually terminated.

An interesting variation in the monitor program is to change Step 4 so that it randomly selects the virtual page to check. This will vary the length of time that virtual pages are on the paging disk before being checked. You would typically run multiple copies of this test program simultaneously. Because the monitor program is verifying the contents of the virtual pages, this will verify the following:

- The virtual page was written to the paging disk and then correctly read back into memory. This means that the tables that map the external paging disk for this page were not corrupted while the page was on the paging disk.
- The virtual-to-real translation tables for this page were valid when it was checked.
- While the page was on the paging disk, it was not overlaid with another page.

Wild Store Monitor

Here is an outline of a monitor program designed to detect a wild store:

- Acquire a large amount of memory.
- Initialize the memory with a specific bit pattern.
- Scan the memory periodically to make sure that the bit pattern has not changed. If it has, capture diagnostic data and terminate with an error indication.

You would typically run multiple copies of this test program at the same time, each with a different bit pattern. For example, one bit pattern could be all bits off, which would be looking for any wild store that turns on a bit. Another bit pattern could be all bits on, looking for any wild store that is just turning off a bit. Now we'll review a real data integrity test program used in testing z/OS.

CASE STUDY: MEMORY AND FILE THRASHERS

In the 1980s, the z/OS SVT team's first thrasher was written in response to a data integrity bug in a prerelease model of the IBM 3090™ mainframe processor. The problem turned out to be related to how the machine was handling a special type of memory used for fast paging and swapping, called Expanded Storage. At the time, no one knew where the problem lay; only that data was being corrupted. After weeks of analysis, the culprit had proved elusive. Then a thrasher was devised and written. It almost immediately caught the problem, which was quickly debugged. Since then, variations on this short, deceptively simple program have been used during the test of many products and features related to storage management, whether on disk or in memory [Loveland02]. In fact, the test cases used in the example in Chapter 7, "Test Plan Focus Areas," for testing a data in memory cache were variations on the thrasher idea. In essence, they were file thrashers. Let's look at both that original memory thrasher, and then how the concept was reused for a file thrasher.

When debugging a problem that is intermittent, devise a test focused on exercising the areas of the software under suspicion. Attempt to turn an intermittent occurrence into one that regularly occurs. This allows you to hone in on the problem and speeds up the debugging process.

Memory Thrasher

Few people outside of the development lab for an operating system probably think much about the possibility of errors in virtual or real memory management. But the concepts contained in a memory thrasher are both simple and powerful. Understanding them may prompt you to think about adaptations you can make for your own testing.

Implementation Details

There are a few basic rules to follow in order to create a good thrasher. First, the processing of the thrasher code should be kept to the absolute minimum to ensure system code, not the thrasher code, becomes the bottleneck. Second, the thrasher should be designed in such a way that multiple copies can be run in parallel as separate address spaces or processes. In z/OS, virtual memory is managed on an address-space basis, and one possible bug occurs when pages from one address space are exchanged with those of another. Running multiple thrashers in parallel is the way to catch such problems. Finally, the golden rule is: trust nothing.

When writing software to test other software, keep your eye on the main objective. Ensure the software under test is being exercised heavily, not your test software. Keep it simple.

Stressing a tightly focused area of your target software is a great way to flush out data integrity defects. Consider running "cloned" copies of a single test program as one technique for generating such stress.

Figure 12.1 shows a pseudocode representation of a virtual memory thrasher. Parameters to control the thrasher's execution are passed in from the user, including the number of pages of memory to thrash through and any delays desired for throttling the thrasher's speed. A template for what will be stored in each page is defined. Note that the first two fields here, PADDR and PASID, are used to identify each page uniquely in a way that the program can independently validate. For PADDR, the page's own virtual address is stored into itself. For PASID, the identifier for the address space within which this instance of the thrasher is executing is saved. These two values will be used to determine if corruption has occurred. The remaining data fields serve a dual purpose. On one hand, they are simply there to provide useful debugging information. On the other, they provide fields that the thrasher can update, forcing real memory frames to be updated.

```
PROGRAM THRASHER(PAGES INT, WAIT1 INT, WAIT2 INT);

Declare PAGESIZE = 4096;                                 /* One page equals 4096 bytes */
Declare MEMPTR, PAGEPTR PTR;                             /* Pointers to beginning of obtained memory table, and individual pages
Declare PAGENUM       INT;                               /* Loop counter, corresponds to pages in memory table */
Declare REFNUM        INT;                               /* Counter of number of times we've looped through the memory table */
Declare 1 PAGEMAP BASED(PAGEPTR),                        /* Template for each page in table */
             2 PADDR INT,                                /* Address of this page in memory */
             2 PASID INT,                                /* Address space ID which owns this page */
             2 PTIME CHAR(8),                            /* Clock from last time this page was updated     */
             2 PJOBNAME CHAR(8),                         /* Name of  job running this instance of the thrasher */
             2 PCOUNT INT;                               /* Number of  times this page has been updated */

GET MEMORY ADDRESS(MEMPTR) LENGTH(PAGES*PAGESIZE) BOUNDARY(PAGE);    /* Get memory table to be thrashed through */
PAGEPTR=MEMPTR;
DO PAGENUM=1 TO PAGES;                                   /* Initialize memory table */
       PADDR=PAGEPTR;
       PASID=MyASID;                                     /* MyASID obtained from system control structure */
       STCK(PTIME);                                      /* Store value obtained from current clock */
       PCOUNT=0;                                         /* Page not thrashed through yet */
       PJOBNAME = MyJob;                                 /* MyJob obtained from system control structure */
       PAGEPTR=PAGEPTR+PAGESIZE;                         /* Go to next page in memory table */
END;
REFNUM=1;
DO FOREVER;                                              /* Repeat until job is canceled */
     PAGEPTR=MEMPTR;
     DO PAGENUM=1 TO PAGES;                              /* Make a pass through the memory table */
        IF PADDR<>PAGEPTR OR PASID<>MyASID THEN          /* Data integrity error detected? */
               Force the program to abend;               /* Force a memory dump to capture state data   */
        ELSE
               DO
               PADDR=PAGEPTR;                             /* Else, update page again... */
               STCK(PTIME);                              /* Store current clock value in this page */
               PCOUNT=REFNUM;                            /* Update reference count for this page */
               PAGEPTR=PAGEPTR+PAGESIZE;                 /* Go to next page */
               IF WAIT1<>0 THEN                          /* Delay between reading pages */
                     Wait for WAIT1 Seconds;
               END;
      END;
      REFNUM=REFNUM+1;
      IF WAIT2<>0 THEN                                   /* Delay between passes through table */
            Wait for WAIT2 Seconds;
END;
```

FIGURE 12.1   A pseudocode representation of a virtual memory thrasher [Loveland02].

When creating test programs to stress software, consider including the ability to input various settings that will direct their behavior. This approach provides a powerful means for reusing a program by altering the testing it performs. When probing for scrambled data, each test must be able to distinguish one bit of data from the next. Look for simple ways for your test case to create unique, predictable data fields that can be easily validated later.

Next, the thrasher dynamically obtains the memory table and initializes it. Note that the size of each entry in the table is related to how the underlying operating system and hardware manage virtual memory. z/OS manages memory on a 4096-byte-page basis, so each entry is 4096 bytes long.

Finally, the thrasher goes into an infinite loop and begins working its way through the table. For each page, it first checks for corruption. If any is detected, it immediately forces an *ABEND* (abnormal end). Typically, the tester would issue an operator command to set a system trap for this particular ABEND which, upon detection, would immediately freeze the entire system so memory could be dumped and the failure analyzed. If no corruption is detected, then the program updates the table entry so the page is changed. It performs any delays requested by the user, and then proceeds to the next page. Note that with this flow, after a page has been updated, it is allowed to "brew" awhile before it is rechecked for corruption. This is necessary in order to give errant timing windows sufficient opportunity to arise, but also means that there will be a slight, unavoidable delay between the time an error occurs and when it is detected.

Test cases that programmatically determine when an error is encountered and assist in gathering diagnostic data are very powerful. Referred to as self-checking test cases, they are more effective than test cases that just exercise a particular function.

Execution

Executing a memory thrasher could not be easier. The program is simply started, and it runs until it is canceled or detects corruption. As stated earlier, multiple instances of a given thrasher are normally run concurrently. Similarly, streams of unrelated thrashers are often run in parallel. In fact, a secondary benefit of thrashers is that they provide an easy method for generating high load/stress with minimal setup requirements, and can provide good background noise while other tests are run in the foreground.

Attempt to create tests that have minimal requirements on configurations and other system attributes. Also, keep the test execution requirements simple. This makes it easy to port the tests from test system to test system, share the tests with other testers, and ensure lots of reuse.

File Thrasher

The data in memory cache support described in Chapter 7 also involved manipulating data, but this time the data resided in files on disk. Nonetheless, whenever data is being manipulated, the potential for corruption exists. For that reason, data integrity monitoring capability was a crucial aspect of the test. So when the team began developing its test cases, they turned to the thrasher concept and looked for a way to adapt it.

Implementation Details

The support being tested involved caching data read by programs as they worked their way through a file. Writing of data by a user while it was being read was not permitted, so the test cases only needed to concern themselves with performing reads. However, something had to initially create a file and prime it with data so the readers would have something to work with. With that in mind, the file thrasher was broken into two pieces: one ran at the start of the test to initialize the file, and a second then read that file back, watching for corruption. Pseudocode for the writer and reader are shown in Figures 12.2 and 12.3, respectively.

```
PROGRAM  WRITEFILE (RECORDS INT, TESTFILE CHAR(8));

Declare WRITEREC              INT;                /* Count of number of
Declare 1 OUTREC              CHAR(200),    /* Template for each record
            2 RECNUM1         INT,                   /* This record's
            2 *                          CHAR(96),            /* Dummy sp
            2 RECNUM2         INT,                   /* This record's
            2 *                          CHAR(92),            /* Dummy sp
            2 RECNUM3         INT;                   /* This record's

OPEN TESTFILE;                                           /* Open the file

DO WRITEREC = 1 TO RECORDS              /* Initialize each record in the
   RECNUM1 = WRITEREC;                      /* Store this record's number
   RECNUM2 = WRITEREC;
   RECNUM3 = WRITEREC;
   PUT (OUTREC, TESTFILE);                       /* Write the record out to t
END;

CLOSE TESTFILE;                                        /* Close the file
END;
```

FIGURE 12.2 A pseudocode representation of a file thrasher writer.

These programs were even simpler than the memory thrasher. The writer filled the file with records 200 bytes in size, with the number of each record stored within itself. That number was the predictable data that allowed the readers to later detect corruption. It was stored at the beginning, middle, and end of the record in order to be able to later detect partial overlays that didn't corrupt the entire record. A design decision could have been to store that record number over and over again

```
PROGRAM READFILE (RECORDS INT, WAITTIME INT, TESTFILE CHAR(8));

Declare READREC INT;                  /* Count of number of records read */
Declare 1 INREC CHAR(200),            /* Template for each record in file */
          2 RECNUM1  INT,             /* This record's number */
          2 *        CHAR(96)         /* Dummy space in record, unused */
          2 RECNUM2  INT,             /* This record's number again */
          2 *        CHAR(92),        /* Dummy space in record, unused */
          2 RECNUM3  INT;             /* This record's number again */

OPEN TESTFILE;                        /* Open the file */

DO READREC = 1 TO RECORDS             /* Read each record in the file */
  INREC =";                           /* Clear the input area */
  GET (INREC, TESTFILE);              /* Read the next record */
  IF    NUMREC1 <> READREC     OR     /* If the record contains the wrong data... */
        NUMREC2 <> READREC     OR
        NUMREC3 <> READREC     THEN
        Force program to abend;       /* Then force a crash to capture state data... */

  IF WAITTIME <> 0 THEN
        Wait for WAITTIME seconds;    /* Pause between reads if desired */
  END;
END;

CLOSE TESTFILE;                       /* Close the file */
END;
```

FIGURE 12.3   A pseudocode representation of a file thrasher reader.

throughout the record, and then later check them all. But this was deemed overkill and would have increased the overhead of the thrasher code, thus breaking the rule of keeping thrasher processing to a minimum.

The reader simply worked sequentially through the file and checked to see if each record correctly contained its own number. If not, it forced the program to crash in a way that could be caught by diagnostic system tools, similar to the memory thrasher. If all was well, then the reader checked to see if it was being asked to simulate a "slow" reader. If so, it waited a bit before proceeding with the next read. When the reader reached the end of the file, it exited.

Execution

Execution was quite simple. The writer was started and allowed to complete. Then multiple copies of the reader were started, each reading the same file, all watching for cases where the caching support under test had corrupted a record. Several groups of readers could be started, each group reading at a different speed so that "fast" readers could over take "slow" readers—a technique that caused problems for the software under test.

Consider an individual thrasher and similar test case as a building block. Combine different combinations and variations of them to create workloads.

Epilogue

The basic thrasher design has been reused and adapted over the years for verifying data integrity in many additional technologies as they have come along, including such z/OS features as Dataspace, Hiperspace™, Coupling Facility, BatchPipes®, Hiperbatch™, and the Unix Systems Services hierarchical file system. Easy to create and run, thrashers have proven themselves to be very powerful and valuable tools in the system tester's arsenal.

SUMMARY

We have discussed just a few of the many ways that data can get corrupted, examined why it is so important to do special testing for data integrity problems, and reviewed some specialized tools that can help with that activity. There are many more software test tools you can leverage to provide further stepping stones for a successful software test. Chapter 13, "Tools—You Can't Build a House without Them," digs into guidelines for buying or building effective test tools.

13 Tools—You Can't Build a House without Them

In This Chapter

- Different tools for different tasks
- Tool categories
- A Case Study: homegrown tool framework
- Build or buy?
- Avoiding the tool merry-go-round

You are about to build your first house and decide to act as your own general contractor. You'll hire all the necessary subcontractors to perform the jobs needed to get the house built. One very important step is choosing a carpenter. You research the available carpenters in your area and find yourself asking, "What makes a good carpenter?" Does a carpenter's selection of tools play a big role in your decision? Probably not. You assume a good carpenter is competent enough to arm himself with the tools he'll need to get the job done right.

A good carpenter is someone who's skilled at *using* the tools of his trade. He is dependable and flexible, able to quickly react and adjust to house design changes on the fly. He has some practical experience building houses. A good carpenter recognizes practical application problems in the design prior to building the house, and provides you with valuable suggestions after reviewing the design. He has demonstrated an ability to uncover and fix problems should any occur during construction of the house. He has current knowledge of local building codes and any other laws or government regulations that may apply. And of course, he must have good references.

It's interesting that while the tools themselves are not really a significant part of defining what makes a good carpenter, no carpenter can perform his job without them. The same can be said for a tester. No book on testing would be complete without a discussion on tools, since they are essential for a tester to perform his work. But, as with carpentry, the art of testing relies on much more than tools—they merely support its approaches and practices.

THE MAGIC TOOL MYTH

Just as the carpenter will have a truck full of implements to perform his tasks, the tester requires multiple gadgets to get his job done. Because different phases of test are designed to find different types of defects, each tool is geared toward uncovering a certain class of problems or supporting a specific test practice. Regardless of any statements made in the marketing material of commercially available test tools, testers will need a mixture of them. There is no single tool that fulfills all of a tester's needs.

Different Tasks, Different Tools

Would you hire a carpenter who only had one tool? It's fun to envision someone trying to screw a bolt into a piece of wood with a hammer, or cut a board with a screwdriver, but it's not fun envisioning your new house being built that way. Software test tools are similar to carpentry tools in this sense; good ones are built to support very specific tasks. Advances in tools may provide additional functions to improve productivity or ease of use, but beware of any widget that claims to be the answer to all your testing needs.

When searching for or evaluating a tool, the focus should be on what tasks it will support and what it can do for you. The emphasis should not be on what the tool does *not* support. Every tool has limitations and drawbacks. Many times, you are better off using a tool that performs a specific task very well but doesn't attempt to do too many things, than using one that does many things, but none very well.

Costs versus Function

Cheaper, better, faster—any tool you decide to use should meet any two of these adjectives. The effects on the third should be considered as well. Let's go back to the carpentry analogy. Say you are a carpenter and are looking for a better hammer. You find an electric nail gun for sale. It's the latest technology in nailing. It very effectively and efficiently drives nails into wood. It appears to help perform nailing tasks better and faster. But it costs more than a traditional hammer. Do the benefits outweigh the additional cost? This is not necessarily an easy question to answer and requires further investigation. After all, ultimately a wood-framed wall built using a nail gun would not be much different than one built by a skilled carpenter using a traditional hammer.

Start by comparing the base cost of the tools themselves. Then consider the additional costs. There are training expenses and additional running costs. The nail gun requires electricity—maybe not a big expense, but one that should be considered. Then there is the potential problem of needing the services of the nail gun in a place that does not have electricity. If this problem will be frequently encountered, maybe buying a generator will fix that issue. But this adds yet more costs for both the generator itself and its ongoing fuel requirements. What appeared to be an easy decision seems to get more and more difficult.

Now reevaluate what your needs are and what the new tool will do for you. Were you looking for a new hammer to outfit a new employee you just hired? Or was your old hammer wearing out from years of use or broken from misuse? What type of carpenter are you? One that frames houses and generally spends the better part of the day driving nails, or one who specializes in making attached decks on houses and mostly uses galvanized deck screws? The first carpenter may be much better off investing in the nail gun, while the other may actually harm his business with an unnecessary upgrade.

Similarly for software testing tools, there will be associated training and running expenses. When new users need to learn about a testing tool, or existing users require education on its enhancements, a training cost is incurred that must be factored into the spending budget. Running costs will also include maintenance of the tool, as well as resources that its operations require, such as accompanying hardware, software, or personnel. Don't forget about those costs—they can break the bank later.

TOOL CATEGORIES

There are many ways to logically group tools that support the software test discipline. They can be organized by test phases, by the test activities they support, or other ways. The specific grouping presented here has no particular significance; it's just one way to tie the many tools together. It is also not all inclusive, nor is it intended to be. It simply offers a general overview of some testing tools commonly used in the software development industry.

Support Tools

There are tools available that will assist in the test process. These tools may not be directly involved in test execution but instead help testers and test teams manage their activities.

Problem Management Tools

The main objective of testing is to discover software defects. When a defect is found, you'll want a tool to help you document it and track it until the defect is debugged and a fix is delivered and verified. Also referred to as a defect tracking tool, the purpose of a problem management tool is to provide a central repository for describing defects uncovered. The tool will identify the defect's current status, such as whether it has been debugged down to the root cause, whether a fix is available, or the fix target completion date. This type of tool can be used by both developers and testers. A good one will be directly or indirectly tied to a source code control tool.

Source Code Control Tools

Traditionally considered a core software development tool, a code library does more than just hold the source code of the software. Its major function is to provide strict controls on a software entity, providing proper serialization of software parts that are created and modified by multiple developers simultaneously. The terms "check out" and "check in" are sometimes used to describe whether a part is in the process of being modified or integrated into the software product. A code library can also work as a tool for testers, as it can provide them with the same ability to keep control of their test cases.

Test Management Tools

Testers quickly discover management's keen interest in their current status. Also called a test tracking tool, this tool gives a test team an easy way to deliver a status update. Many times, this type of tool will show how current testing progress maps against what was planned. In other words, it tells you whether you are ahead of or behind schedule. Some test management tools also keep track of the individual testing tasks planned and can identify which ones have been attempted. They can also track whether those attempted tasks succeeded or failed. Some will even identify the defect tracking tool problem number(s) associated with a failed test and automatically monitor the status of that problem via an interface with the defect tracking tool. Of course, no test tracking tool is complete without the ability to automatically generate fancy charts and graphs that make managers drool. Read ahead and you'll see an example of using this type of tool in Chapter 18, "Managing the Test."

Test Planning Tools

There are various types of widgets in this category. They range from text editing software used for test plan development to fancy reviewing tools that assist in the review process. These reviewing tools typically let reviewers append comments directly into a formatted test plan document, automatically notify the test plan owner, and support a disposition of the comment (e.g. accepted, rejected, update completed). In many cases, they will assist in complying with quality certification standards such as ISO9001.

Other tools to assist in test planning can be built or purchased. A very easy one to build is described in Chapter 5, "Where to Start? Snooping for Information,": a simple checklist to guide a tester through investigation, planning, and execution activities. When challenged with the potential of having to test many combinations of hardware environments or other variables, there are optimization tools to help you identify the minimum number of configurations required to achieve maximum coverage. These are just a couple of examples out of the many tools available.

Source-code-aware Tools

These tools are typically geared for the developer and are most appropriately used during the unit test phase. They are mentioned here because testers should at least be aware of them and advocate their use by development. Also, there are some cases where a tool best suited for unit test can also be used for some purposes in other test phases.

Code Coverage Tools

A code coverage tool does what its name states. It reports on the source code statements that have been executed after tests have been run, as well as those that have not been executed. In addition, these tools give statistics on the number of times a statement was executed and the percentage of statements executed. Some code coverage tools will also show the ranges of statements not executed. Traditionally run in unit test, these tools have also been used by function testers and system testers to get a view of the code coverage attained when they run their test cases and workloads. A number of code coverage tools require the tester to recompile or actually modify the product software to enable them to extract the pertinent path information. Consider this a running cost.

Static Code Analysis Tools

Code analysis tools programmatically scan source code and identify common coding mistakes. These tools do not require that you execute the software under analysis. Some common coding errors these tools attempt to identify are use of uninitialized variables, memory leaks, and out-of-bounds array access. In some cases, the source code scan is accompanied by an analysis service, in which you contract out the analysis to a vendor. Some types of errors identified by static code analysis tools can also be identified by specifying certain options on some compilers. Again, it's normally the development team's responsibility to have this analysis done, but you can gain some valuable insights by reviewing the resulting reports. For example, you may be able to identify parts of the software that tend to be more error prone than others. Based on this knowledge, you may wish to zero in on these parts during your test.

Test Execution Aids

There are many, many tools in this category, far too many to list here. This class of tool assists in the actual execution of tests and can also ease the burden of creating test cases. We'll describe two types: end-user simulators and frameworks.

End-user Simulators

This is a generalized way of describing many tools. From GUI automation to large systems load and stress, these tools provide a way to automate entering work into the system in ways similar to those of the software's real users. Considered the "bread and butter" of many system test teams, they can supply a way to simulate many thousands of end users simultaneously entering transactions. Such tools can drive very robust applications through quite simple and natural means. For instance, a tool might do nothing more than simulate the keystrokes or mouse clicks of an end user on a Web page. Those keystrokes or mouse clicks invoke "real" transactions that call "real" applications that require access to "real" data. By simulating hundreds to thousands of such users, the tool can push significant loads against the targeted software stack.

Frameworks

Many very powerful tools do nothing. Of course, this is an unfair characterization of frameworks, but it illustrates their nature. Frameworks are tools that provide services or encapsulated, invokable functions for use by test cases or test scripts. They eliminate busywork so the tester can focus on creating only the code needed to exercise the items he wishes to test. Frameworks provide the foundation for those tests, or offer services that can reduce the complexity of establishing certain environments. Many frameworks are easily extended by allowing the user to plug in new callable services. This is one reason why frameworks are so powerful and potentially long-lived. They allow the tool to be enhanced by its users so it can evolve over time and keep current with new technology. Later in this chapter we'll describe a sample framework in detail.

Tester Niche Creations

The *Merriam-Webster Online Dictionary* defines a tool as "something (as an instrument or apparatus) used in performing an operation or necessary in the practice of a vocation or profession." Using this definition, testers typically build many small tools as they perform their daily duties. These tools are often born out of frustration or boredom due to repeatedly executing mundane tasks. Or, they are the result of a tester trying an innovative way to focus a test in a particular area. These tools are usually scripts, execs, or other small programs designed to fill a niche in the team's test suite. The thrashers described in Chapter 12, "Data Corruption," fall into this category.

Just a Sampling

This is just a very small subset of the many software test tools available. It would be impossible to describe all the tools that exist. If you know exactly what you want to achieve, you can likely find a tool to help you get there. By fully understanding your test responsibilities and adhering to best practices, the specific tools you'll need will be apparent. Locating them should not be difficult.

Tools You Won't Find on the Open Market

Although there are many software testing tools available commercially, it probably isn't realistic to expect them to fulfill all of your needs. Test tool suppliers are in business for the same reason your company is—to make money. As a result, they must have positive business cases to develop and support new test tool offerings. There will be times when your requirements won't meet this standard, and so you'll have to create the necessary tools yourself. Let's look at a couple of examples.

Tools for Testing New Technology

If the software you are testing is groundbreaking new technology, it may be impossible for a test tool supplier to support your testing needs. They can't support what they don't know exists. Even if you disclose to them prior to announcing the new technology, you can't assume that they will alter their own strategies and development plans immediately. By the time they are done analyzing their own business case to decide whether to support the new technology, your testing will most likely be complete. If your test plan was dependent on the tool company supporting your new requirements, you could be in a precarious position. This is a case where you'll often have to develop your own custom tools.

This is not to say that existing tools cannot be used for testing new technology. For instance, the end-user simulators described earlier are basically ignorant of the software technology they are driving. In this case, it's the scripts created by the testers that can be updated to ensure the new function is tested appropriately. The end-user simulator can act as a test harness for your scripts and does not need to understand the underlying function of the software. Of course, you can come up with a scenario where even this is not the case. If the end-user simulator enters work into the system over a limited number of network protocols and the software function you are testing is the implementation of a new network protocol, then you'll need to find other ways to drive the software. If you obtain a thorough understanding of what it is you will be testing and you know the capabilities of the tools you use, you won't be caught by surprise in a scenario like this and you can put plans in place to address it.

Tools for Testing Unique Functions

For white-box or gray-box function testing, your productivity and effectiveness can be improved with test tools that understand the target software. But there may be cases where your needs are not ubiquitous enough to warrant any external test tool supplier supporting them. You'll have to fill the void with in-house tool development.

Let's look at one such test tool and the functions it supplies. This tool loosely falls under the category of a framework described earlier and is used mainly by function test groups responsible for testing components of the z/OS operating system.

CASE STUDY: A HOMEGROWN TEST TOOL FRAMEWORK

The Component Test Tool (CTT) was developed to provide a framework for testers of the IBM mainframe's operating system. CTT's origin lies in a creative approach to testing a component deep in that operating system. A significant software rewrite planned for the Recovery Termination Manager (RTM) was going to require a huge investment in test case coding. An obvious approach would have been to code a common test case model, then for each new test case copy that model and modify it as needed. But by doing this, there is the risk of propagating common errors and adding complexity when establishing environments for each test case.

The situation motivated an experienced test leader and his team to search for a more efficient way to validate the RTM. The team needed a means to provide simplification, extendibility, workload distribution, exploitation of system services as part of normal tool processing, and multisystem capability. The result was the CTT.

Simplification of Complex Environments

CTT provided testers with a set of services they could use to create and modify test cases quickly and efficiently. The major strength of CTT was its support for establishing a wide variety of system operating environments quickly, consistently, and, most importantly, correctly. The tool provided a set of functions, or "verbs," that allowed the tester to easily create test cases in extremely complex environments. And with a single invocation of a verb, CTT performed all of the messy tasks needed to establish these environments [Loveland02].

When faced with the need for many similar test cases to establish complex environments, consider creating a framework that consolidates that complexity in a single place, so development of the individual test cases becomes simpler.

For example, most operating systems set priorities for different types of work. On the mainframe, something called a service request block (SRB) represents a unit of work that carries a higher-than-normal priority. Unfortunately, establishing and executing the SRB operating mode can be an involved process with many steps. CTT simplified that process by hiding it behind a single verb. This freed testers to focus on the services being tested in SRB mode, rather than on this tedious setup work.

A framework can provide a small set of high-level commands that perform tasks that are routine but tedious and error prone.

Figures 13.1 and 13.2 outline a traditional programming approach to establishing an SRB mode environment and a CTT SRB mode implementation, respectively. The code in Figure 13.1 implements the scheduling of the SRB using a high-level programming language. The details aren't important. Just note the volume of code and complexity involved—and the opportunity for error.

The code in Figure 13.2 makes use of the CTT test case infrastructure. The interesting part is the function named SCHEDULE. This single verb performs the entire set of tasks outlined in Figure 13.1 without requiring the programmer to understand all of the details. Clearly, CTT made it easier to develop test cases and eliminated worry about the complexities of the underlying environment. Consolidation of the complexity of system or application services into a single interface is a characteristic of leading software testing tools.

Extendability

Constantly depending on the test tool support team to provide new function to all interested test teams quickly results in work prioritization. Software test tools must be self-extendable by their users in order to lower the reliance on the tool support team. CTT was structured with *plug-in* capability to make it extendable by its user community. Let's examine how the technique was implemented.

Find ways to make a framework easy for users themselves to extend. An interface for pluggable, user-written modules is one effective technique.

```
/*Code fragment to schedule SRB (Service Request Block) Routine */
DCL CVTPTR PTR(31) LOCATION(16);
DCL SRBREG REG(6) PTR(31) RSTD;
DCL SRBPTR PTR(31);
DCL ASCBPTR PTR(31);
DCL SRB_ADDR PTR(31);

DCL MYSRB CHAR(LENGTH(SRBSECT))BDY(WORD); /* Srb storage */
DCL SRB_PARMLIST BDY(DWORD);/* SBR parameters */

  ?MODESET KEY(ZERO) MODE(SUP);
/* GET NON-SWAPPABLE */
  GEN(SYSEVENT DONTSWAP);
/* LOAD THE SRB    */
  ?LOAD EP("SRBRTN*") LOADPT(SRB_ADDR)
      GLOBAL(YES,F) ERRET(BADLOAD2);
BADLOAD2:
 IF SBR_ADDR=0 THEN /*If load failed */
   DO;      /*Terminate*/
     RETCODE=16;
     ?WTO("Load failed for SBR routine SRBRTN") ROUTCDE(11);
   END;      /*End of load failed */
ELSE DO; /*Sbr loaded*/
     SBR_PARAMLIST="B;/* Clear out parameter list*/
   /*SETUP SBR SRBRTN*/
     SRBREG=ADDR(MYSRB);/*Get addressability to SRB*/
     RFY SRBSECT BASED(SRBREG);
     SRBSECT BASED(SRBREG);
     SRBSECT="B;/*Clear out SRB*/
   /*Initialize the SRB control block*/
     SRBPTR=ADDR(SRB);  /*Set address of SRB */
     SRBID="SRB";     /*Initialize acronym   */
     SRBPASID=PSAAOLD->.ASCBASID;/*SRB is to run in Home addrspace*/
     SRBASCB=PSAAOLD
     SRBPTCB=PSATOLD; /*Purge tcb affinity*/
     SRBEP=SRB_ADDR|"80000000"X;/*INDICATE AMODE 31*/
     SRBPARM=ADDR(SRB_PARMLIST);/*Set up SRB parm list*/
     SRBRMTR=ADDR(CVTBRET); /*No Resource manager*/
/****************************************************************/
/*Actual call to the system to schedule the SRB for execution. */
/*Additional complexity on scheduling the SRB is introduced    */
/*when different types of system locks are required.           */
/*This is the most simplistic case.                            */
/****************************************************************/
 ?SCHEDULE SRB((SRBPTR)) SCOPE(LOCAL) LLOCK(NO)
    FRR(NO) MODE NOHXM);
END;/*End of SBR Loaded*/
GEN(SYSEVENT REQSWAP);/*  GET SWAPPABLE    */
?MODESET KEY(NZERO) MODE(PROB);/*Return to unauthorized state*/
```

FIGURE 13.1 SRB schedule program segment [Loveland02].

Implementation Details

The design and implementation of CTT allowed for quick and convenient extendibility. CTT is comprised of two functions, parsing and processing. During the
parse phase, the input stream of statements is deciphered and interpreted. CTT
parses the entire input stream and, if there are errors, reports on all of them and

```
INIT TESTCASE=SCHEDULE,ASID=MAINSID,
     MAINID=MAINTASK;/*Identify the testcase*/

/**********************************************/
/**Sample CTT deck to Schedule an SRB and   */
/**wait for the SRB to end its processing   */
/**********************************************/

STARTDEF TYPE=MAIN, ID=MAINTASK;/*Start of main task */
  SCHEDULE SRDID=SRB1, ASID=MAINASID;/*Schedule SRB*/
  WAIT WAITID=WAITER1; /*Wait for SRB to complete*/
ENDDEF TYPE=MAIN, ID=MAINTASK;/*End of MAIN task*/

STARTDEF TYPE=SRB, ID=SRB1; /*Start of the SRB*/
  POST WAITID=WAITER1,ASID=MAINASID;/*Post MAIN task*/
ENDDEF TYPE=SRB, ID=SRB1;/*End of SRB*/
```

FIGURE 13.2   CTT SRB schedule program segment [Loveland02].

stops execution. If the parse completes successfully, CTT builds control structures representing each individual input statement. These control structures are linked into a double-threaded structure that is an ordered representation of the input statements.

A high-level command input language can offer a rich user interface for a framework, but it implies that a parser will need to be reused or developed.

After parsing, CTT begins processing. The CTT uses a simple dispatching algorithm that traverses the queue and examines the control structures, each representing a particular input statement. One of the data items within the control structure element is the address of a program to be called to perform the functions associated with the element. The control structure element contains all of the parameters and options specified on the input statement. The process program, which is called by the dispatching algorithm, interprets the data passed via the control structure element and performs the actual function requested. Figure 13.3 shows the CTT dispatching approach.

To perform actions and coordinate work, a framework will typically require at least a crude dispatcher.

This implementation is key to the extendibility of CTT. Both the parse program and process program that are called by CTT are simple plug-ins. Testers wishing to implement new or improved CTT verbs or functions can simply specify an input pointer to a set of verb definition files. These files specify the name of the parse and process routines that CTT is to load and utilize for the specific verb. At any time,

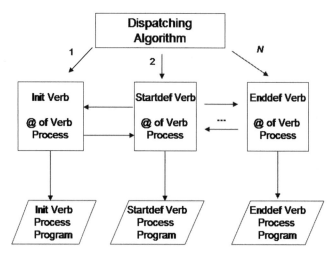

FIGURE 13.3   CTT dispatching algorithm [Loveland02].

testers can develop their own verbs or functions for use in the CTT framework. As these plug-ins mature, they are then integrated into the base tool framework for the benefit of all users.

By creating a user-extendable framework you can turn the entire test community into part of the tool's development team, greatly speeding the availability of new features.

CTT also provides its users with a call interface to other programs. The important aspect of this function is a precise set of data parameters between CTT and the "called" program. The data parameters contain pointers to return and reason code indicators so that the target program can inform CTT of success or failure.

Ensure a framework can always report on the success or failure of test cases it manages.

Another benefit of this capability is that the tester can take advantage of CTT's support for establishing complex execution environments and then call a target program of its own. This gives the tester a way to simplify his target program and let CTT perform all of the complex tasks of establishing a particular operating mode.

Extend a framework's reach by enabling it to programmatically invoke external test cases.

Workload Distribution and Multisystem Capability

Once the original RTM testing was completed, the CTT continued to evolve along with the technology it was designed to test. When IBM began developing its mainframe clustering technology, Parallel Sysplex, the CTT expanded its capabilities to include multisystem environments. This new and improved CTT allowed the tester to distribute portions of a test case across systems in the cluster. The multi-system capability allowed testers to validate cross-system functions and processes that were, otherwise, very complex to build and implement.

Structure a framework so it can be easily adapted to meet unforeseen future needs.

```
//CTTDECK JOB_
     .
     .
     .
//CTTIN DD*
INIT TESTCASE=CTTDECK.SYSTEMID=SYS1,
   CTT functions (verbs) to be performed on a system SYS1

INIT TESTCASE=CTTDECK.SYSTEMID=SYS2,
   CTT functions (verbs) to be performed on a system SYS2

INIT TESTCASE=CTTDECK.SYSTEMID=SYS3,
   CTT functions (verbs) to be performed on a system SYS3
```

FIGURE 13.4   Provides a template for a multisystem CTT test case.

The implementation allowed portions of the multisystem test case to be distributed in the cluster regardless of the number of systems currently active. Testers were able to target specific parts of a test case to a specific system by simply identifying the actual system name in the SYSTEMID parameter of the INIT verb. If the CTT test case was coded for more than the current number of active systems in the cluster, CTT would intelligently distribute portions of the test case across the currently active systems. This helped promote CTT's portability and reuse across different test configurations.

Consider portability issues when creating a framework in order to maximize its appeal and usefulness throughout the test organization.

Exploitation of System Services

In order to provide this multisystem communication capability, CTT itself made use of the very clustering services it was being enhanced to help test. Figure 13.5 gives an overview of the natural exploitation of these services. The primary ones used included those for monitoring members within a defined cluster subgroup, and those designed to communicate among the members. Message passing among the members was the key means of coordinating actions. By using new services of the software under test to accomplish its mission, the CTT went from a simple framework to an exploiter in its own right. This role as exploiter provided yet another option for test coverage.

A framework can contribute to the testing of new software features by making use of them itself.

NOTE

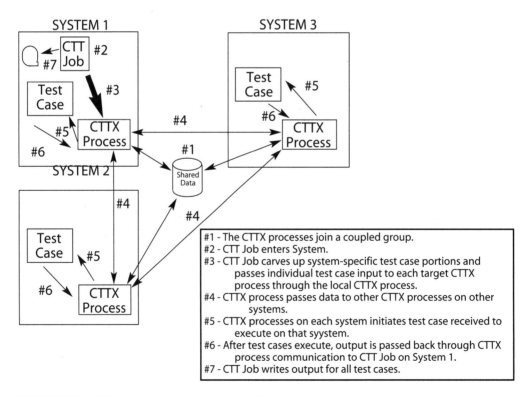

FIGURE 13.5 CTT and coupling services exploitation.

New Technology and Tools

With the introduction of the IBM eServer™ zSeries z900, mainframe technology began to provide larger memory capacity than ever before. As a result, the test tool landscape needed to provide support for the new frontiers in real and virtual memory. CTT was no exception. It expanded to exploit the new hardware to provide the test community with the framework to exercise its functions.

As with hardware, each time a new software product is produced or planned, development teams must look to their testing brethren and work together to ensure that the proper tool support is in place to help validate the product.

Epilogue

The Component Test Tool was originally designed as a framework to ease the burden of coding a large volume of test cases when preparing to test a new software release. CTT had to be written in-house, because the area it addressed was too specialized for a tool vendor. Because it was written in a flexible, extendable way, it has been able to evolve over the years to meet new testing challenges. To this day, it still continues to thrive and help mainframe testers spend less time on tedious, repetitive coding and more time on finding bugs.

BUY VERSUS BUILD

The title of this section could very well be "Buy versus Buy." Whether you spend resources to build a tool or to buy one, you are paying someone. The payee may be different, but it boils down to money spent. There is no right or wrong answer about which option to choose. It is a matter of what makes the most business sense in each case. However, there are some general guidelines you may wish to follow.

Tools to Buy

Unless you are in the software test tool business, your first instinct should lean toward obtaining testing tools from external sources rather than spending a lot of time and effort building them. You can either purchase the test tool from an outside vendor or find an existing, supported tool that is widely used throughout your company.

Tools that support tasks and practices that are common to most test teams, or that are in support of activities not directly related to the software being tested, should be obtained externally. A good example is tracking status. Every test team has to do it. Suggesting that your test tracking requirements are so unique that you need your own homegrown, customized tool for tracking is a difficult argument to win. Your time is much better spent testing than writing and supporting a test tracking tool. It's this line of thinking that is needed when you are faced with the "buy versus build" decision.

In addition, tools that provide complex functions and can support your test requirements are best purchased. End-user simulation tools are a good example. It would be very difficult and most likely not a good use of your time to try to build them. These complex, powerful tools are best left to test-tool experts and full-time developers.

Tools to Build

Whether you explicitly decide to build tools or not, you *will* be building them. It's just a natural byproduct of testing. By its nature, software testing requires testers to create various scripts and other test tools. It's unavoidable. You'll also find that nontest tools will be built as part of the overall test effort. For example, testers will automate mundane tasks—you can pretty much count on it. These efforts should be embraced and rewarded.

The other tools you cannot avoid building are ones that are required to help you test new technology that cannot be efficiently tested with existing external tools. The CTT just described is a good example. Focused test drivers like the thrashers mentioned earlier should also be built.

AVOID THE TOOL MERRY-GO-ROUND

Tools are so essential to software testing that it's very easy to get entangled in the tool decision process. In their quest for perfection, it is not unusual for testers to continually question whether there are better tools available.

Identifying the Real Problem

Testers and test teams are under constant pressure to reduce the time needed for a test at the same time that they are wrestling with more and more complex software. A natural reaction is to blame a lack of tool support as the major reason for being unsuccessful at handling these conflicting demands. But if proper attention is paid to test planning and preparation, the tools required will be identified as a matter of course. Many times, the frustration with certain tools is a symptom of other issues, rather than any real technical issues with the tools being used.

Optimizing Your Use of Existing Tools

Identifying, investigating, and evaluating tools are important responsibilities of a test leader. But it's important to recognize how much time and effort is spent doing so. Of course it is very important to keep abreast of new test tool technology and strategies should be put in place to ensure you don't fall behind. But this activity needs to be balanced with existing test responsibilities. It's important to exhaust the use of the tools you have and augment them with other creations if needed. It may hurt the process more than help it if you keep from fully utilizing the tools you already have because you're spending too much time on endless tool evaluations.

SUMMARY

Just like any carpenter, a tester needs a toolbox full of tools to get the job done. There are both tool requirements and many solutions available for all aspects of software testing. But like a good carpenter, a good tester is not defined by his tools, but by his skill at using them. Quality tools are not free, whether you build them yourself or buy them, and you'll need to make some difficult business decisions about how to best address your tool needs. Sometimes building your own tools is unavoidable, and some tools will naturally be developed as you execute the test process.

We've seen that some test tools provide a framework for driving test work through the system. But what is the content of those tests? Can they align with real customer activities? In Chapter 14, "Emulating Customers to Find the Bugs That Matter," we'll look at emulating customer workloads to expose the bugs that matter most.

14 Emulating Customers to Find the Bugs That Matter

In This Chapter

- Approaches for porting customer applications
- Customer-oriented goals for tests
- Managing the test lab as a production environment

"Customer-like testing" is an oxymoron. It's a common term many test teams use to describe their efforts. But customers of information technology use software to do something useful—solve a problem, become more productive, help their businesses perform, or create a competitive advantage. Software customers do not explicitly attempt to remove defects in their production environments. In fact, they strive to avoid them. So, if attempting to find and remove defects is not customer-like, how can any test activity with that goal be described as such? In this sense, "customer-like testing" is self-contradictory.

That in no way suggests testers should not attempt to emulate customers in their quest to find and destroy bugs. Putting software through the same paces in the test lab that it will undergo in customer shops should be one of your primary objectives. Designing and implementing tests targeted for typical usage aims you toward the defects that would most affect your customers. You'll remove the bugs that matter.

As noted in earlier chapters, each test phase is geared toward finding different types of defects, and should be focused on the right set of objectives. The notion of emulating customers applies to all test phases. It's as much a matter of having the customer mindset as anything else. However, in many cases the test phases best suited to having specific, documented customer emulation objectives are SVT and Integration Test (if one exists). Techniques for emulating customers during testing can be divided into three categories. The first is defining *what* you run in your test, the second is *how* you run it, and the third is *managing* the test environments.

DETERMINING WHAT TESTS TO RUN

Customers' production software rarely runs in isolation. It must fit into a complex, intertwined environment. It must inter-operate with many other individual pieces of technology that are brought together to create a complete IT infrastructure. Testers ignore this reality at their peril.

In some cases, taking an application the customer runs in its production environment and porting it to your test lab is a good way to find problems not exposed by other testing. And since it's a real application, any problems it finds automatically fall into the category of defects that matter. On the other hand, there are times when creating artificial applications or workloads that are modeled after real applications are cheaper and more effective. This is particularly true in the realm of general-purpose software, where the range of customers spans many industries. In such cases, it is far too large an undertaking to mimic every customer's applications for testing. On the other hand, creating a composite workload patterned after a variety of actual environments can be quite effective. Let's examine both the porting and modeling approaches.

Porting Customer Workloads: the Challenges

An executive of a software development company is playing golf with an executive of one of his biggest customers. In between drives, chips, and putts, the customer describes a set of problems his team has seen with the latest release of the software. The software development executive apologizes and commits to port the customer's workload to the test lab in order to re-create and resolve the problems. Both agree that it is a wonderful idea and head off to the nineteenth hole.

Was the idea as good as it initially sounded? Perhaps. If implementing the idea results in a cost-effective test improvement, it is. However, if the implementation proves expensive and actually *reduces* test effectiveness, it's not good—for the software company or the customer. What may seem like a terrific idea on the golf course can sometimes prove to be just the opposite on the test floor. The likely success or failure of porting a customer workload into a test lab is dependent on a variety of factors. Many of these may not be obvious at the outset of the project. Let's take a look.

Customer Application Attributes

First, it's important to understand the nature of customer applications. They are written to perform business logic and accomplish tasks for the organization. The functions they perform are intended to meet the requirements of some business unit or process. The applications are not written with the goal of uncovering defects, and most likely will not have attributes that are desirable in a test application. For example, they are not designed to be run repeatedly to test functions or detect problems and capture diagnostic data. So while a particular customer application may happen to be good at exposing a certain bug or class of bugs, it may not be overly useful in helping the test team isolate and diagnose those bugs.

Capturing Data

An application won't trip over bugs until it is invoked. Simply copying the application to your test lab is not enough. You'll also need to drive realistic activity against it. This implies you may need to capture both the initial state of critical pieces required for the application to run and the actual runtime activity of the application. For example, the state of the data in a database is key for application transactions to execute successfully. The initial state of the database needs to be synchronized with the beginning of the transactions. Depending on the situation, you might also need to collect information on the flow of activity to the application in order to replicate that same flow in automated test scripts. This is fairly trivial to do for a GUI application on a personal computer. It becomes more difficult to achieve for a large enterprise application that receives a continuous stream of input from local users on channel-attached terminals, remote users coming in over the network, remote devices such as ATMs or point-of-sale kiosks, other applications, and simultaneous input and activity from batch work.

Additional Complexities

In addition, large, real-life applications have other components that must be captured. The state of the security environment, the security repositories, and user information and permissions are needed. The real time and date of the activity might be important to the application. The application may require pieces of information from the database of another application running in a separate environment. It may pass and receive data to and from that other application. These types of applications are typical in large IT environments and they routinely support hundreds to thousands of concurrent users. Any piece of the puzzle that is not captured can significantly impact the later execution of the workload in the test environment. Unfortunately, this type of issue is often not discovered until after significant time and effort has been spent on the porting activity.

Confidentiality Concerns

There are also confidentiality issues to address. The contents of the data to port may contain very sensitive information. For instance, the personal information of the business's customers might be included—names, addresses, phone numbers, credit card numbers, or Social Security numbers. Very strict data protection procedures may need to be created, reviewed, and approved. Many details like the physical location of the storage drives; backup capabilities and security requirements on the backup media; and rules on storage sharing, test system access, and tester access need to be documented. Any of these issues could become an insurmountable hurdle to proceeding with the port.

What Would You Get?

All of this information gathering and synchronizing can be done, and in fact, has been done. It's not impossible. But what are you left with when you are finished? You have a point-in-time snapshot of a piece of a production environment that you can replay. That can be considered a good thing. The snapshot can be used for very specific test objectives such as proof of concept activities or specific performance measurements. Using it for general testing of robust, complex software has its downfalls, however. The environment, its data, and its infrastructure can be copied, but without the customer's usage flow you're not accomplishing much from a test perspective. Sometimes building the workload from scratch can be just as effective at finding the same bugs the customer experienced—along with the side benefit of being useful for a long time.

What is Missing?

We've looked at what you get after all the data is collected, but what about what you don't get?

The Big Picture

One thing you won't get is an entire view of the application. The activity in large IT environments similar to the one described in Chapter 2, "Industrial-Strength Software, It's Not a Science Project," is very dynamic. What happens on Monday isn't exactly the same as Tuesday. The activity that occurs the first week of a month differs from that of the last week of the month. The same is true about end-of-quarter and end-of-year processing. The type and level of activity you end up with depends on the days you collected the data.

Updated Code

It's also important to note that application programmers are just that, programmers of applications. This means they create, enhance, and maintain their applications. They continuously update them. So, it is safe to assume that very soon after an application is ported to a test environment, it no longer is the same as the application running in the customer's environment. A tester would be fooling himself if he thought what he had a month after collecting the data was a current view of the application. Be aware that after you have your copy of the application, you will only be gaining the benefit of what it does up to that point. Anything new that the customer's programmers do after that point is no longer part of the benefit you see.

Randomness

Another element important to test workloads that you won't get with customer application ports is the capability for randomness. The activity from the ported application often needs to be replayed in the same sequence as it was when initially gathered. The speed of the transactional input can be varied, but only on a global scale that keeps the sequence of events the same. So every replay is basically redundant, resulting in the workload's gradually losing its effectiveness in finding defects. Software can get "grooved" to a static workload, which is not the result you want.

Maintainability

In a moment of crisis, you may be tempted to dump a customer's entire application environment blindly to portable media and restore it in your test lab. Certainly this is one way to ensure that you capture not only the application, but all of its associated data and configuration information. It also creates a starting point at which the application and its data are well-synchronized. However, the result may prove difficult to maintain. A lack of documentation on the database structure and the application's dependencies on it, for example, may make the database difficult to prune or upgrade. If you don't understand the internals of the application, it might be impossible to adapt it later when its supporting infrastructure is upgraded and features it relies on are deprecated. Be wary of the lure of a raw dump and restore of a customer environment. In some situations it might provide a quick fix, but don't expect it to deliver long-term value to the test team after the crisis is over.

Return on Investment

After investing all the time and effort involved in porting a large application, you want a good return on that investment. Snapshots of an application should be able to be replayed for a substantial period of time, right? Not necessarily. An experience from a real application port will demonstrate this potential pitfall.

Example: The Aging of a Ported Application

A large application was ported from a company in the insurance industry to a software test environment. It was the "claims" application. This application is used to process the claims made by insured customers, performing some very complex tasks like automatic fraud detection. After a period of time, transactions that used to work began to fail. In this case, the problems were not the result of system software changes. The transactions began failing because claims were being made against policies that had expired. Policies were expiring because the premiums for the policies were not paid. Policy management was done by a different program, the "premiums" application, and that application was not ported.

Modeling Customer Workloads: Techniques

When a direct port of a customer application does not seem likely to achieve your goals, what other approaches can you take? We'll use the term modeling loosely here, but you can build your own stripped-down applications or test cases that are modeled after customer usage. Additional attributes geared toward test requirements can be folded into these test programs. For example, you can create workloads that generate activity similar to your customer's application and supports user controls that dynamically alter execution or the sequence of events. Give yourself the ability to randomize some sequences or capture diagnostic data.

Start by looking for an existing test application you have that uses the software under test in similar ways as the customer application. The two programs will likely be quite different, but if they hit similar pressure points in the target software, you may be able to adapt your existing test version to mimic the real customer example.

If you aren't trying to replicate a particular customer's problem but simply want to make your test workloads more representative of the real world, consider creating a composite customer profile. Obtain activity data from a sampling of your customers. Use some of the customer reconnaissance techniques outlined in Chapter 5, "Where to Start? Snooping for Information." Break the problem down into its base elements and look at them in excruciating technical detail. Are there spikes in the activity when business opens? Or is there more of a saw tooth characteristic to the workload? Be sure that your sampling includes customers who frequently report defects.

Then for SVT, for example, consider using the aggregate of all the team's various test cases, etc. as the "production workload." Learn the general attributes that workload demonstrates. This will be your starting point, your baseline. Now begin a compare-and-contrast exercise with your SVT workload. Are there ways it can be modified to align with the composite customer profile?

Systematic Approach

What data you review and what activity you strive to generate depends heavily on what it is you are testing. But the general approach can be the same. You'll want to take a systematic approach using empirical data. Identify key characteristics of the way the software is driven—pressure points and rates of activities that are measurable and externalized in some way, either by the software under test or related tools. Then define corresponding activity goals for your existing workloads. Make targeted changes to the workloads, and then measure them. Iteratively modify and remeasure. Keep a close eye on the activity your workloads generate and enhance them until they converge with your customer sampling.

Activity Goals

Most operating systems have many system activity measurements that can be monitored via performance reports, operator commands, and system monitoring tools. These measurements allow for easy ways to gather data from customers and define test goals of system activity based on that data. The testers can also use the same performance reports and operator commands to measure their workloads against those goals and make modifications based on the results. We'll describe a few examples for a system test to trigger ideas on what is available for your own situation.

Input/Output Rates

I/O activity can be viewed in many ways. Goals for I/O activity can be defined at different levels of granularity, such as the total number of I/O requests per second across a single system. Another example is the total number of I/O requests per second across all the systems participating in the same cluster. You can get more specific and define goals for I/O activity to a particular storage drive, again from both a single system and from multiple systems that share the same drive (when such sharing is supported.) Getting even more granular, you can define and measure goals for I/O activity against a particular file on a storage device. And for network or SAN-attached storage drives, you can define I/O utilization goals across the attachment medium.

You'll also want to ensure you have a good mix of different I/O types. Your mix would include attributes like read/write ratios against a database, so create workloads that perform X number of writes of data for every Y number of reads. Since caching is an important part of the technology, you'll want to have goals for that also. You can look at cache hit percentages and cache misses. This applies to both hardware and software caches, if any. Linux systems, for example, buffer file I/O in otherwise unused memory.

For all of these examples of I/O activity goals, it's important to correlate activity numbers with response time goals. You'll want to ensure that the activity numbers created from a review of the customer data are matched with a test hardware configuration that can support the desired activity requested and performs like customer environments.

Memory Usage

Most operating systems allow you to monitor different forms of memory usage. Simple console commands usually reveal how much memory is currently used, free, shared, or being used for caching or buffering. More sophisticated tools can often track the ebb and flow of memory usage over time. Likewise, some middleware programs can monitor how their exploiting applications are using memory. Web application servers, for example, can usually display changes in Java heap size as the load on an application increases. These kinds of memory usage statistics are important to include in your analysis. You can set test activity goals based on them. You might set a goal of driving the Java heap size to a particular threshold X times an hour, for instance, or target a specific system paging or swapping rate.

Shared Memory

Some software takes advantage of shared memory segments, which allow multiple processes to access common control structures and data. Examples of such memory areas include IPC shared memory in Unix and Linux, and the Common Storage Area and System Queue Area in z/OS. Goals on the use of these shared memory segments can be set and monitored.

Buffer Utilization

In addition to system-wide memory utilization goals, you can set goals for specific functions or subsystems. Many functions have their own cache or in-memory buffers for fast access to information and the ability to avoid I/O. For example, a distributed secure sign-on solution might maintain all user authentication and authorization information in a central server's repository, but cache portions of it as needed on each local client system to improve response times. Utilization goals for such caches can be created and measured. Some functions even support the ability to monitor buffer management activity, e.g., the number of times data was cast out of the buffer to make room for a more recently referenced item and the number of times the entire buffer filled up.

Resource Contention

In large clustered systems, where each system runs on an SMP, serialization is essential to successful operations. Varied resources on the system will be serialized for defined periods of time to ensure integrity. Some resources are "popular," so contention is anticipated and acceptable. The number of resources in contention, how long the contention lasts, and the number of waiters for the resource are monitored. Goals can be set for the amount of contention occurring as well as the average number of waiters. Average wait time is another reported item that can be modeled by a set of SVT workloads.

Other Activity Numbers

Some general system activity goals can be set, but still provide value in guiding some test objectives (e.g., the total number of active processes or address spaces on a system.) Other examples include the number of batch jobs that start and stop in a given period, the number of concurrent interactive users, and average CPU utilization.

Putting It All Together

Reviewing data generated by multiple customers will allow you to identify common themes and trends. You will want to find the high watermarks and use them as your baselines. Once the baselines are set, you can begin measuring the activity from your tests and compare the rates to those baselines. The ultimate goal is not just to achieve the baseline rates, but to exceed them, to "turn up the heat." In a system test environment, you'll be able to use a combination of test cases, thrashers, and workloads running together to achieve the activity goals and demonstrate the capability of the system, while putting yourself in the position to uncover the bugs your customers would shudder to see.

How Many Potatoes?

Using the techniques and approaches described in this book, you should be able to "test the breakage." This means running a test in a way that will eventually crash some software, which could be a good thing. But how do you ensure that the crashes you cause are the result of a software design or coding problem versus trying to put ten pounds of potatoes into a five-pound bag? Very sophisticated software can do amazing things, but it cannot create new hardware resources out of bits and bytes. Modeling your workload activity after your customer's gives you a much better understanding of how many potatoes should be able to fit in the bag.

IT'S NOT JUST WHAT, BUT HOW YOU TEST

The primary type of software discussed in this book is code that is made up of many components and developed by many programmers. The software under development may consist of multiple new functions. Typically, the testing of the new functions is parceled out to individual testers. This is appropriate, particularly early in the development cycle before all the pieces have had a chance to mature and stabilize. But once that stabilization has occurred and the pieces have come together, the way final tests are run can be slanted toward emulating customers.

Assigning Tester Roles

At some point in the test, you can take an approach beyond simply assigning individual testers to specific new functions. Here is where an end-to-end view of the solution can be examined. Take a close look at where the software fits into the bigger picture. Determine how the software will get integrated into a production environment, and how it will be operated and managed over time. Get the entire test team to participate, and assign roles to testers modeled after customer IT support roles.

In Chapter 1, "The Testing Challenge and Those Who Take It," a short description of typical IT support roles was presented. IT shops are managed by teams of professionals, each fulfilling specific responsibilities. Have the test team emulate this structure. Decide which role each tester will play—operator, systems programmer, network specialist, database administrator (DBA), or performance analyst. Spend time viewing the behavior of the software from these different perspectives. Work as a team to test the software with a production mentality. The roles you assign to team members will depend on the software you are testing and your team's individual skills. Think in terms of how the software will be used by your customers and how it integrates into the IT environment. The examples that follow are a subset of the roles typically found at large IT installations.

Systems Programmers

The systems programmers can perform all the setup and customization tasks using the documentation that comes with the software. They might also act as the support staff for the other team members, creating and documenting the procedures for managing the systems over the long haul. They can develop and perform maintenance procedures, provide hardware configuration management, and offer support for local customizations. The systems programmers may also be responsible for the data backup and archiving procedures, log management, change control, software installation, problem determination, and availability management, and also own their automation. While performing these tasks, they will obtain a good understanding of how the software performs from a real-life perspective.

Networking Specialists

The networking specialists can own and manage the network. They should pay particular attention to any networking functions provided by the software under test and ensure all of the latest features are enabled. Another role for them is to look at the integration of the software's networking capabilities with many other pieces outside of the specific test bed. The network specialists might, for example, create a portal to enable the rest of the team to remotely monitor and control the target software, or link it to a shared patch download repository.

Security Specialists

The security specialists control all aspects of security for the entire IT environment. They are responsible for the security of the network and manage the firewalls and all other protected resources, such as files and databases. They work with all of the other IT team members to provide the level of security required or mandated. These specialists also might take the approach of integrating the software's authentication and authorization mechanisms with an external application managing single sign-on across the environment.

Database Administrators

The DBAs own the data and define and manage the attributes of the databases. They need to understand the database requirements of the software under test as well as the applications built to drive the new functions. They can then work with the systems programmers to define the backup and archiving requirements of the pseudoproduction environment. The DBAs also provide the care and feeding of the databases, all the while noting the database server software's behavior and how it interacts with other software in the environment.

Performance Analysts

Every customer wants to squeeze the maximum amount of work out of their computing resources. That's where the performance analysts come in. These experts capture data on resource consumption, tune systems to achieve peak performance, and project future capacity needs based on recorded performance trends. Most industrial-strength software product teams have testers responsible for measuring performance in search of possible bottlenecks. However, such experimentation is normally done in unconstrained environments under carefully controlled conditions. Ask those same testers to perform the role of performance analyst in a customer-like, pseudoproduction environment where the conditions are anything *but* well controlled. That experience may open their eyes to weaknesses in the software's performance-data-gathering capabilities and lead to improvements that customers will greatly appreciate.

Application Programmers

The application programmers have a key role in this environment as well. They provide the much-needed programming skills to build the infrastructure and framework within which the business will operate. Without them, you aren't going to accomplish much. Similarly, the test team will be coding test cases, workloads, and tools that establish the testing fabric within which the test will be conducted.

Testers as Educators

A valuable byproduct of taking an approach similar to the one just described is the hands-on, real-life experiences obtained by the test team. This experiential knowledge gives the testers an excellent foundation. They are now better able to relate to the software's users and observe software behavior from a different perspective. If fact, the test team can become an acknowledged competency center of hands-on knowledge that can be of great value to the development, service, and customer communities. Testers also become a resource for educating customers, using language and experiences the customers can relate to, and offering hints and tips for things to do and to avoid. This can be done via documentation the test team creates or direct discussions with customers. A huge side benefit is the common bond that develops between the testers and customers. This elevates the perception of the contributions of test and adds to the team's credibility.

Mirroring Customer Production Objectives

Typically, there are major differences between test environments and customer production environments. Beyond the environmental distinctions are differences in how the code is executed. These stem from the contrasting objectives of testing versus production. Recognizing what the differences are enables you to shift the objectives of the test to more closely align with customer production objectives. Let's examine two typical ones.

Continuous Execution

A common test requirement is to set the environment to a known state. Often, testers spend the first part of the test carefully initializing storage devices, allocating new files, and creating databases primed with specific data. Once the environments are set up properly, the testing begins. But customers do not initialize their environments, and they do not have the luxury of "starting clean." Their only opportunity to start fresh is at the very initial deployment of a new application. After that occurs, the environment enters the world of continuous operations. Initializing databases, for instance, is no longer an option.

Can you imagine your bank reinitializing your checking account on a regular basis? Although it's appropriate for most tests to depend on a known starting state, some amount of testing should be geared toward examining continuous operations and understanding aging effects. For example, looking at the software's continuous operations may uncover potential memory leaks that could exhaust that memory at the most inopportune time, or other problems that only occur after extended execution.

Diagnostics versus Recovery

Another significant difference between the objectives of test and production is illustrated by the way testers and customers respond to a problem. When a problem is encountered during test, the tester goes to any length required to gather enough diagnostic data to be able to thoroughly analyze and debug it. His entire focus is on exterminating the bug. That's not the case in a production environment.

Most customers have a documented, agreed-upon Service Level Agreement (SLA) associated with their production environments. The SLA normally includes attributes such as transaction response time goals, availability commitments, and the like. It is not unusual for the IT professionals who support a production environment to have their job appraisals and even bonuses tied to how well the systems comply with the SLA. In essence, they have a vested interest in achieving SLA targets.

With this in mind, you can see why the objectives and actions of a production support staff will differ from those of a typical tester when a software defect is encountered. The customer's most important goal is availability, so its staff focuses on restoring service and isolating the problem from other production workloads. Their concern is recovering from the problem. Obtaining diagnostic information is important to them, but not at the expense of application or end user availability.

This presents an interesting dilemma to testers. Is it more important to do whatever it takes to remove the defect, or to understand, gain experience, and prove that the software can recover from errors? Well, it's important to do both. Almost all testing should be focused on finding, debugging, and removing defects. But some time and attention should also be spent on observing the downstream affects of a defect. Explicit scenarios should be defined that drive the end-to-end failure recovery first and gather diagnostics afterward. This is the point at which you can identify any First Failure Data Capture (FFDC) deficiencies and provide feedback to design and development on the capabilities of the software to actually support high availability and continuous operations. You can examine the ability of the software to identify when an error occurs, its ability to provide guidance to operators and system programmers on what has occurred, and what recovery actions to take.

This is different from explicit recovery testing described earlier in this book. To truly experience these situations and react in the same way customers would, you need to be surprised by the error, not artificially inject it yourself. One approach is to play "hide a bug." Have one member of the test team act as the operator or system programmer and have lots of workloads and test case streams running in the background to achieve the systems activity goals described earlier. Have another member of the team inject a mystery error unbeknownst to the operator. Perhaps a networking cable is pulled or a critical service killed. The tester operating the environment now can experience firsthand the software's capabilities to support customer needs. Observe the effectiveness of the error messages presented—did the operator take the most appropriate recovery actions? Was the problem easily recognized and isolated? If not, why not? What were the effects on the workloads and test cases running? How long did it take the operator to accomplish complete restoration of service?

Scale and Systems Management

For reasons of cost and perceived efficiency, test lab configurations are often relatively small. A single test environment may contain only a handful of systems. In such tiny configurations, difficulties with coordinating the software's actions across multiple systems are easily overcome, and therefore easily ignored. Testers may not even realize a systems management hole exists in the software's support.

Customer production configurations, on the other hand, can be enormous. Hundreds of systems might be working together on a set of shared tasks. In such large environments, weaknesses in the ability to control and manage the software across multiple systems become glaring. Imagine a cluster of Web application servers in which a simple configuration update requires the user to logon to 50 systems individually to make the change, rather than issuing a command from a single point of control from which it is propagated automatically around the cluster. If testers spend a portion of their time with configurations that approach even a fraction of true customer-like scale, they will be forced to confront these manageability issues head-on simply to get their testing done.

MANAGING THE TEST ENVIRONMENTS

Another opportunity you may have to more closely emulate customers is to approach the overall management of your test environments in similar fashion to customer management of IT environments. Many of the tasks you need to perform to create and manage test environments are the same set of tasks customers deal with on a daily basis. Although test environments tend to be much more dynamic and ever-changing than typical production environments, there are still some things you can do to emulate customers and gain their perspective.

Centralizing Support

There are not many software development companies or organizations that develop only one piece of software. Many times there are multiple test teams that test different software in the same lab. When this is the case, an opportunity arises to emulate customers by centralizing many of the management activities of that test lab.

Asset Management

The physical assets required by the test teams can be managed centrally. Although the test lab may support multiple teams, you can view it as a single entity. Managing all the hardware requirements, ordering the hardware, installing the hardware, and keeping track of inventory are some responsibilities that can be assigned to the asset management team. Another set of responsibilities can be controlling the power and cooling requirements of the test lab and scheduling electrical work by outside vendors.

How does asset management help a software test team emulate customers? It provides the capability to take more of an end-to-end view of a realistic environment. One challenge all companies face today is how to control costs. Centrally managing hardware assets can do just that. It opens up the possibility to most efficiently use the hardware in the lab. Specifically, it lets the sharing of hardware resources to occur more easily. Instead of each test team obtaining its own hardware, all of the requirements can be pooled, and fewer pieces of hardware may be needed. This is how many customers manage their hardware requirements. It then allows the test team to operate under customer-like constraints and see how their software behaves in a heavily shared environment. Feedback should be given to the development teams in the event that the software does not fit seamlessly into the shared environment.

Centrally Managing Data

There will most likely be large quantities of data generated from testing as well as large amounts of data needed to perform testing. In this case, the data includes logs of all types, diagnostic data such as memory dumps, test databases, files holding code to be tested, and the test cases themselves. Though not identical to mission-critical production data in IT shops, it can still be viewed and managed as such. Consider the aggregate of all this test data as production data. You'll want to use similar techniques to back up the data, archive it, and restore it when needed. Again, it allows you to see how your software relates to typical data management activities in production environments. You can expose your software to realistic data management tools and backup automation activities. For example, what happens to your software when a piece of data it requires has been automatically archived since it was last referenced? Does it seamlessly wait for the recall and then proceed normally, or does it react negatively and take inappropriate actions?

This approach also promotes efficient use of resources, such as backup media. It encourages the use of common tools and approaches to address common issues across multiple test teams. Individual testers will be able to move from one test team to another without having to learn a completely new set of data management tasks. Automation need only be developed once and can be maintained centrally.

Testers can gain more experiences with more realistic environments, instilling a customer-like mindset.

Taking a Customer's View

A common theme throughout this chapter is the differences between typical software test environments and objectives versus real-world deployment of software. Recognizing those differences is the first step toward building a capability to address them. There is more to validating software than running individual tests and seeing if they work. Understanding the daily struggles of customer software support personnel and building empathy for them makes a tester think in completely different terms about the nature of software. A tester who has developed this skill will consistently ask himself "How would a customer react to this?"

Customer empathy will provide you with a great foundation for understanding the importance of taking an end-to-end view. You'll see how the software you're testing has to fit into a much bigger environment and be able to withstand all types of external stimuli. You'll be prepared to fully prove the software is ready for the demands of a production environment. There may be costs associated with this technique in terms of time, effort, and equipment. As always, you will need to balance this against the potential cost of frequent service calls and unhappy customers. Experience shows that for complex software packages that must handle highly intertwined production environments, the payback is often quite real.

SUMMARY

Testers strive to find as many defects as they can, and customers want to avoid defects at all costs. These diametrically opposed objectives create challenging issues for testers, yet are not contradictory with the idea of emulating customers. Porting real applications from customers to use as a tool for driving new software can be a good means of reaching some test goals but there are lots of cases where that is not the total answer. Other approaches can prove just as, if not more, valuable at finding the defects that matter. In an SVT, very specific software activity goals can be set from in-depth review of customer data. Some test time should be spent looking at production aspects of software such as continuous execution and restoration of service after a failure. Viewing the test lab as a production environment also instills more of a customer mindset in testers and exposes them to additional demands.

We have discussed enough about preparation, planning, and thinking about testing. At some point, you'll actually have to perform the tests. It's time for the main event. Chapter 15, "Test Execution," will describe some critical issues to consider when executing tests.

Part
V

Executing the Test

Bugs can be elusive little critters. They hide in the dark recesses of sophisticated software and resist detection. If they do surface, it may be at inopportune moments when your attention is directed elsewhere. A good test will roust bugs from their hideouts, snare them in a finely-crafted net, and cart them off to oblivion. A sloppy test, like a torn net with gaping holes, will let bugs escape. You'll want your net to be tight and unforgiving.

Even with strong planning and preparation, executing a test isn't easy. It's a complicated, chaotic affair that demands care and attention. The next four chapters will guide you through the process. We'll look at structuring activities around different test execution sequences, from traditional to iterative to artistic. You'll see how to detect when a bug is tangled in your net, and approaches for diagnosing it. If your testing gets bogged down due to insufficient hardware, we'll reveal several ways to expand your options through the magic of virtualization. Or, if the hardware you require is so new that it's still under development when you're ready to begin, you'll see how simulators and prototypes may be able to save the day. You'll also learn techniques for controlling the inevitable chaos associated with testing in order to keep your execution on track. Finally, we'll discuss the tester's weapons for getting bugs fixed, and what you can do if the end date arrives but your testing isn't finished. Now toss out your net, it's time for a bug hunt.

15 Test Execution

In This Chapter

- Test execution flow
- Artistic testing
- Iterative testing
- Detecting problems
- Diagnosing problems
- Testing the documentation

Y ou stride down a narrow, shadowy corridor. The silence is eerie, broken only by the soft padding of your own footsteps on the beige, industrial carpet. Ahead, a lone steel door blocks your path. Your fingers squeeze its cold, sculpted handle, then yank. The door swings open, and out rushes the mechanical hum of machines. You step into the computer room and see that ahead, a crowd has gathered. Developers, planners, and managers shuffle about, their movements tentative, uncertain. You approach. Suddenly, a finger points your way. The others look, and stiffen. The throng slowly parts; all conversation hushes as you pass through. On the other side, you reach your destination: a swivel chair, resting before a gummy keyboard and dusty monitor. You sit. The crowd edges closer. Your gnarled, wizened fingers rise to the keyboard, and hover. The time for testing has come.

The beginning of your actual test may not be quite this dramatic, although after all the studying, digging, planning, reviewing, preparing, and scheduling, it might seem that way. Executing a test is the best part, the point where all your advance work pays off. But there are several variants and techniques to consider. A fairly mainstream sequence of events usually occurs, although its flow can vary. There are also some more unusual testing approaches which are very useful for certain situations, but their execution models are quite unique. No matter what your test execution looks like, you'll need to be able to spot problems when they happen, and then figure out what to do with them. And be careful not to overlook the documentation—bad books can cause a customer just as much trouble as bad code. Let's look at each of these eclectic areas, all of which may eventually touch you during the execution of a test.

TEST EXECUTION SEQUENCE

Different tests and test phases have their own ebb and flow. No single sequence of events is right for every case, but there are some common characteristics we can examine. Let's pick the SVT phase as an example. Figure 15.1 shows a typical flow.

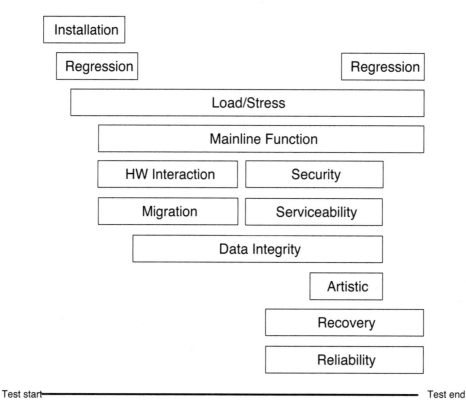

FIGURE 15.1   Typical system verification test sequence.

Establishing a Baseline

You can't do much with software until you install it, so at least a portion of your installation testing must get done immediately. After that, the first order of business is to validate that entry criteria have been met and to establish a stability baseline. Running an automated regression test case suite at moderate levels of stress is a solid means for achieving both goals, and so it's the first test in the sequence. Once most of the regression tests run without error, a natural next step is to increase the regression workload's intensity. This signifies the onset of load/stress testing and morphs the regression suite into the first stress workload. More workloads will follow as the target software is beaten and battered over the course of the entire test, with load/stress acting as either its own focus area or as a backdrop against which other testing occurs.

Mainline Activities

Once the software proves it can handle a heavy load, that load can begin to serve as background noise for attacks on new or changed mainline function. Other tests can begin at this point as well. If support for new hardware is part of the test, you may want to start that work now to allow for the possibility of long turnaround times for fixes to defects you find in the hardware itself. It's also logical to begin migration/coexistence testing as early as possible, since you may be able to cover much of this testing as you migrate your own test systems from the software's prior release. Security and serviceability testing can also commence at this point, or wait until later as shown in Figure 15.1.

If data integrity is a concern for the software, it's prudent to allow considerable time to explore it. Problems in this area are notoriously tricky to solve, so they can significantly elongate the test process. However, since new mainline functions are often the focus of data integrity worries, it is frequently best to wait until those mainline functions have proven they can survive some initial, basic tests before progressing to the more sophisticated integrity attacks.

Late Cycle Tests

Recovery testing is typically done toward the end of the test, since people usually want to see that the mainline code is working smoothly before they start to sabotage it deliberately. We'll look at artistic testing in a moment, but since it relies on skills that are built early in the test, it's reasonable for artistic tests to occur after those skills have been acquired. So it too normally occurs in the latter half of the cycle.

There's little point in attempting reliability tests early in the cycle, since it's unlikely the software will be stable enough to survive extended runs. Be careful, however: any number of things can go wrong in a reliability test planned to last for several days, from hardware failing to logs filling up and freezing the system to someone tripping over a power cord. Allow time to attempt this test several times before achieving success. Also, if regression test suites have not been included in the daily stress runs, or if the defined regression tests include some manual activities, then it's a good idea to re-execute them near the end of the test. This ensures previously-tested support hasn't suffered collateral damage from a steady stream of fixes.

Staying Flexible

There's no magic to this sample flow. You might choose to do all migration testing last, or before starting your initial regression tests. If a main feature of the new software is its ability to recover from failures, then it makes sense to begin testing recovery at the same time as other mainline functions. Maybe your window for artistic testing should be wider than we show here. Or perhaps you won't have any predefined window for artistic testing, but will jump into artistic mode whenever the results of your planned tests suggest you should. The point is not to pay homage to some specific sequence of activities, but rather to think about what makes sense for your test, and choose a flow that is not only effective, but efficient.

ARTISTIC TESTING

The renowned British economist, John Maynard Keynes, was once accused by a critic of changing his stance on a subject. He reportedly responded, "When I get new information, I change my opinions. What, sir, do you do with new information?" [Schoch00] Keynes could just as easily have been talking about artistic testing.

We first touched on artistic testing, also known as *exploratory testing,* in Chapter 7, "Test Plan Focus Areas." It recognizes that you'll always know more about a piece of software at the end of a test than you do at the beginning. Rather than ignoring that reality, artistic testing exploits it. It encourages you to take new information and insight that you acquire during the test, and use it to spontaneously devise fresh scenarios that were not considered when the test plan was originally conceived. It's a creative process that Bach defines as simultaneous learning, test design, and test execution [Bach03].

Artistic testing is a test focus area whose content isn't actually devised until the execution phase is well underway. There are several different paths you can follow and you may not know which is more appropriate until the moment for artistic testing actually arrives. Let's briefly look at each.

Structured

One approach is to pause for a moment, step back, and reassess the testing underway. Is it becoming apparent that the existing test plan misses an important area of the software? Or are there areas that are covered, but insufficiently? Are there environmental or configuration enhancements needed to fill gaps in the testing? Are the test workload suites sufficient, or should they be tweaked or different combinations tried? Brainstorm the possibilities, and jot down your ideas. These notes then become your artistic testing road map. This structured approach is almost like informally creating a new, minitest plan, but without all the formal documentation, reviews, and signoffs. As you pursue your new road map, additional quirks in the software may become apparent. Follow them, and see where they lead.

Investigative

It's likely your test plan will provide fairly broad, even coverage of the target software's functions and subfunctions. Once the test is underway, you'll typically find that some functions are working quite well, and others are more troublesome. These problem-prone areas represent soft spots, portions of the software that for one reason or another are weak.

The second approach to artistic testing is to probe the soft spots. Investigate those very specific areas. Poke and prod some more. Dig deeper. Use your intuition. Be creative. Go where the software and its problems lead you. The theory here is that bugs in a section of code are like cockroaches in a house—the more you find, the more likely there are others lurking in the dark. The simple fact that you have found an unusual number of defects in one area suggests there are more to find. The investigative approach encourages you to react to conditions the software presents to you, trying wild combinations of things on the spur of the moment that would never have occurred to you during the formal test plan development process.

Customer-like Chaos

Artistic can be defined as "showing imagination and skill." These are just two of the many traits of an effective tester. We can take that imagination and skill and combine it with spontaneity. What we get is organized chaos.

With this approach, the entire test team simultaneously uses the software for its intended purpose, each in his own way, making up tasks as they go. Focus areas might be divided among the team, but otherwise there is little coordination of actions. This mimics the kind of random usage that the software may see in the production environment. Such chaos is likely to force the execution of code paths that more structured testing may miss. Better yet, if that chaos can be oriented around the kinds of activities likely to occur in a customer environment, the defects it uncovers will also align with those that might occur in production. This approach fits well at the end of a test, as a final check of the software after all planned tests have been completed.

Case Study: The Power of Chaos

A fundamental linchpin of the mainframe clustering technology called Parallel Sysplex was contained primarily within a single component of the operating system. This component provided underlying services for others to use. A large number of components of the operating system and platform subsystems were enhanced to exploit those services to extend the technology's reach.

The first exploitation of those base services was done by two other key system components. These base and exploiting components turned out to be a target-rich environment for testers. Even after each of the individual components had reached their respective FVT exit milestone, bugs kept popping up. It became clear the full software package wasn't ready to move forward to the next phase of testing (SVT). This was a real predicament.

Executing to a test plan is important, but so is keeping a close eye on the experiences gained during its execution. When those experiences suggest more testing is needed, be flexible. Develop and perform additional test activities based on the new insight.

The FVT test team members pondered how they could stabilize the environment. They decided to take an artistic approach and define some organized chaos. The primary technique was to drive the entire package of components with random use and operational tests. These tests included exercising system services in all components, performing command-driven operations, injecting program errors, and removing systems from the cluster, all while other testers were acting as users. Each day, testers were assigned a different area on which to focus, infusing variability and randomness to the activities. These spontaneous and pseudorandom operational tests drove a set of unique paths that had not been driven in the isolated FVT environments. In fact, the operational tests drove paths similar to those that customers were expected to use.

Consider aligning artistic test scenarios with likely customer activity. It's an excellent way to extract the most critical defects.

This randomized approach proved successful at uncovering a significant number of important defects across the three targeted components. The integrated, artistic test strengthened the code before its entry to the SVT cycle. Sometimes you just need to pull all the tricks out of the bag and try anything and everything to drive out the defects that matter.

When faced with the need to quickly augment the planned test, work closely with other testers and help each other, if possible. Most importantly, be creative and try new approaches.

AN ITERATIVE APPROACH: ALGORITHM VERIFICATION TESTING

Algorithm verification testing (AVT) was described in Chapter 3, "The Development Process." It represents a purely iterative model for software testing that is as much a way for development to refine their design as it is a test. For an AVT, take all the earlier discussion about test execution sequences and throw it out the window. Rather than sequences, an AVT is defined by a constant loop of experiment, refine, and experiment. In terms of execution, however, there's always one big question with an AVT: how do you know when you're done?

The Test Completion Quandary

The measure of progress for a traditional test follows a classic pattern, the so-called "S" curve, as shown in Figure 15.2. It represents the successful completion of test scenarios over time. Progress is initially slow as the test begins to ramp up. Soon, scenarios begin to get completed very rapidly, and the S curve steepens. As the test

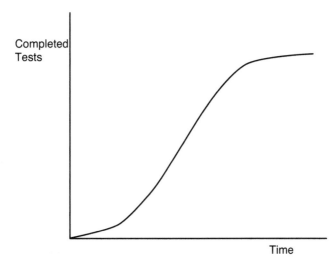

FIGURE 15.2 Classic test progress S curve.

winds down, successful completion dwindles while scenarios await the last batch of fixes, long-running reliability tests wrap up, and so forth. Software project managers around the world are intimately familiar with this curve, and are quite comfortable projecting results from it. For an AVT, however, it's useless.

In an AVT, each experiment unveils a new behavior that requires adjustment to the algorithm. With each adjustment, the results from prior tests become suspect and must be revalidated. These retests may bring to light more new wrinkles to be accounted for—and force subsequent retests. This iterative loop suggests that no experiment can be considered truly complete until all are successful, or very nearly so. As a result, a plot of the test progress shows it appearing to limp along for quite some time, until finally everything comes together and it spikes up. This flow is depicted in Figure 15.3.

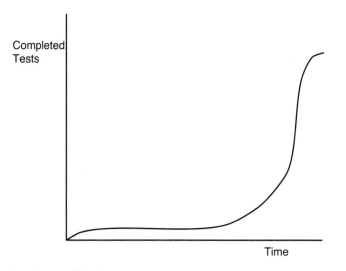

FIGURE 15.3 Algorithm verification test progress curve.

If you are involved in an AVT, one of the challenges you'll face is educating people that they can't superimpose their classic test project management template on your activity. Status tracking must be approached differently. Although you will have crisply defined experiments, you can't project when they will succeed. This concept may blow some managers' minds. But because in this model the test and design are so intertwined, testing can't complete (or even show significant progress, in classic terms) until the designers and developers close in on the correct design. In effect, attempting to project the end of an algorithm verification test is the same as attempting to project a moment of invention.

In reality, an AVT could continue almost indefinitely, because it's always possible to do a little more tweaking to further optimize a complex algorithm. But eventually a point of diminishing return will be reached. The trick is recognizing when you've hit that point. You have to learn to see when something is operating acceptably, rather than perfectly. This is not a job for purists. The best approach for knowing when you're done is to have one or more experts on the algorithms specify detailed criteria up front about how good is "good enough," and then stick to it.

Status tracking in this environment is tricky, and it's unlikely you'll get far with an approach that just says, "trust me." A useful technique is to try to chart progress against defined goals, but with soft and movable target dates. Break the definition of the test into logical chunks. For each chunk, you can track whether code is available, testing is underway, and if a particular algorithm has met some predefined exit criteria. Unfortunately, while this data will show a lot of movement early in the test, soon it will tend to stagnate as all code is available and tests are underway, but few algorithms are meeting criteria. You can solve this problem by providing backup data, to reassure people that progress is indeed being made. List activities performed since the last round of status, accomplishments or progress, and any current obstacles. This kind of information will keep everyone informed, so your test will seem less like a black box.

Case Study: Testing a Workload Manager

For many years, predecessors to the z/OS operating system included a powerful component that managed system resources to optimize performance. It allowed the system programmer to specify, in tremendous detail, exactly how resources should be handed out to different classes of work. However, the fine-grained control that made it so powerful was also its greatest weakness. A system programmer was forced to specify a mind-boggling array of arcane tuning values: performance groups and periods, working set sizes, multiprogramming levels, dispatching priorities, dispatching algorithm variants, contention indexes, I/O priorities, time slice groups, and so on. The system programmer had to do the tuning using operating system terms rather than human terms. The definitions were also static, limiting the system's ability to adapt dynamically to changing workflows and other conditions. They were static in another sense as well: once established, many customers hesitated to go back and modify them. The complexity level was so high, any thought of change generated a fear of unintended consequences.

A New Component

In response, a new component was devised that would allow the system to *self tune*. This new component was called the *Workload Manager* (WLM). It only asked the system programmer to tell it, in simple human terms, the performance goals to be achieved and a business importance for each goal. In fact, these goals were expressed in terms similar to those found in a standard service level agreement (described in Chapter 2, "Industrial-Strength Software—It's Not a Science Project"), such as the desired response times and throughput rates (or *velocities*) for different types of work. WLM would then feed that input into its sophisticated algorithms to dynamically tune the system, make tradeoffs, and adapt ongoing processing to meet the specified performance goals.

WLM is a part of the operating system that acts as the 'traffic cop." It makes decisions about which vehicles are allowed on the highway and how fast they can go. When the highway is not crowded, its job is easy. When there is a traffic jam, it ensures ambulances are not delayed getting to the hospital by moving other vehicles off the highway or routing the ambulance through streets that are not congested.

As you might imagine, replacing a set of arcane and sometimes conflicting operating system performance controls with a completely different set was hard. But the task of devising algorithms that would self tune the system to meet requested goals under many conditions was more than hard—it was mind-numbing. A series of hypotheses was encoded into algorithms, but no one could be sure those hypotheses were correct. The only way to validate them was to exercise the code as early as possible. Unlike a traditional test, the intent was not to validate that the code matched the specification, but to validate that the specification itself was correct. It was like prototyping, but done on what would eventually be the real product code. It was a classic case of iterative development.

The testing effort described here was not focused on finding traditional bugs in the software. It was focused on helping the design and development teams learn about the decisions of the traffic cop. Detailed reviews of the actions of the traffic cop and the resulting traffic flow were performed and, if needed, the traffic cop would be retrained to make better decisions.

A Unique Team with Unique Tools

A standard FVT and SVT were performed against WLM to exercise externals and other basic function. But because those tests could not expose the subtleties of the algorithms, highly specialized tests were needed. These were incorporated into an AVT, which started about the same time as the FVT and finished along with SVT.

The AVT team carefully constructed a series of experiments. Each was designed to present a different situation for the algorithms to handle in order to observe how they reacted. But it wasn't enough to study the results from the outside. The team needed to look at the actual internal values that fed into the algorithms to ensure everything was truly operating as expected—or to diagnose problems if they were not. So the team developed a specialized tool that periodically captured every relevant internal control structure. They paired it with a customized reporting tool that could present that data in meaningful ways, tailored for each experiment.

Special testing efforts may need special tools. Define the needs and requirements of specialized tooling when planning. Include the cost of the tool development when determining what the test will require.

Balancing Test Shots with Analysis Time

Because the AVT needed to be run on native hardware, and time on the test mainframes was precious, the team had to be prepared for each experiment. Goals were crisply defined, tools were tweaked, and workloads were primed. The AVT was also very single threaded. All variables that could affect the algorithms were interdependent, so each iteration required changing only one variable at a time. Despite tight schedules, daily test runs were not done. Why not? Because any single experiment could generate more data than there were people-hours to analyze it before the next day. The rule of thumb was two eight-hour test shifts per week, and never more than three.

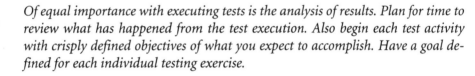

Of equal importance with executing tests is the analysis of results. Plan for time to review what has happened from the test execution. Also begin each test activity with crisply defined objectives of what you expect to accomplish. Have a goal defined for each individual testing exercise.

Result analysis was a group activity, bringing together the designers, developers, and testers to discuss what they were seeing. If actual results did not match expectations, new theories were proposed. Once a single flaw was noticed in any sequence of events, all subsequent results in that experiment were considered suspect. When a fix to that flaw became available, the change it introduced would potentially invalidate experiments that had previously succeeded, so everything needed to be rerun with the new fix.

A clear and formal pipeline for turning around fixes was critical. The team depended on a continuous build process to fold fixes into the experiment engine. All known fixes and design changes had to be incorporated before the next experiment, or there was no point in running it.

Creating extremely close working relationships among testers, developers, and designers is a powerful approach for quickly and effectively validating and improving complex software. Be an ambassador for this approach and work to make it a normal part of the development process.

Finding the End Point

The team uncovered many surprising results, due to obscure interdependencies in system operation that the designers or developers didn't fully appreciate. Many iterations involved simple code tweaks, but some also required very significant design changes, even very late in the cycle. As the deadline approached and test tracking charts showed little apparent progress, there was concern by project managers. Finally, a breakthrough occurred and the late spike in measured progress promised in Figure 15.3 was achieved. The celebration could begin.

TIP

Prior to beginning an AVT, prepare project managers for the unusual test progress curve they will likely see unfold, so they won't be surprised.

Epilogue

Throughout the course of the AVT, the entire WLM team's rallying cry was reminiscent of the Hippocratic Oath: "First, do no harm to the system." They worked together to devise targeted experiments, create custom tools, analyze results, and iteratively move forward one fix at a time. As a result, the team was able to stay within the bounds of their motto while delivering complex, yet high quality, new function. When WLM was delivered to customers it proved to be quite robust, and served as a strong base upon which the mainframe's ability to self tune has been expanding ever since.

CATCHING PROBLEMS

Regardless of the type of testing being performed, the whole point of doing it is to find problems. Therefore, it is critical that testers take care to detect when a problem has actually occurred. How can you be sure you aren't missing any?

The Evidence Trail

Sometimes the fact that an error has struck is clear, but other times it might take some digging. Most bugs leave behind a trail of evidence. Let's review several possibilities.

Test Case Failures

The most straightforward evidence that a defect has surfaced is when a test case fails. A well-designed test case will test a specific function and verify the results. If the results are not correct, then the test case should collect the necessary documentation of the failure and signal that a failure has occurred.

You will probably want to purchase or develop a tool to automate the monitoring of the success or failure of test cases. If a test case runs without detecting an error, the tool can delete all of its output and just add it to the "success" tally. This automation will be most useful when you are doing automated runs of hundreds or thousands of test cases. You'll want to know when a test case fails, but won't want to spend a lot of time reviewing the output of those that didn't. By filtering out all unnecessary output, this tool will be a great time saver and ensure that the failures get noticed.

Abnormal Termination

For certain types of failures, the test case will not finish normally but instead will abnormally terminate or crash. The operating system or software component will terminate the current unit of work before it has an opportunity to provide an error return code or issue an error message. Such crashes occur for different reasons, and each typically has a corresponding failure code. These codes are normally documented in a system codes manual, which includes a description of the type of failure each termination code depicts.

When a crash occurs, a memory dump is typically generated. The dump is a snapshot of memory at the time of the error and includes many operating system control structures, registers, and memory areas related to the failing unit of work.

On some systems, there will be messages in the console log or system log alerting the operator that a dump has been taken, but on others, the dump may be quietly stashed away somewhere without any notification. Make sure you know where dumps will be stored, and watch for them.

Wait States

The most obvious indication that something has gone drastically wrong is when the operating system goes into a permanent wait state. This occurs with catastrophic errors when the operating system has determined it can not safely continue. The various kinds of wait states are usually defined by wait state codes documented in a system codes manual. A wait state code will identify what the failure was, but is unlikely to explain what caused it. In order to debug such a failure, you will probably need to use a standalone utility to capture a complete memory dump prior to rebooting the operating system.

Error Logs

In some cases, it's possible an error occurs but the software determines a dump is unnecessary, so it simply recovers from the failure and continues on. This variety of failure is usually written to an error log, which may look different depending on the systems and products you use. Testers must review these logs often to see if any "silent" failures are occurring.

Messages

System messages often reveal a lurking defect to the alert tester. When you execute a scenario or run a load/stress job stream, monitor the system log for any message that seems strange. Don't assume that because you don't understand the message, it isn't important. Quite the contrary is true. Look up the message to make sure it is not a clue that something unexpected has happened. Some testers focus narrowly on the immediate task at hand, and miss bugs by ignoring "extraneous" messages that they didn't think concerned them. A good tester doesn't stick his head in the sand, he questions everything.

Another type of defect to look for is incorrect information in the messages themselves. Always be on the lookout for these kinds of problems. They are most noticeable in messages issued in response to commands you enter. Is all of the information in the message correct? Is it complete, or is something important missing?

Carefully examine all error messages. Do they lead you to the correct understanding of the problem? Do they supply enough information? If not, you might have found a valid usability or serviceability bug.

PROBLEM DIAGNOSIS

After a problem has been detected it needs to be diagnosed. Problem diagnosis is broken into two phases: Level One and Level Two. All problems will go through level-one problem determination. If they are not found to be duplicates of an already-reported problem, level-two problem determination will commence.

Level-one Problem Determination

In this first phase, the tester will examine the documentation collected for the problem to get a basic grasp of what happened. He will then do some research to determine if it is a duplicate problem. Level-one examination includes the following:

- If an error message was issued from the system, look it up in the system messages manual. Try to discover more detailed information about what it means and (hopefully) determine the module that detected the problem.
- In the event of a crash, look up the termination code in the system codes manual to learn what it signifies. From the resulting memory dump or related messages, try to determine in which module the failure occurred and the location of the failure within that module.

- After a test case detects an error, look at the test case to understand which function was being tested and what the surfaced error really indicates.
- When there is a return code from a function that signaled an error, look it up to find out what it denotes.

After collecting this information, use it to search your problem-tracking database for a match with problems that have already been reported. When checking for a true match, you will often need to be very specific. For example, when the same kind of program interruption occurs at the same location in the same module, you have a match. Conversely, you wouldn't want to claim a match if the same program interruption occurs in two different modules, as it is unlikely to be the same problem.

When you find a match, there is still more research to do. For example, you need to determine if there is a fix available. If not, maybe all you need to do is increment a count of the number of occurrences of the problem in your tracking database. This sort of "duplicate occurrence count" can come in handy for prioritizing bugs. If multiple testers are hitting this problem and it is blocking the progress of further testing, you may need to inform development that they should place a higher priority on resolving it.

If a match is found and a fix is available, has it been installed on your system? If not, why not? If the fix has been installed, it means that this may be a new problem, or that perhaps the fix did not resolve the original problem.

If you don't find a match, you may still need to do more searching. If the software under test is a new release of an existing software system, the problem may actually be a bug in the *previous* level of the software. Perhaps the bug has lain dormant, but is now exposed by conditions created by new or changed code in the new release, or by a fresh test case. In this scenario, search for problems on the previous software level, which may be in a different database or defect queue. If you find a match, you'll have to do the same kind of fix-status analysis that was previously outlined.

Level-two Problem Determination

If, after all of this searching you do not find a match, then it would appear that you have found a new problem. It's time to move into the level-two problem determination phase. Here you need to diagnose the problem down to the line of code that is its root cause. This level of problem determination typically requires the tester to have some additional skills. Among them are:

- Insight into the architecture and instruction set of the computer the software is running on

■ Detailed knowledge of the internal structure of the software under test
■ Experience with the programming language that the software is written in
■ A thorough understanding of the debugging tools available for the system

Level-two problem determination is a lot like a detective solving a crime. As Sherlock Holmes said in *The Sign of the Four*, "When you eliminate all that is impossible, whatever remains, however improbable, is the truth!" All of the evidence is reviewed and theories are developed as to what caused the failure. Then comes the hard part—exploring each theory until the cause is determined. This is typically an iterative process, in which a theory is developed to explain the symptoms and then is either proved or disproved. When a theory is disproved, it is either modified or replaced with a completely new one. The process is repeated until the guilty party is found.

Analyzing the Memory Dump

Reviewing the evidence often involves analyzing a memory dump that was captured at the time of the error. The initial questions that need to be answered are:

■ Where did the failure occur (exact offset into a program)?
■ Why did it fail?
■ How did the program get to the point where it failed?

Once these questions are answered, you need to start backtracking from the point of failure to find out where the incorrect information originated. As you are doing this, keep in mind that the defect may be in the section of code that surfaced the failure, or that code may be a victim of bad information generated somewhere else.

The debugger will typically begin by obtaining a *program listing* for the software in question. This listing shows the low-level assembly and machine language instructions that make up the compiled program, along with the offset of each such instruction from the program's beginning. Ideally, it will also show the high-level programming language statements that the assembly language instructions were derived from by the compiler. Detailed program listings such as this allow you to see what the computer was actually executing as it worked through the program, and can normally be generated by using particular options at compile time. For example, the GCC compiler found on Linux systems [GCC] can be invoked as follows to generate a complete program listing in file "listing" for program "foo.c":

```
gcc  -Wa,- ahls -o foo foo.c > listing
```

Alternatively, if you are debugging a module for which a listing wasn't generated at compile time, you may be able to generate one from the program's object code. For example, the following will disassemble an object code file on Linux systems to std out, and if the program was originally compiled with the -g option, the resulting listing will even include the corresponding high-level language source statements:

```
objdump -S  foo.o
```

Once a debugger has the program listing, he will review it to understand the flow through the program leading up to the failure, while also looking at the memory dump to see what was contained in registers and memory locations when the failure struck. This process often involves "playing computer" in reverse, which means working backwards from point of failure, doing what the computer did for each instruction. For example, when the instruction is to load a value into a register, you actually calculate the memory location and look at the value in that location in the memory dump. As you are doing this backtracking, you are developing a theory that matches the evidence that you have gathered so far. Continue backtracking while either validating or disproving the theory. You will normally reach a point where you can prove a theory.

Some problems are relatively simple to solve. For example, a program may suffer an interruption because it tried to reference an invalid memory location. This condition might have been caused by the caller of the program initializing a parameter list incorrectly. But some problems are far more difficult to solve and may require the tester to set traps and re-create the failure multiple times.

TESTING THE DOCUMENTATION

Test execution is not just about the software itself. Bad documentation is as likely to cause problems for your customers as is bad code. If a crucial step is left out of installation instructions, the install will fail. Even worse, the install may appear to succeed, but key features of the software will be inoperable. Or, if the software provides a great new feature but the documentation doesn't tell the user how to set it up and invoke it, the feature might as well not even exist.

Software users rely on documentation. The documentation could consist of manuals, release notes, or help panels. Whatever the form, the content had better be correct. Sitting around a table and reviewing documentation is important, but just as in a code walk through, errors will slip past. By far the best way to discover these errors or gaps is through testing. However, this doesn't necessarily mean you need any special activity. If you put some thought into it, your test execution can cover the code and the text that describes it, all at the same time.

Key Target Areas

There are four main focus areas when testing documentation:

- Instructions
- Examples
- Messages
- Samples

If specific instructions are provided for certain activities, its likely you will have test scenarios defined for those same activities (if not, you probably should consider expanding your scenarios). When executing those scenarios, follow the documented instructions exactly, looking for errors or omissions.

Similarly, step-by-step examples may be provided to explain GUI screen inputs, clarify syntax for commands or other interfaces, show expected outputs, or illustrate other important points. If so, then it's very likely you will need to exercise those same areas when you test the software. Mirror those examples in your tests. Watch for inconsistencies that might confuse the user, as well as outright errors. Keep in mind that any user following these examples closely will be trying to understand how something that's new to them works. Any inconsistency could prove perplexing, and therefore is important to fix.

When you hit a problem, for example, an error message, you should verify that the documentation for the message is correct. The meaning of the error message may be obvious to you, because by now you are very familiar with the software. But a typical user most likely will not be as knowledgeable. So check to see if the error message documentation adequately explains the error and what should be done to address it.

Finally, samples are sometimes documented for such things as initialization or tuning parameter input files. When these are supplied soft copy via a companion CD-ROM or Web download, many customers will try to plug them in as is. If they are only documented in hard copy text, some users will implement only excerpts, and others will go so far as to type them into their system verbatim. In either case, you'll need to try these samples during your test execution to make sure they are valid.

The approach for managing documentation defects you'll find should be decided up front. Some organizations treat defects in manuals the same as those in code, using common defect reporting and tracking tools for each. Others use more informal means for managing documentation defects. Either way will work. The important thing is to acknowledge that these defects will exist, testing can find them, and that a feedback loop for reporting them must be in place.

SUMMARY

Test execution is where the real fun begins, and there are many ways in which it can unfold. A classically sequenced model can be organized in multiple ways, depending on what is most efficient for your project. An algorithm verification test has its own unique flow that is intimately linked with the design and development processes. Artistic testing encourages you to design new tests during the execution phase, funneling fresh experience with the software into new scenarios created on the fly.

No matter which execution model you follow, you won't be successful unless you know how to detect when you've actually found a problem. Strong testers don't just blindly report suspected problems to their developers—they spend at least enough time doing level-one debugging to correctly identify the failing module and check for duplicates. And no test is complete unless it examines the documentation as well as the code.

No matter what the nature of your test, in order to execute it you'll need access to computers. But what if your team doesn't have enough hardware available to do the job? Chapter 16, "Testing with a Virtual Computer," shows you a way out of this dilemma through the magic of virtualization.

16 Testing with a Virtual Computer

In This Chapter

- Subdividing a real computer for testing
- Using a virtual computer for testing
- Combining partitioning and virtualization
- Leveraging virtualization to automate complex test scenarios
- A Case Study: a closer look at z/VM

What is one thing that all software testers require before can they attempt a single test scenario? They must have a computer system on which to run their software. Indeed, for large, complex software projects they usually need more than one.

Unfortunately, as wonderful as computers are, they cost money, and that's something test teams often have in short supply. But that doesn't reduce the need to create a variety of suitable environments for performing a thorough test. Maddeningly, computers often woefully underutilized during testing, particularly unit and function verification testing. Wouldn't it be amazing if there were a way to harness that unused capacity to create several test environments from a single computer? If you think so, then you're not alone. Let's examine how it's done.

PARTITIONING

One technique for creating multiple test environments from a single computer is to *partition* it into multiple, distinct entities. There are different ways to go about this.

Physical Partitioning

From the early 1970s until the late 1990s a number of high-end IBM mainframes had the capability to be electrically split into two separate computers. This allowed the customer to either run the computer with all of the CPUs, main memory, and I/O paths as one big system image or split it into two smaller separate computers. The split was done on an electrical power boundary so that either side could be powered off without affecting the other. The split was typically down the middle. When operating in split mode, the two sides were completely independent and different operating systems could be loaded on each, as shown in Figure 16.1. Similar approaches are now available on high-end Reduced Instruction Set Computers (RISC) and Intel systems. This subdividing is called *physical partitioning*.

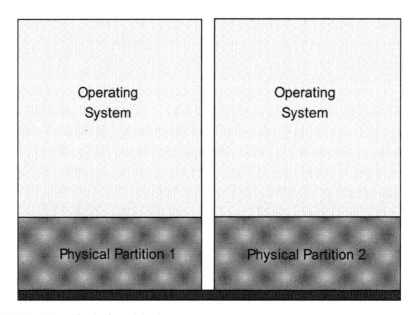

FIGURE 16.1 Physical partitioning.

The details of the implementations vary by manufacturer. The maximum number of partitions (also known as *domains*) typically varies from 2 to less than 20. Some allow loading of any operating system that is supported by the underlying hardware, while others only support a single, specific operating system. All offer a very coarse granularity for the division of resources, which cannot be shared between partitions and must be allocated in whole units. For example, a single CPU must be assigned to one partition; it can't be split or shared among them. The partitions can only communicate with each other through external connections (e.g., networking), as if they were physically discrete machines.

Logical Partitioning

A refinement of this concept was developed in the 1980s on mainframes and is called *logical partitions* (LPARs). LPAR capability is now available on other classes of computers as well, typically at the higher end. They provide a way for the customer to divide the real computer into a number of smaller, logical computers, as shown in Figure 16.2. All of the LPARs images don't need to be the same size. The customer configures how many CPUs, how much main memory, and how many I/O paths are connected to each LPAR image. Both the CPUs and the I/O paths can either be shared by some or all of the LPAR images or dedicated to a single LPAR image. The maximum number of LPAR images that can be defined within one computer is typically 32 or fewer. Each LPAR image is isolated from every other LPAR image, creating what is almost like a series of independent, smaller computers.

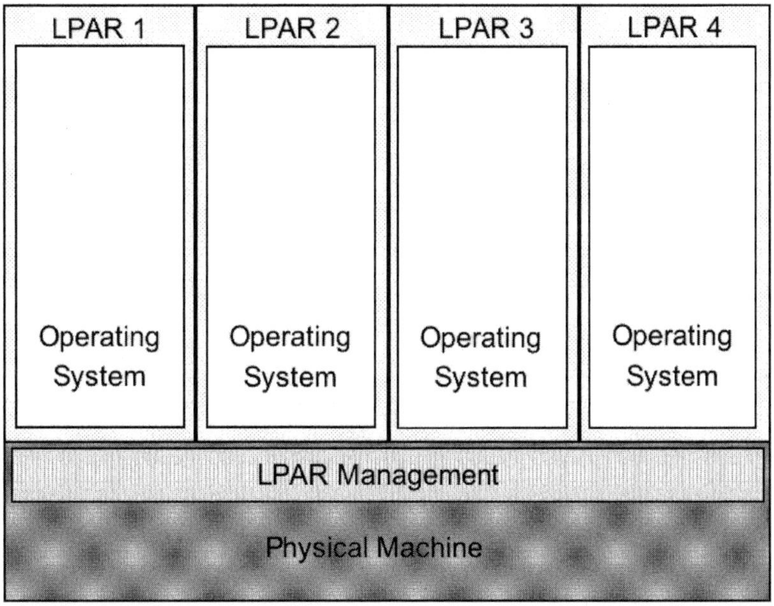

FIGURE 16.2   Logical partitioning.

Usually operating systems don't require any special modifications to run in an LPAR. The magic is handled through a microcode layer on the hardware. This extra layer between the native hardware and the operating system software allows resources to be mapped to the logical partitions with much greater flexibility and granularity than is available through hardware partitioning. There also may be the capability for LPARs on the same machine to communicate with each other through internal pipelines (implemented with hardware assists) which reduce the need for external networking hardware.

Software Partitioning

Finally, there is *software partitioning*. This approach employs control software that works in concert with a specific operating system to subdivide its resources. See Figure 16.3. These software-defined partitions are capable of running distinct instances of a specific operating system. User Mode Linux (UML) is a popular example. UML implements the platform-dependent portion of the Linux kernel (the *arch* layer) to run on the Linux software "platform," rather than on a specific hardware platform. Essentially, it ports Linux to run on top of Linux. This linkage means that each UML partition is limited: it can never run anything but Linux. On the other hand, like Linux itself, UML isn't tied to a specific hardware architecture,

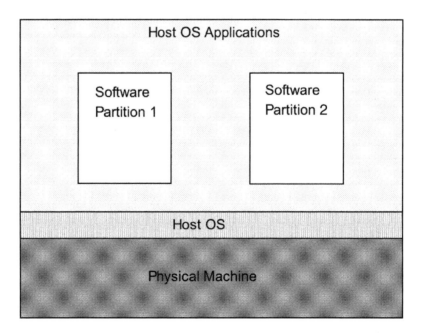

FIGURE 16.3   Software partitioning.

so it can be easily ported to multiple physical platforms [Dike01]. In addition to the UML partitions, the host Linux can also run more typical applications. Proprietary approaches for software partitioning are also available, such as HP-UX™ Virtual Partitions from Hewlett-Packard™.

VIRTUALIZATION

So far, we have looked at some techniques for subdividing a computer into a number of smaller images. Now we are going to look at another solution to supplying the testing environment, which has some additional capabilities. This solution gives each tester one or more *virtual* computers to test on. The virtual computer would appear to the software running inside of it to have all of the resources that are available on a real computer. For example, it would have a certain amount of main memory, virtual I/O devices, and one or more virtual CPUs, each of which would have all of the hardware facilities of a real CPU. The intent is to provide an environment that appears to the operating system, middleware, and applications to be a real, physical computer so they can run unchanged. Not only that, but the virtual computer may have the ability to *emulate* hardware that might not actually exist on the underlying physical machine.

Emulation

One way to build this virtual computer environment is to write an application that emulates the hardware platform on which the software under test will run. This emulator needs to decode each instruction and then do exactly what the instruction is designed to do. It runs as an application on a host operating system, so from that perspective it seems similar to the software partitioning approach shown earlier in Figure 16.3. But, unlike the software partitioning approach, the emulated environment is not tied to a particular operating system. Assuming it faithfully emulates the targeted hardware architecture, it can support any operating system enabled for that architecture.

Typically, an emulator does not run on the same hardware platform as the one being emulated. The intent is usually to provide a machine of one architecture on top of a machine of a different architecture. For example, the FLEX-*ES* emulator from Fundamental Software, Inc. emulates z/Architecture™, Enterprise Systems Architecture/390®, and System/370™ on an Intel Pentium® processor. Likewise, the open source Bochs emulator can run on a RISC-based system and emulate the Intel x86 architecture.

Multiple instances of an emulator can often run on a single physical computer, each supporting a single emulated computer. Each emulated computer can run its own instance of an operating system that is supported by the emulated architecture. However, there will sometimes be a one-to-one correspondence between emulated resources and physical resources, such as CPUs. This limits the possible number of emulated computer instances [FUND].

The greater the difference between the emulated architecture and the hardware platform the emulator runs on, the greater the complexity of the emulator, and the slower it will run. For example, if the smallest unit of addressable main memory (for example, an 8-bit byte) does not have the same number of bits, or if when a word of memory is loaded into a general-purpose register the bytes are not loaded in the same order, the emulator will be that much more complex and slow. The major problem with this approach is the performance penalty introduced by the blanket layer of interpretation between the virtual and physical computer. Assuming similar processor speeds, the software under test could end up running from 10 to 100 times slower than it would on a real computer.

Hypervisors

Another approach to building a virtualized environment is to run the virtual computer natively, suspend it any time it executes an operation that would affect the state of the real CPU, and emulate that operation before returning control to the virtual computer. The software that does this is called a *hypervisor*, or *virtual machine monitor*. A hypervisor gives each user his own virtual computer, also called a *virtual machine* or *guest*. The virtual machine that each user gets appears to have a certain amount of main memory, a defined number of CPUs, and a list of I/O devices at various device addresses. The hypervisor handles the mapping of physical resources to emulated logical resources that are assigned to these virtual machines. It provides very fine-grained control over resources. Also, there doesn't need to be a one-to-one correspondence between physical and logical resources, although the closer that mapping is, the better the performance will be. For example, a virtual machine could be defined with more CPUs than actually exist on the physical computer, or with only 10% of a single CPU.

Sugerman et al. note that unlike an emulator, a hypervisor gets out of the way whenever possible to let the virtual machine execute directly on the hardware, so virtual machines can achieve near-native performance [Sugerman01]. However, that means a hypervisor running on a machine of a particular architecture can only support virtual machines of that same architecture. A single hypervisor can also support multiple virtual machines concurrently, with the maximum number ranging from dozens to hundreds depending on the underlying hardware platform. Each guest can run a different operating system, or different versions of the same operating system, if desired. Also, virtual machines on the same physical computer can often communicate with each other at memory speeds, through *virtual net-*

works managed by the hypervisor. Operating systems typically don't require any special modifications to run in a virtual machine—they think they're running on a real computer.

Virtualization through hypervisors is not a new concept. It originally grew out of work done on IBM mainframes in the mid 1960s [Creasy81]. Early IBM announcement materials for the technology drew a comparison between virtualization and light streaming through a prism. It suggested that just as a prism could break a single beam of white light into multiple beams of different colors, so could virtualization break a single mainframe into many virtual computers [Varian97]. Similar technology has now penetrated other server classes as well, and its availability often reaches from the high end to the very low end of a given server line. There are a couple of different approaches for implementing virtualization via a hypervisor. Let's briefly look at each.

Native Hypervisor

A *native hypervisor* runs directly on the server hardware, as shown in Figure 16.4. It's essentially an operating system with hypervisor capability. This closeness to the hardware maximizes its control over system resources while minimizing performance overhead. However, it puts the burden for supporting devices on the hypervisor, adding to the hypervisor's complexity and cost. This technology is

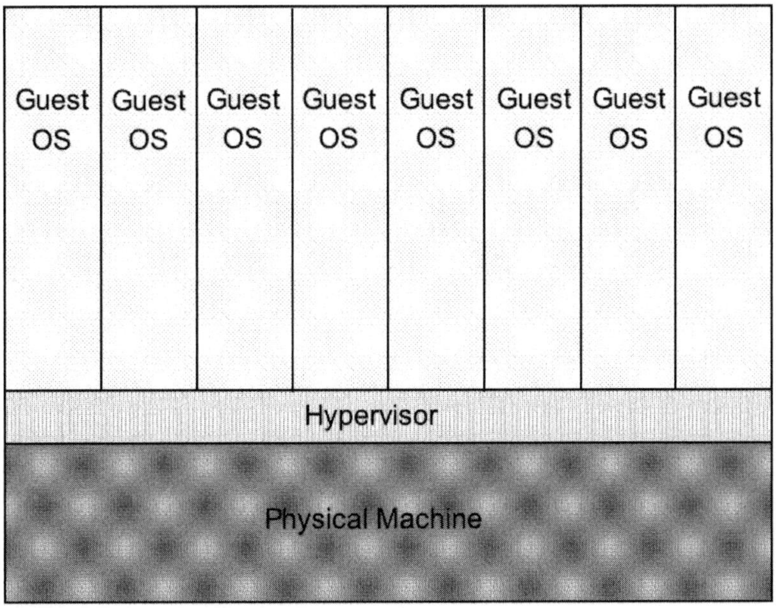

FIGURE 16.4 Native hypervisor.

typically quite robust, performs well, and is suitable for production use. Examples include the IBM z/VM mainframe hypervisor and the VMware™ ESX Server™ hypervisor for Intel servers.

Hosted Hypervisor

The complexity involved in supporting a full suite of hardware devices can be avoided by offloading this chore to a host operating system. That's the technique used by a *hosted hypervisor*, which coexists with a host operating system on the same machine. Sugerman et al. describe an architecture for this, in which support is split between a hypervisor component that virtualizes the CPU, and an application component that runs on the host operating system and handles I/O for the guest [Sugarman01]. A driver loaded into the operating system connects the two. See Figure 16.5.

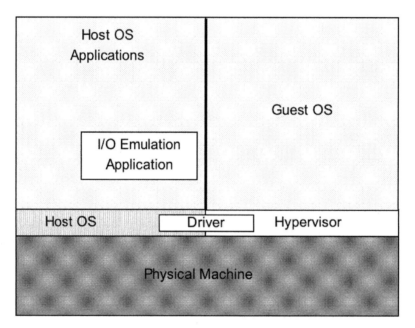

FIGURE 16.5 Hosted hypervisor.

There is a price to be paid for the convenience of leveraging the host operating system for device support. The hosted hypervisor gives up a degree of control over system resources. It also incurs additional performance overhead due to the heavyweight context switching between the host operating system and hypervisor worlds, particularly for I/O-intensive workloads. Examples of this technology include the VMware Workstation and GSX Server™ hypervisors, which both run on top of either Windows or Linux host operating systems on Intel hardware.

PARTITIONING AND VIRTUALIZATION COMBINATIONS

It's worth noting that partitioning and virtualization technologies are not mutually exclusive. They can be combined in various ways to further maximize the utilization of a physical computer. For example, a single server could be divided into a dozen logical partitions. Several of those LPARs could each be running a native software hypervisor, which in turn subdivides each LPAR into dozens of virtual machines. This approach is depicted in Figure 16.6.

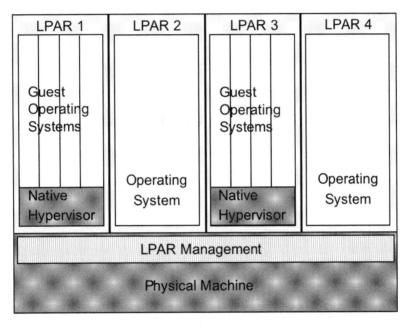

FIGURE 16.6 Virtualization within logical partitions.

Another possibility is to have a native hypervisor create several virtual machines, and inside one (or more) of those virtual machines, run another copy of that same native hypervisor—creating a second level of virtualization. Such an approach is commonly used to test new versions of z/VM prior to putting them into production, for example. Combinations such as these can indeed prove quite powerful.

WHY GO VIRTUAL?

Now that we have seen several ways that a virtual computer can be built, let's examine some of the additional capabilities that are often available in these environments and can aid testing.

Testing across Multiple Operating Systems

It's common for some types of software to run on multiple operating system plat-forms. For example, a database or Web application server might run on several fla-vors of Windows and a variety of versions of Linux from multiple Linux distributors. Multiply those operating system variants by the number of testers who need access to them, and the resulting number of computers needed to fully test the software can easily exceed the test team's budget.

One approach to addressing this problem might be to limit the number of systems available to testers, compromising test coverage to stay within budget. Virtualization offers the opportunity to avoid that compromise. It can give each tester a single machine upon which he can test with multiple operating system environments at once, each running in its own virtual machine. The virtual machines would be completely independent, so that a failure on one would not in-terfere with tests running on the others—just as if they were separate, physical ma-chines.

Going one step further, several testers could even share a single physical ma-chine that has pools of virtual images in operation, with each pool running the de-sired suite of different operating systems. Each tester would get his own pool, and would access the various virtual machines over the network. It would appear to each tester as though he had his own private suite of operating system images upon which to execute his tests.

Multinode Testing

What about tests that require multiple systems working in concert, such as client/server or Web services networks? Multiply the number of required network nodes by the variety of supported operating systems and by the size of the test team, and the machine requirements could fly off the scale. Most teams would not test every possible combination in such a case, but would instead pick and choose some meaningful subsets. Nevertheless, the number of machines required could be large and, combined with the necessary networking switches and routers, could eas-ily exceed the team's hardware budget.

Again, virtualization can come to the rescue. A collection of virtual machines could be interconnected through a virtual network, all within a single, physical computer. The hypervisor could emulate Ethernet connections between the guest images using memory-to-memory data transfers, creating a mininetwork operating entirely inside that computer (without requiring any additional external network-ing hardware). On z/VM these virtual networks are referred to as *guest LANs;* other hypervisors use different names for the same concept.

Rapid System Provisioning

Another possibility that virtualization offers testers is that of quickly provisioning new system images. Large software packages often go through many build cycles during the testing phase to incorporate bug fixes. In some organizations, these builds are even done nightly. Once the build is done, the updated software package must be reinstalled on every system where it is being tested. Ideally, the new build could simply be reinstalled or updated on top of the previous one, and testing could continue. Unfortunately, depending on the nature of the software, this may not work well. Either the software will not support this sort of reinstallation, or the reinstall/update process may not clean up all the places in the system where bits of the previous version were installed. The latter situation is particularly true early in the test cycle, when the software's update process itself is not yet stable. The resulting intermingling of code from old and new builds on the same system creates an unstable situation that could lead to "phantom" bugs that generate confusion and waste time.

To protect themselves from problems that partial or garbled installations might cause, some test teams follow a policy of only installing new builds of the software under test on *clean* systems, where the software has not previously been installed. While this eliminates phantom bugs, it forces the team to reprovision the entire operating system environment each time they pick up a new build.

Virtualized environments offer a shared disk environment, along with facilities for easily copying operating system images from one virtual machine to another. This gives the tester the ability to maintain a set of base operating system images and generate replicas or clones of these system images on other virtual machines for the actual testing. When a new build arrives, the old virtual machine images can simply be deleted and replaced with a fresh replica. This frees the tester from maintaining multiple system environments and allows more time for testing.

Saving Test Environments

Some hosted hypervisors allow testers to make a point-in-time copy of a virtual machine that can be saved as a file on the host operating system, and referenced or reverted to later. This ability to bring a test environment up to a particular state, save that state, and then reset to that state over and over again could be very useful for repetitive testing activities. It could also be used to save the virtual machine environment after a problem has occurred, then send the captured image to another team member or developer for use in debugging.

Debugging

Some hypervisors offer robust capabilities for setting breakpoints and traps for use in testing and debugging. For example, a breakpoint could be set so that when an instruction at a specific location is executed, a value at another memory location is displayed on the console, and the execution of the guest is resumed. By managing breakpoints at the hypervisor level, the entire system image (including the guest operating system) can be frozen when a breakpoint hits, offering the ultimate in control over the debugging environment. Also, the fact that breakpoints are being set and hit is invisible to the software stack running in that guest—even the operating system doesn't realize it's being temporarily stopped and resumed by the hypervisor. This is a very important difference when compared to the artificial environment typically created by an interactive debugging tool. Also, the interactive debugging function is ordinarily going to use services of the guest operating system. That means, for example, the interactive debugger cannot be used to set breakpoints in those parts of the operating system because it would cause unexpected recursion.

Automation

Hypervisors often provide scripting capability, which allows the user some level of programmatic control over the virtual machine. This support offers enticing opportunities to automate tests that otherwise could only be performed manually.

CASE STUDY: A CLOSER LOOK AT Z/VM

To get a better feel for how a hypervisor operates, it might help to take a closer look at one. For example, let's examine the granddaddy of them all, z/VM, and how it is used in testing z/OS.

Hardware Architecture

To understand this discussion, it will be helpful first to understand a little about the underlying hardware infrastructure upon which z/VM is deployed. The zSeries architecture has two classes of CPU instructions and two states that the CPU can operate in: problem state or supervisor state. It is a basic design principle that there will always be an operating system running in supervisor state and it, in turn, will run application programs in problem state.

Privileged Instructions

Privileged instructions are a carefully grouped subset of the CPU instructions that can only be executed when the CPU is in supervisor state. The remainder can be executed when the CPU is either in problem or supervisor state. This grouping allows the operating system to isolate and protect itself from problem state application programs and similarly each problem state application program is isolated and protected from all others. An example of a privileged instruction is the one that sets the time-of-day (TOD) clock. There is one TOD clock per CPU, which the hardware continuously updates with the current time. Any program can view the contents of the TOD clock, but we would not want to allow problem state application programs to update it. In the latter instance, every other program that viewed it would see the altered and possibly wrong value. Privileged instructions such as this are reserved for the operating system's use.

Program Interruption

If the execution of a privileged instruction is attempted while the CPU is in problem state, it will be suppressed, and a *privileged operation exception* program interruption will occur which the operating system must handle. Building on this function, z/VM was developed as a hypervisor operating system capable of running other operating systems in a virtual machine in problem state. Because the virtual machine operates in problem mode, z/VM can recognize any time the guest attempts to alter the CPU state.

z/VM Structure

z/VM has two main components—the control program (CP) and the Conversational Monitor System (CMS). CP is the resource manager of z/VM. It creates the virtual machines in which users can run either CMS or other guest operating systems.

In early versions of z/VM, CP ran the virtual machines in problem state directly on the real machine until an interrupt caused CP to regain control. One such interrupt was a program exception. In this case, CP had to determine the reason for the exception generated by the virtual machine. Some program exceptions would be passed to the guest operating system; others, which could be caused by the guest operating system executing a privileged instruction, required further checking. If the guest operating system was in virtual supervisor state, then the instruction needed to be simulated by CP. If not, the program interrupt was passed to the guest operating system.

To further improve the performance of virtualization, in the early 1980s a processor-assist feature was added to the mainframe architecture. One function of the assist was enabling a guest to execute both problem and supervisor state instructions, with the latter behaving differently when required to preserve the integrity of the guest environment. The processor assist eliminated the need for z/VM to emulate privileged instructions, and so reduced the performance overhead of running guests.

CP Commands

A little more background on CP is helpful before we dive into an example of how z/VM has been used by testers. There are a number of CP commands that can be used when operating the virtual machine to simulate the external controls on a real mainframe processor. Some of them are:

Start: to start a virtual CPU

Stop: to stop a virtual CPU

Display: to view the contents of a main memory location or register

Store: to modify the contents of a main memory location or register

IPL: to load the guest operating system into memory and begin executing it

There is also a CP command to set a breakpoint:

Trace: to set a breakpoint and define what to do when it is reached

Debugging

The CP trace command allows you to set breakpoints to stop execution of the guest at key trigger points, and display and alter main memory and any register available to the guest operating system. You can then either resume the execution where the virtual machine stopped or at another memory location. There is also conditional logic within the breakpoint function to allow programmatic control over its flow. The setting of breakpoints under z/VM can be combined with scripting capabilities to create a powerful tool for test automation.

When choosing your virtualization solution, be sure to look for functionality that will allow you to establish breakpoints to stop and then restart program execution. This capability gives you flexibility for debugging all types of problems.

TIP

Tools for Automation

Let's explore an example of using z/VM to automate complex test scenarios that have traditionally been quite difficult to automate. The example is based on the capability of stopping the virtual machine during execution of the guest operating system, which relies on using z/VM's support for breakpoints or traps. In order to follow the example it will be helpful to understand how these traps work.

Using Trace Traps with z/VM

Special z/VM instructions are designed to be invoked from the guest operating system to stop it and drop the virtual machine into CP mode. Once in CP mode, you can then enter commands that set *trace traps* (z/VM terminology for breakpoints) within a given program. After the trace traps are enabled, you can then resume the guest operating system. When the program is entered and the trap springs, CP regains control and can either stop execution of the guest operating system or perform an action identified on the trace trap.

Modifying Memory

You can also display or modify memory of the guest to learn whether processing is occurring correctly or to inject errors. Modifying guest operating system memory is primarily done during unit verification test, where the focus on a single program's processing is important. Function verification testers generally don't modify guest memory since their primary goal is to create all situations using external means. However, there are times when such modification is necessary, particularly in recovery testing.

Testing in a virtualized environment can benefit from the ability to modify guest memory. Look for that capability to enhance your functional testing.

A Study in Automating Intricate Scenarios

So how can we leverage the capability to stop the guest operating system on demand? We can integrate it with z/OS operating system functionality to build an automated recovery scenario that, without a virtualized environment, would be nearly impossible to automate.

Use virtualized environments and their functions to automate otherwise manual scenarios.

The Original Way: Exploiting Basic Virtualization

For many years, the general flow of FVT recovery scenarios within components of z/OS was in two phases:

Phase I: Prepare to inject the error.
Phase II: Inject the error and monitor recovery.

Phase I involved three basic steps:

- Randomly stop the guest operating system.
- Set a trace trap inside a targeted program using CP commands.
- Restart the guest and generate appropriate system activity to cause the trap to spring.

The purpose of the trap was simply to freeze the system at a particular point in the targeted program's execution in preparation for phase II. Each of the steps was performed manually. When the trap sprang, phase II began. The tester would inject a programming failure through a variety of techniques. This was mostly done by overlaying the next execution address in the operating system's program counter to zero. It just so happens that for z/OS, the value at location zero is never a valid instruction. After the guest operating system was resumed, it immediately tripped over this invalid program counter value and an *operation exception* program interruption occurred.

At this point, the recovery routines cleaned up the execution environment, gathered diagnostic information for problem resolution and, in most cases, retried the failed processing. The tester's responsibility in this manual approach was to ensure that the operation was retried (if appropriate), see that the proper dump data and trace records were saved for later analysis, and verify that the system and this component or function could continue to service requests.

This ability to freeze the entire operating system, poke through its memory, inject errors, and then resume was quite powerful. In some sense, it was like a scene from a science fiction movie, in which the lead character can stop time. Everything around him is frozen, but he is still able to walk around, snoop in people's houses, and cause mischief. That's the power of virtualization. But the FVT team wanted to go one step further and leverage this power to automate the otherwise purely manual scenario.

The New Way: Virtualization + Automation

This recovery scenario involved two distinct environments. First, it required actions to be taken from the hypervisor's shell environment (CP), such as setting trace traps, injecting errors, and resuming the virtual machine. Second, it required knowledge of the state of what was running *inside* the virtual machine, such as where the program to be trapped was loaded into memory.

Automating a scenario that spans multiple environments is normally quite difficult. However, in this case both environments were closely connected. The guest operating system environment was running inside a virtual machine envelope, around which was wrapped the hypervisor environment. This closeness made the possibility of understanding and acting across the two environments conceivable. Still, any tool that hoped to control the entire scenario needed to possess two qualities:

- Visibility into the state of the operating system running within the virtual machine
- Ability to invoke hypervisor actions

One tool that could accomplish both would be a hardware-based capture/ replay tool that would sit outside the system under test and tap into the system's monitor and keyboard cables. It would "see" what appeared on the monitor by intercepting data streams flowing across the monitor's cable, and "type" commands by injecting them into the data stream flowing from the keyboard's cable. By running on external hardware, the tool itself would not be affected by transitions between the hypervisor shell and the virtual machine. In some sense, it would be like an automated human reading the screen and typing commands.

Such tools do exist and they work, but the FVT team felt the virtualized environment offered a more elegant approach. Figure 16.7 outlines the flows involved.

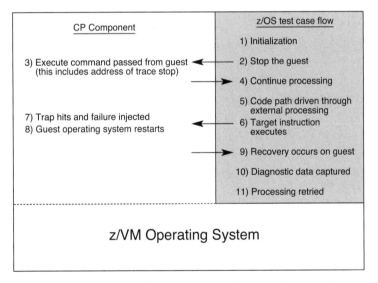

FIGURE 16.7 Automated recovery scenario using virtualization on z/VM.

As mentioned earlier, the z/VM virtualization support includes a means for the software running within the virtual machine to tell the hypervisor to stop that virtual machine and invoke a command or series of commands. The z/OS FVT test team created a custom tool that exploited this feature.

The New Phase I: Preparing to Inject the Error

The custom tool ran on the z/OS guest. It invoked a special instruction that stopped the virtual machine, and also specified CP commands to be issued after the virtual machine dropped into CP mode. These embedded commands could, for example, set a trace trap and resume the virtual machine. This technique gave the team an automated approach for the first step of the scenario.

Look for virtualization support that will allow you to stop the guest system to perform a command or series of commands.

But how did the automated test case find the targeted program's address in order to set the trace trap correctly? Because the tool ran on the instance of z/OS under test, it could search system memory and control structures to locate the program and place its address into a variable. Knowing this address, the embedded CP command could set a trace trap at a desired offset past the targeted program's starting address, then inject a program failure (as described earlier), and finally resume the guest operating system. The tool had now created a trace trap within a specific routine in the operating system without any manual intervention by the tester.

Combine the capability of virtualization with tooling that can use information of the guest machine to provide powerful automation.

The New Phase II: Injecting the Error and Monitoring Recovery

Now, a test case needed to somehow drive the relevant code path through the targeted program. If the test case did this successfully, the trap sprang, the guest operating system was stopped, and CP executed the action identified on the trace trap command. In this case, that entailed placing a value of zero as the next address to execute and then resuming the guest operating system.

After the guest was resumed, an operation exception program interrupt was immediately generated. This appeared as a true failure condition inside the targeted program from which the system had to recover. In turn this drove the RTM processing to give control to recovery routines that were in place to protect the targeted program. The recovery routines then funneled diagnostic information into processor memory dumps, trace files, or log files. After the debugging information was gathered, the recovery routine indicated, in most cases, to retry the processing that originally failed.

No Automation, Compromised Quality

Without the capability of virtualization and breakpoints, this type of recovery scenario would have been nearly impossible to create on the native zSeries hardware platform. But virtualization provided the infrastructure and tools not only to create such a scenario, but to automate it. This capability proved to be a tremendous help in finding the problems that matter to customers in support of continuous availability.

Extending the Automation Even Further

The team took this one step further and added results checking. They used the full capability of the custom tool's support for dropping the guest operating system into CP mode, displaying system memory or invoking specific commands, and finally, resuming the guest operating system. The tool's interface into CP from the guest z/OS operating system allowed the tester to specify a variable into which the command's response was placed. The tool then parsed the response and validated that the expected values were present. The control flow, including this step of verification, is illustrated in Figure 16.8.

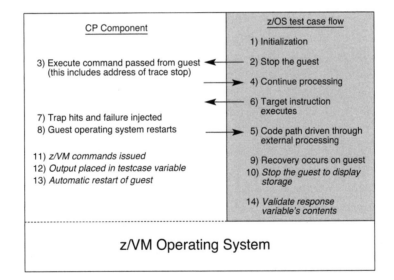

FIGURE 16.8 Process flow for integrating z/VM commands into z/OS test cases.

This custom tooling capitalized on the power of the virtualized environment to provide an efficient and dependable way for automating complex mainline and recovery scenarios. In addition, it allowed for automated verification of product control structures and key data during test case execution without noticeable interruption.

Not only can you automate complex scenarios but you can automate the validation of their results. Extend the automation to include self-verification techniques.

TIP

SUMMARY

The ability to subdivide a single physical computer into many smaller test environments is very powerful. It can significantly expand the number of images available for testing across operating systems or multinode configurations. It offers opportunities for rapid system provisioning and saving snapshots of test machines. It also presents a wide variety of possibilities for debug and test automation.

Even if you do take advantage of virtualization, there are situations when it's hard to begin testing because some portion of the underlying infrastructure you need is not available. In Chapter 17, "Simulators and Prototypes," we'll see how you can begin testing before all the pieces exist through the use of simulation and prototypes.

17 Simulators and Prototypes

In This Chapter

- Simulators and prototypes
- What to do when the hardware isn't ready
- Tools for dealing with schedule mismatches
- The perils of simulation
- A prototype case study

Software development isn't a paint-by-numbers process. It's often a messy business where different pieces of a puzzle need to magically come together at the right moments, when it may seem impossible to do so. This is particularly true when the new software under development also requires new hardware. In this chapter, we'll discuss the challenges that specific scenarios create for test. In particular, we'll review some of your options should you find yourself in a position where you need to start testing and the hardware you are dependent on is not yet functional.

SIMULATORS AND PROTOTYPES: WHAT ARE THEY?

Let's define a couple of things before we start, the first being a simulator. A simulator is a piece of software or hardware that mimics some other piece of software or hardware. In order to do that, the simulator's external interfaces must look as much like the real thing as possible. But a simulator might be mostly an empty shell that does only a subset of what the real thing will do.

The second item is a prototype. Across a variety of engineering disciplines, a designer will often create a prototype when he wants to explore various design options. A prototype is a crude, stripped-down version of something to be delivered later. It's used to explore certain characteristics of the real thing. Software engineers use prototypes to evaluate the merits of different algorithms, for example, or to see how different elements will interact when they come together. Unlike a simulator, a prototype's main mission is to do real work. It's not expected to be high quality or necessarily even perform well, unless exploring performance is its main objective. A prototype is a quick-and-dirty way to see how aspects of the ultimate deliverable should eventually run. It's similar to how hardware engineers will build a prototype or model of a new piece of hardware to use for testing before the real product goes into manufacturing.

THE CASE OF THE MISSING HARDWARE

Let's assume you get into a situation where you have software to test but the necessary hardware is not in sight. This is most likely due to time constraints. This is common when time-to-market is a key driving force. To shorten the elapsed time of a project, you need to do as many things as possible in parallel—and that can mean that hardware and software are developed simultaneously. Hence we experience the problem of "nowhere to test" whenever the hardware development takes longer than the software development or the hardware is not stable when it is first married with the new software.

Sequence of Events

The following is a likely scenario:

- The design team creates a proposal for a new hardware device.
- A very detailed specification is developed that defines how the new device works, what commands can be sent to it, what it does with each command, what kinds of errors it can return, etc.
- The hardware developers take the specification and build the first prototype device or engineering model.
- In parallel, the software developers take the same specification and code the software to support the new device.

Nowhere to Test

You're ready to start your UT and FVT, but the prototype machine isn't ready yet. If you have the luxury of waiting, you can delay any testing until the first prototype is ready. Since it will elongate the overall project schedule, this is most likely not a viable option. On the contrary, you'll probably be under pressure to do some amount of testing before you get the working hardware. Now it's time to be creative.

SIMULATION

When you can't wait for the new hardware, consider simulation. This technique allows you to construct a tool that mimics the real hardware while doing a minimal amount of work. The simulator absorbs input from the software and responds as defined in the specifications, so from the software's perspective it appears as though it is interacting with real hardware. Sometimes a simulator will need to do some limited amount of real work in order to react properly to the input it receives. For example, if it is simulating an I/O device that has data storage capability, then it may be necessary for the simulator to also store data. But that real work is merely a byproduct of its simulation activities, not its main objective.

A powerful capability of simulators is having a command or parameter interface that can be used to modify how the simulator responds to input. For example, an external switch could cause the simulator to return an error condition on the next command it receives. Or, a parameter to adjust the I/O response time could be used to simulate a hardware device timeout. Both of these capabilities can be extremely useful in your UT and FVT.

The advantages of using simulators are not confined to the hardware realm. They can also be quite valuable when the development schedules for two different software packages that interoperate with each other don't align. If one package needs the other in order to begin testing, simulation may break the logjam. In some sense, even simple stub routines and scaffolding (discussed in Chapter 3, "The Development Process") are forms of simulation. Both receive input passed to them and respond in a manner within the bounds of what the caller expects. They are, in effect, simulating a software module that hasn't yet been created.

For the purposes of our discussion, we'll focus on the more specialized case of software simulation of new hardware. You'll find that many of the concepts apply equally well to simulation of new software.

Impersonating New Hardware

If you decide to build a simulator, you should already have a specification for the function in question. The specification should describe what actions the hardware will perform, and what will pass back and forth on the interfaces between the software and hardware. Your tool should mimic this interface traffic. Treating the new hardware as a black box, the tool doesn't need to do everything the new hardware will, it just needs to react the same way on the defined interfaces.

Attributes

Whatever tool you develop must:

- Be low in cost. You can't spend an excessive amount of resources on building this tool, because it may be a "throwaway" item that is no longer needed when the real hardware is functional.
- Survive a cost-versus-elapsed time tradeoff to ensure the tool is worth developing.
- Precisely match the interface specifications.
- Have the capability to be built in a timely manner. The tool will only help you if it is available to fill the gap between code readiness and the availability of functional hardware.
- Be easy to use. If the tool is difficult to operate, then people will tend to avoid it.

Example: Testing an I/O Driver

Say your team's challenge is to test the I/O driver for a hypothetical, three-dimensional graphical display with a joystick. The overall project objective is to design and build the display and the software I/O driver to support the hardware. Your job is to test the I/O driver. The project plan predicts that the I/O driver will be coded long before the first graphical display is functional. This sounds like a perfect opportunity to create a tool that will simulate the graphical display. That way, you can start your I/O driver testing sooner.

What Does Your Simulator Need to Do?

In this example, the simulator should:

- Accept all valid commands that can be sent to the display. The tool should do a reasonable amount of validity checking of the data that is sent with the commands.
- Reject all invalid commands with the correct error codes. The simulator should also be designed to record these errors in an error log. This is recommended because you'll more than likely need to investigate why something is attempting to send these invalid commands to the display.
- Respond to commands with the same kind of timing that the real display will have. This probably means you will need to insert some timing delays in your simulator.

- Comply with any rules demanding that certain commands only be performed in a particular order.
- Send joystick input to the I/O driver in the same way the real hardware will. If collisions can occur between commands sent to the display and input sent from the joystick, your simulator needs to be able to create that scenario as well.

Degree of Simulation

You have a choice to make with your simulator tool when establishing the extent of simulation you need to do. One option is to discard the display data because your tool only needs to respond on the interface like the real graphical display will. Another possible option is to convert the three-dimensional data into two-dimensional data and display that on a normal graphical terminal. The latter option requires more work, but it can help you surface specific kinds of defects earlier or ensure the integrity of information targeted for the display (e.g. the display data may be correct except the image is upside down).

Using the Simulator to Test

Your simulator is written and ready to go. You've modified the operating system so that any commands that would normally be sent to the new three-dimensional display device are sent to your simulator instead. Now you can begin doing UT and FVT on the I/O driver. When you are debugging new problems discovered in this environment, you need to keep reminding yourself that the problem could either be in the code you're testing *or* in the simulator code. You'll probably go through several iterations of development correcting defects in the I/O driver or the simulator. As you gain experience with your simulator you may decide to enhance it to make it even more beneficial.

Dialog among the Teams

The I/O driver, the hardware, and the simulator are all based on the same specification, but each of the development teams may have interpreted the spec slightly differently. Therefore, it's important that there be a continuous dialog among the three teams to resolve any differences (differences that might have been discovered by the testers). Through this continuous dialog, and by developing the hardware and software in parallel, the teams will gain the advantage of being able to enhance the original specification earlier in the process. Naturally, this is faster than waiting until the hardware and software first come together. The earlier in the project these kinds of changes can be made, the faster and cheaper they are to achieve.

Shifting to Real Hardware

You have been using your simulator to do as much testing as possible and now the new graphical display is ready to try. How well things work when you first attempt to use the new display depends on several factors:

- The degree of testing performed on the I/O driver using the simulator
- How well the simulator matched the real display
- The hardware team's thoroughness in testing the new display
- Whether each team's implementation of the specification matches

There's no doubt that you'll eventually need to do a fair amount of additional testing on the real hardware when it's available. In the meantime, your simulator will be judged a success if it closely mirrors the real hardware and allows you to compress the overall project schedule.

THE PERILS OF SIMULATION

Simulation can be a very valuable tool for the test team when schedules don't line up. But there are dangers that await a development organization that relies too heavily on a simulator if it deviates from the way the real hardware works. Let's take a look at a classic case of such overzealous use of simulation.

Case Study: When Simulation Meets Real Hardware

Most operating systems support the use of page or swap files on disk, which act as a kind of overflow area for memory. Unfortunately, performing I/O to disk is always much slower than accessing memory. For this reason, designers are always looking for ways to improve disk I/O performance. In the mainframe world, one of the earliest such improvements was made when cache was added to the disk hardware. This dramatically improved the read time for data that had been recently referenced and was still in the cache by eliminating the need to actually search for and retrieve the data from the physical disk—a (relatively) slow, mechanical process.

NOTE

Cache is high-speed memory that is often added to disk hardware to improve read/write performance.

In the mid 1980s this idea was improved upon by adding some special, lower-cost memory to the CPU called *expanded storage*. The operating system could use this memory as an internal cache for paging. In effect, expanded storage added another layer of cache, which often eliminated disk I/O for a paging operation. This internal cache was not accessible to the operating system through normal instructions. Instead, new instructions were added to copy pages back and forth between normal memory and expanded storage. This hardware support was first delivered in a new family of mainframe processors.

Testing Dilemma

Naturally, software support was required in the operating system to exploit this new hardware feature. The new code was developed at the same time that the processor hardware itself was being built, which was scheduled to be ready at approximately the same time as the start of SVT. This timeline put UT and FVT in a bind. Without the hardware, they had no way to test the new code. Yet due to tight schedules, the system test team was counting on those other tests to get the code reasonably stable prior to the onset of load/stress testing.

Solution: Simulation

Faced with this dilemma, the team decided to create a simulator that would be based on the use of a virtualized environment. Additions were made to VM, the mainframe hypervisor discussed in Chapter 16, "Testing with a Virtual Computer," to imitate the new instructions for copying pages to and from expanded storage. The development effort was not too large, and because the requirement was foreseen well in advance, the simulator was completed before the operating system code was even written.

When faced with a major schedule mismatch between codependent products, consider "imitating" one of them with a simulator.

TIP

The development team took advantage of the simulator's early availability. Developers checked their new code against it every step of the way. In effect, they used the simulator as an architecture-compliance tool, making sure that the code they wrote adhered to the new expanded-storage architecture by running it against the simulator. This approach kept development moving briskly, and before long the code was ready for FVT. The FVT team ran a battery of tests against the expanded storage support, using the simulator in lieu of actual hardware. Several bugs were found and fixed, and eventually the code was deemed ready for SVT.

The use of a simulator in a virtualized environment successfully allowed UT and FVT to be done before the hardware was ready, so the overall project schedule could be met.

NOTE

Software Meets Hardware

The hardware was ready on schedule. It too had survived a series of tests, in this case by hardware engineers using their own specialized tools, and now was ready to face its toughest challenge: supporting the real operating system. A joint test was arranged. The system test team gathered its new operating system code and brought it over to the new machine. There, SVT members met their hardware test counterparts. They loaded the software into the system. The hardware engineers made final checks of the hardware. Finally, the moment of truth arrived: it was time to boot up the new software on the new hardware for the very first time. Anxiously, both sets of testers looked on. The suspense didn't last long. Almost immediately the operating system crashed.

The teams were stunned. This wasn't supposed to happen. Prior testing had been thorough, and a smooth bring-up was expected. The software testers took a memory dump and examined it. Quickly, they discovered the failure had occurred the very first time the operating system attempted to execute one of the new instructions for expanded storage. Oddly, the error indicated there was a problem with the instruction itself. Further investigation soon revealed the cause: the operating system code had the operands for the new instruction reversed.

The Big Flaw

How could the earlier testing have missed such an obvious error? Suspicion fell on the simulator. A comparison was done of the specifications describing the new hardware architecture and the simulator's emulation of that architecture. Indeed, it turned out that the simulator was built incorrectly. It was erroneously designed to expect those operands to be backwards, so it only worked when the operating system reversed them.

Never rely solely on a simulator for testing software.

That explained why the error escaped. But why wasn't it detected when the simulator was first used during UT? A sheepish developer admitted that he hadn't bothered to look at the actual hardware specifications. Instead, he'd simply written his operating system support to match the simulator.

Each of the three teams (hardware developers, software developers, and simulator developers) should have built their respective components to match the design specifications, rather than matching how one of the other teams built their component.

Be wary of stretching the use of a simulator beyond its intended role.

The problem was easily fixed and testing quickly resumed. Overall, the simulator was quite useful for its intended purpose. It enabled the team to complete early testing and to find and fix several bugs. Only when it stepped outside of its true role, by being used as substitute for the product specification rather than as a test tool, did it lead to trouble.

PROTOTYPES

Prototypes are not only useful for software and hardware designers. There are occasions when they can be helpful to testers as well. When hardware and software schedules don't line up, and a simple simulator isn't sufficient to fill the gap, a prototype can sometimes save the day. It can provide the tester with temporary hardware upon which to test until the real hardware is available.

A hardware prototype is not something the test team can usually create entirely on its own; help from other teams is needed. Also, the situations in which such a tool plays a role are fairly specialized. Most testers will never have a need to test on a hardware prototype. Nevertheless, it's an interesting concept; one that may give you perspective on how testers can react to a seemingly impossible situation by expanding their vision of what is possible and then making miracles happen.

In this next example, we'll look at using a prototype to emulate a new processor architecture. By necessity, the case study requires a certain amount of technical discussion about the architecture being emulated. If this is beyond your need or interest, you may want to skip ahead. But if you'd like a glimpse into how an effective prototype can be built and exploited for testing, or you are simply curious about how this kind of thing is done, then read on.

Case Study: A 64-bit Server Prototype

When the IBM System/360™ mainframe was introduced in 1964, it supported the ability to use memory addresses that were a maximum of 24 bits long. With that many bits, you could address a maximum of 16 megabytes of memory, which was a lot in 1964. Eventually the need to access more memory arose, so the mainframe hardware and software were adapted to support 31-bit addresses. A 31-bit address can access at most 2 gigabytes of memory, which also seemed like plenty at the time. But the day finally came when 2 gigabytes was insufficient, and the decision was made to add hardware and operating system support for 64-bit addresses.

Memory addressing is a big deal for servers and operating systems and, to a lesser extent, middleware and applications. The changes required are in the very guts of the system, affecting such things as memory managers and interrupt handlers. The actual composition of the hardware instructions that make up a compiled computer program have to change to account for the increased address size. Even the CPU's general purpose registers (GPRs), often used to calculate memory addresses, must increase in size to hold all 64 bits. Doing all of this in a compatible way that allows older, 24-bit and 31-bit applications to work correctly together with the newer 64-bit ones on the same machine makes the job even more difficult.

In the face of such dramatic change, thorough testing is crucial. However, the software team rarely has time to wait for the real hardware to be available before it begins. Let's see how z/OS development solved this problem.

The Challenge: Parallel Development

At the same time that the hardware engineers were designing and building the new chips for the 64-bit processor, the z/OS software developers were working on the changes to the operating system to support the new processor.

The Operating System as a Test Tool

The hardware team planned to do extensive testing of all the new 64-bit support using its own customized tools. However, experience had shown that no matter how much testing was done on a new processor using architecture verification tools, it was never enough. Additional problems always surfaced once the operating system was run on the new processor itself. In effect, the z/OS operating system made a great hardware test tool.

In order to hold the hardware delivery date to customers, it was critical that the hardware test team had a stable level of z/OS already running in 64-bit mode when they were ready to verify the new processor. That meant that the z/OS team needed to find a way to test the 64-bit support before the new machine was functional.

 Deadlines for creating interdependent products in parallel can generate a testing requirement for a prototype of one of those products.

Testing 64-Bit Mode before a 64-Bit Machine is Built: Possible Solutions

The team proposed and investigated several possible ways to perform early testing of the 64-bit software support. The biggest hurdle for any of the possible options was the changes implemented in something called the *dynamic address translation* (DAT) tables. DAT tables are built by the operating system to describe to the CPU how a virtual memory address translates to a real memory address. Because real memory addresses were increasing to 64 bits, there were major changes to the layout of the DAT tables.

Option One

One possible solution was based entirely on virtualization. The idea was to modify VM to emulate the new architecture completely. However, because VM itself would still be running on a 31-bit machine, the hardware would not understand the format of the new 64-bit DAT tables. That would force VM to simulate the use of 64-bit DAT tables and do all of the virtual-to-real address translation processing for each instruction. It was determined that the performance of the guest would be so slow that it would not meet the testing needs.

When designing a prototype, don't ignore performance considerations. The prototype must perform well enough to be useful in its intended role.

Option Two

The team also considered modifying an *existing* machine to use DAT tables in the new format. This option wouldn't have been practical on a machine where hardware managed the DAT function, because it would require the engineers to redesign and build new processor chips. But in this particular case, one of the earlier-generation machines used firmware for the DAT function. This opened up the option of modifying the firmware so that it could handle DAT tables in both the old and new formats. It would also be possible to update the firmware with some of the new architecture instructions.

When selecting a base upon which to construct a prototype, review a wide range of possibilities. You may be surprised by a choice that can make the development job much easier.

The remaining new instructions, those that could not be added to the firmware, needed to be simulated. The logical approach was to modify VM so that it would simulate the changes to the GPRs, the new instructions, and the like. With this combination of changes to VM and to the firmware, some simulation could be performed by VM, and the DAT work would be handled by the hardware prototype.

Consider the use of simulation with your prototype. Combining the two techniques can result in a very efficient approach.

The Choice

Given these benefits, the obvious choice was option two. The 64-bit prototype was built as described and operational for more than 12 months before the first real machine was scheduled to be powered on. The z/OS developers made extensive use of the 64-bit prototype and were able to complete UT, FVT, and some limited SVT of z/OS. The UT and FVT team members had all of the VM capabilities that they were accustomed to. While the performance of the guest z/OS was not great, it was acceptable on the 64-bit prototype. It certainly allowed for the functional verification of the operating system.

Success or Failure?

This combination of a special hardware prototype and VM doing some simulation was judged a great success. When the real machine was declared stable enough to try, the team was able to boot z/OS in 64-bit mode on it within two days. By that second day, they were able to run batch jobs and log users on.

Much more testing continued after this first boot. The hardware testers now had a stable 64-bit operating system that they could use as a tool for pressuring the new machine. And z/OS testers continued their SVT, now on the real hardware.

SUMMARY

Simulators and prototypes are not needed every day. But when the need does arise, they can be lifesavers. Either one can help you shorten the elapsed time of a project by imitating new hardware before it is built, and allowing you to overlap software testing with hardware development. For a successful outcome, it is very important that a simulator mirrors the responses of the new hardware as closely as possible and that it is only used for its intended purpose. No matter what hardware environment you rely upon, you'll face chaotic situations during the testing cycle. In Chapter 18, "Managing the Test," we'll explore ways the tester can gain control of the chaos and be the master of his testing domain.

18 Managing the Test

In This Chapter

- Testing the correct code
- Reining in testing chaos through run logs
- Avoiding oversights with an end-of-day checklist
- Techniques for tracking problems and scoring defects
- Measuring success as a weapon for getting bugs fixed
- Practical solutions when a test fails to meet its end date

Chaos, disorder, confusion: sounds like a typical day of software testing. From a distance (say, in a magazine article—or a presentation to your executive management), testing may appear to be a sleek killing machine, methodically working its way through one scenario after another, smashing bugs with ruthless precision. But look more closely and the glossy veneer begins to fade.

- A step is omitted on page 13 of the user's guide you're following for configuring a networking application. But it's not until hours later, when you reach the critical point in a test and the application won't connect to a partner system, that you begin to suspect something is wrong.
- While working through a well-planned recovery scenario, suddenly more things than expected begin to fail. The system console lights up in a meteor shower of error messages. The first in a series of 50 tests uncovers a severe bug that blocks all the others. Instantly you're behind schedule before you've really

begun. Your end date is a week away, testing is behind, and the list of open bugs keeps growing. Management insists that delaying the software's roll out would be catastrophic, but is eager to hear what other suggestions you might have.

The notion that the act of testing software really isn't a neat and tidy activity should not be surprising. Chaos theory teaches us that the world is always more complex up close than is seems from a distance. Benoit Mandelbrot, the father of a branch of chaos theory known as fractal geometry, once made this point by observing that, for example, clouds are not spheres, mountains are not cones, and bark is not smooth [Mandelbrot83]. Why should we expect software testing to be any different?

Once you accept that the testing process is messy, you can take steps to rein in the chaos. There are certain problems and difficult situations that most testers are likely to face. There are also techniques that can be used in the face of these troubles to maintain some measure of control. With some forethought and care, you can even harness the chaos to work for you, rather than against you. Or, in the words of Shakespeare's Polonius, "Though this be madness, yet there is method in't."

TESTING THE CORRECT CODE

A new tester was once handed what seemed like a good introductory assignment. An existing piece of software was being updated, not with new functions, but with new algorithms to improve its performance and efficiency. To test this update, he could make use of test cases and scenarios from prior tests, minimizing his upfront preparation needs while also teaching him how to find and access that archived material. But the required testing wasn't trivial. Indeed, it was fairly time-consuming, and would give him a good introduction to the test environment as well as his team's processes and techniques.

Once the new code became available, he grabbed it and dutifully began his work. Two weeks into the test, everything was going smoothly. While all those around him struggled through problem after problem on other new functions of the software, his testing sailed along without hitting any such roadblocks. *This testing thing is easy*, he thought. After a month of testing he finished, a full two weeks ahead of schedule. Unfortunately, he hadn't found a single bug, but he shrugged that off. After all, it wasn't his fault if the software happened to be rock solid.

Then it happened. Another tester on his team accidentally stumbled over what turned out to be a major bug in his assigned code. The defect was a glaring error. Our young tester was embarrassed and dumbfounded that he hadn't caught it. His test plan had been thorough, and his execution flawless. What had gone wrong? A tickle of worry began to gnaw at his gut. Quietly, he did a little investigation. He dumped one of his target modules on his test system. Then he did the same on the test system of a teammate. The module had an eye catcher at the top that was human-readable in a hexadecimal memory dump. The eye catcher contained the module's name and the date it was last compiled. He compared the two dates. In an instant his stomach began to churn, his hair follicles stood on end, and a bead of sweat started trickling down between his shoulder blades. The dates didn't match. In fact, the date from his system was over a year old. He'd just spent a month testing the software's prior release.

Protecting Yourself

Though this story may seem like an extreme case, smaller-scale instances of testing the wrong code happen to testers every day. In this example, a complete rebuild of the new software was done every six weeks, with individual fixes for problems found by a tester applied daily as needed. But many software projects follow weekly, or even daily, build cycles. With that much churn, it's not only possible, but probable that you'll find yourself in a similar situation unless you take great care. If the software you're testing has line mode commands or GUI actions to show the exact version of software on your test system, use them every time you pick up a new build. Or, dump a sample of the actual executable code like our tester did, but do so *before* your test, rather than after. Protect yourself from the embarrassment of being told the spiffy "new" bug you're so proud of was fixed two weeks ago and your system is down-level. Always confirm that you are really testing what you think you are.

RUN LOGS: KEEPING TRACK OF WHAT'S GOING ON

A day of good testing can be both exhilarating and chaotic. It's rewarding to watch as an intricate scenario you devised reveals a devastating bug, and fun to follow a trail of error messages and unexpected results to the hidden lair of a new defect. But it's also often muddled and confusing. Despite having a strong plan in place, testing is often not a linear activity. There may be some serendipity involved. To understand the twists and turns that testing can take, it may help to consider a few situations in which you might someday find yourself.

On the Trail of a Bug

Say you start down a planned 20-step test path. Part way through, you realize you missed a step. You go back and try to insert the missing step, but some other action you've since taken makes that impossible. So you undo that action, and then try again with the missed step. Again, a previous action blocks your path, so you undo it too. Now the omitted step can be inserted successfully. You celebrate with a trip to the vending machine. On the way back, you run into a friend who regales you with a story about his run in with a grizzly on a recent backpacking trip to Alaska. Finally you return to your test system and redo that last action you undid, but forget to first redo the prior one. BANG! A bug hits. Excited, you collect documentation on the error and file a bug report. A week later, the developer (or you, if you are doing your own debugging) realizes more information is needed to debug the problem. First, of course, you need to re-create it. How exactly did you do that?

Testing lore suggests that over half of the bugs found in any large-scale test are not uncovered by exactly following a detailed plan step by step, but rather through these kinds of subtle and unplanned deviations. Whether this is really true is unknown, but at times it certainly seems that way. In the case of artistic testing, it's that way by design.

Keeping the Test System Afloat

Testers also do a lot more on their systems than run through test scenarios and uncover bugs. Often, considerable set up, configuration, and other preparatory work are needed before a scenario can even begin. This puts the tester in the position of being a systems programmer or administrator. Such people aren't paid highly because their jobs are easy: things go wrong, documentation is unclear, and hardware fails. In other words, problems arise, and the tester must figure out solutions. It's why many testers acquire the same skills as system programmers and administrators. This investigation takes time, sometimes a lot of it. It's not unusual for a tester to spend the better part of a day resolving an issue that isn't directly related to the software being tested, but must be overcome before further test progress can be made.

Unfortunately, it's also not unusual for the same or similar problem to pop up again, weeks later. When this happens to you, it's a safe bet you'll remember hitting the problem previously. But will you remember how you fixed it? Or will you tap your fingers on the desktop, mumbling to yourself, "I *know* I saw this three weeks ago. What did I do? . . ."

What if you were not the first one on your team to encounter the problem? What if one of your teammates saw the same thing on his test system a few days earlier? Will you even know about it, or will you waste time tackling something that he has already solved? Will you be forced to poll your entire team every time you trip over something odd, just to ensure you are really its first victim?

Surviving in a Shared Environment

You might find yourself working within a pool of test servers shared by your entire team. Or perhaps you have your own dedicated test system(s) that are tied into a common pool of Storage Area Network (SAN) servers to hold your test data. Most likely your test system also hooks into one or more Internet Protocol (IP) network switches or routers that are shared with your teammates. You are all probably pulling fresh copies of the software under test from the same build server. Sadly, shared resources are just as likely to fail as dedicated ones, but the impact is more widespread.

When a failure hits, someone has to do something about it. If it's a hardware failure, this may involve gathering some diagnostic information and contacting the appropriate support team. If the build has a problem, you might follow a similar approach to notify the build team. But what if you spend an hour of precious test time collecting failure documentation and tracking down the right person to whom you should report the problem, only to find out one of your teammates beat you to it—three hours earlier? If only you all had a common place to post problems, actions, and resolutions for such things, so time wouldn't be wasted.

The Power of Run Logs

If you can't prevent events such as these, at least you can keep track of them. That's where *run logs* come in. A run log is simply a tool that each team member uses to note the activities that occur during a shift of their testing. Think of it as a daily, online testing diary to which the whole team contributes. It forms a collective memory of the team's activities that can be referenced by any tester, any time. It provides a valuable aid for testers trying to re-create defects, solve system administration or configuration problems, coordinate the resolution of issues related to shared resources, or simply remember how something was previously done. It also can be an effective communication pipeline among team members working different shifts, or as a way to share important global information among teams. It's especially useful for SVT and integration test, but there's no reason an FVT team can't benefit from a run log as well.

The actual tool used to contain these run logs isn't terribly important. Teams have successfully used everything from a series of flat files on a shared disk, to a private online forum, to a customized database in a groupware application such as Lotus® Notes®. Whatever tool is chosen, it should at a minimum be sharable by the whole team and enable multiple testers to create their own discrete run logs simultaneously. Ideally, it should also time stamp each entry you make, and allow simple searches of the entries from all testers from most to least recent.

Run Log Input

Good input is the key to a good run log. Every time you begin or complete a task, you should make a quick note in the run log. If you're executing a scenario with multiple steps, make a brief entry about each step just prior to running it. If you have to back up and redo something, note that too. When you hit an unexpected error (i.e., a likely bug), cut and paste any relevant error messages or other interesting information into the run log. If you create a problem record at that time, note the problem number in the run log too—that will help you quickly find the entry later if needed, either for further debugging insight into the circumstances surrounding the error, or for re-creating the bug to gather more diagnostic information.

Similarly, if you trip over a system or application problem that takes you a while to resolve, list that in the run log. Describe the symptom clearly, so that others experiencing the same problem will find it and your resolution when they search. Also, if you make configuration, tuning, or other changes to any shared servers or other common resources, highlight them in your log too—you might even want to indicate changes in bold or in color so they catch the eye. In the event that your changes have unexpected downstream effects that impact others on your team, your log entry can help them unravel the mystery of "what changed?"

Good Run Log Technique

By far the best way to use a run log is to update it as you go. Sometimes people new to run logs decide they want to wait until they are finished with a scenario before creating an entry for it. Their thinking is that by waiting they can make the entry clean and perfect. This is hogwash. It misses the whole point, which is to keep track of an often muddled and confusing sequence of events that led you to a potential bug, or helped you solve some other issue. If you want to create a beautiful how-to guide for your fellow testers, do so as a separate document. The best run logs are often the ugliest. They capture information that might at the time seem trivial, but in hindsight may prove quite useful. This is actually very similar to commenting code. It's best done as you go along, while each step is fresh in your mind. If you're paired up for team testing of complex software, an effective approach is to split up the tasks. Have one person execute a scenario while another describes what is happening in the run log. This way, both testers stay involved and the test is also well documented.

A Secret to Withstanding an Audit

Is your project subject to auditing by an outside agency to ensure compliance with some set of standards, such as ISO 9000? If so, then you may be asked to provide documented evidence proving claims that you did in fact complete test scenarios. Run logs provide an excellent source of such proof.

Create a summary section at the top of your run log. Include your name and the list of scenarios (or other tasks) you plan to execute on that day. When the day's work is done, go back up to the top and note which tasks were fully completed, partially completed, failed, or not attempted. When an auditor later asks you to prove that you completed scenario RCV0041, you can simply search your run logs for it. Up pops an entry with a summary section which clearly lists that scenario as fully completed, followed by the step-by-step description of what transpired as you executed it. If the summary section from the first hit on your search doesn't show RCV0041 as fully completed, just keep searching until you find the entry that does. The full history of that scenario's execution is right there at your fingertips.

We've discussed how the input to a run log is more important than the tool you use to create it. Still, it is worthwhile to consider recording your run logs with a tool that also allows a direct connection to your status tracking database. If marking the success or failure of a scenario within your run log also directly updates your team's status, you've added convenience and saved time.

AN END-OF-DAY CHECKLIST

At the end of a vigorous day's testing, you might be inclined to wrap up quickly and head out the door. But what if you come in the next morning refreshed and ready to dig into a problem you had hit, only to discover that you forgot to save a critical memory dump or system log? No problem, you can just go back to your test machine and retrieve that data—unless someone else has reused that machine for another test and wiped everything out.

Just as a grocery list helps you remember what food to buy, a simple end-of-day testing checklist can go a long way toward helping you avoid an oversight that you will later regret. Formality is not important here. The checklist need not be anything more than a few reminders scratched on the front page of a notebook. It can include anything that you or your team deems important. For example, a checklist might include:

- Were any memory dumps taken? If so, have they been archived?
- Have system logs been scanned for potential bug symptoms? If any anomalies were found, have those logs been archived?
- Have appropriate problem records been opened for problems found?
- Has a run log been completed?
- Does the summary section include all attempted scenarios, with an indication of whether they were completed or not?
- If any problem records were opened, have they been noted in the log?
- Were any problems encountered with servers or other physical resources shared by the team? If so, have those problems been reported to the proper people for resolution?
- Does a new build appear to have problems? Have they been reported?

This isn't rocket science. The trick, however, is to actually create and follow such a list, rather than just assuming you will remember everything. Doing so provides another weapon in your arsenal for maintaining control in the face of chaos.

GUARDING THE TREASURY: PROBLEM MANAGEMENT

Problems are the tester's pot of gold. You hope that all your planning, preparing, and testing will result in a nice big cache of potential defects. But a good tester doesn't just report a problem and forget about it. He must take ownership.

Staking a Claim

Ensure a problem is reported to the proper people. If someone other than you is responsible for debugging it, check with them periodically to assess their progress to see where your problem is in their queue. Be a squeaky wheel. However, it's wise to use discretion. How frequently you follow-up should depend on the problem's severity and its impact to further test progress. Constantly nagging others over low-severity problems will quickly make you a pariah in the organization. But hot problems demand fast turnaround, and you have every right to push for a quick resolution if your problem deserves one.

Once the problem has been debugged, a fix will need to be generated. Monitor the status of fixes for all of your defects. Once a fix is available, it's time to do your part. Be prompt about applying it and verifying it does indeed resolve the problem. When you're satisfied that the fix works, don't delay in marking the problem as resolved.

The Right Tool for the Right Job

To keep track of the constant ebb and flow of defect status, most teams record and monitor problems in a database that has been customized for the task. Each problem record or trouble ticket should include such information as:

- The person who reported the problem and will be responsible for verifying the fix
- The date it occurred
- The software's build version
- Severity and impact
- Who is assigned to debug it
- Its current state (e.g., unassigned, opened/assigned, in debug, re-create requested, fix being created, fix available, fix under test, closed)
- Description of the problem, the circumstances surrounding its detection, and its consequences
- Diagnostic data (e.g., memory dump, system logs, traces) attached or referenced
- Whether or not a bypass is available
- Fix designation or number
- Resolution description

- Whether or not the defect was new and unique
- A count of the number of re-creates needed to debug it (as a trigger for investigation into weaknesses with the software's first failure data capture capabilities)

Problem Scoring

The issue of problem severity versus impact is interesting. Many teams simply score a problem's severity on some predefined scale, such as one to four. The score of a defect depends on how its *symptoms* would affect a customer's operation. A score of one might mean the product is essentially inoperable, is corrupting data, or experiencing some other critical symptom. Two and three would be progressively less severe scores, with a four indicating a minor issue such as incorrect message wording.

This kind of scoring is both common and quite valuable for prioritizing debug and fix-creation activities. Unfortunately, by focusing purely on symptoms, information is lost. While the problem's symptoms might only rate it as a severity three, it may touch an area that is central to a new function and therefore block the execution of many test scenarios. For that reason, some teams augment problem severity with the notion of problem *impact*. The problem's impact score depends not on its external symptoms, but rather on the degree to which it is blocking test progress. This extra information enables prioritization decisions to be based on a more complete picture of the damage the problem is causing.

Database Access

The problem tracking database should be accessible to both the test and development teams—or should it? If the development team is responsible for debugging all reported problems, then they'll certainly need access to the problem records. But what if the test team takes ownership for debugging the problems they uncover, as suggested elsewhere in this book? In this case, it might make sense to create a two-tiered problem reporting structure. Tier One would be reserved solely for tester access. Any *suspected* problem would be recorded here. Once the problem has been debugged, if it turns out to be a valid, unique defect, then it would be promoted to Tier Two. The problem description in this second tier would be concise and to the point. It would focus on the actual lines of code in error, along with an explanation of contributing factors and resulting symptoms.

Benefits

There are a couple of benefits to the two-tiered approach. First, by isolating the first tier to the test team, it encourages testers to record any anomaly they feel is a potential problem. They don't need to know at that point if it's a defect, only that it's something that requires further investigation. Since the audience for these records is limited to the test team, testers are not inhibited. They can create as many entries as they like, without worrying about flooding the development team with lots of reports that may ultimately go nowhere. Because everything is captured, subtle errors won't be lost or forgotten.

The second benefit to the two-tiered approach is that the second tier will contain almost nothing but valid, unique bugs. It won't be cluttered with user errors, test case problems, nonreproducibles, and so on. It's not unusual for some of these "nonproblems" to make up over half of what a prolific test team reports. With the two-tiered approach, the development team doesn't have to waste time weeding through this chaff, and can instead focus on the wheat—real defects.

GETTING BUGS FIXED

Let's assume your testing is so successful that you uncover an ever-growing mountain of bugs. The biggest problem then becomes getting them fixed. Without fixes, a good tester eventually becomes a victim of his own success. As the heap of bugs mounts, so does the list of test cases for which progress is blocked. Eventually all testing avenues become choked with defects, and there's little for the tester to do but watch the clock as the end date nears and testing stagnates.

You need a weapon to solve this problem. For many teams, the weapon of choice is a set of well-honed measurements. Good metrics don't necessarily serve up convenient answers so much as lead people to ask the right questions. Unfortunately, when used improperly, measurements can become a source of endless busywork, paper shuffling, and fancy charts with a value far below their cost. But when used correctly, a good measurement can succinctly communicate to those running the project which defects are putting the end date in jeopardy, so the key ones are fixed promptly.

Measuring Success

If you find yourself fascinated by the world of measurement techniques for test projects, you're in luck. There are countless books devoted to software testing processes, each touting a variety of software metrics, reliability models, and predictive analysis techniques (for an excellent example, see Kan [Kan02]). Such an in-depth discussion is beyond the scope of this book. We'll stick with a simple yet effective approach that captures effort expended, effort remaining, and effort blocked, while also highlighting the impact of defects on testing progress.

A Bare-bones Approach

Your test plan will have a list of variations or scenarios to execute. Perhaps the simplest technique for measuring your progress is to count how many variations are successful each week and plot them on a graph over time. However, this method omits important information. It does not account for variations that have been attempted but are not yet successful, so it does not present a complete picture of the testing effort that's been expended so far nor the effort that remains. It also does not draw attention to tests that are blocked or the defects that are blocking them.

A Multistate Approach

A better approach is to view each variation as being in one of five states:

> **Not Attempted:** The variation has not yet been tried.
>
> **Attempted:** Work has begun on the variation, but isn't finished. This state may indicate an elaborate variation that requires considerable work, one that was started but became sidetracked due a setup error, or one that stumbled for some other reason still under investigation.
>
> **Failed:** The target code failed the test due to a defect.
>
> **Blocked:** A defect has been hit by another variation which will also affect this one. It's pointless to attempt this variation until the defect is fixed. A variation might also be marked as blocked if delivery of the code it is intended to test has been delayed.
>
> **Successful:** Everything worked as planned.

Other states are possible. For example, you might include an "unblocked" state for variations that were previously blocked but now are available to execute. You could also include a "fixtest" state for variations that were previously marked as failed but now have fixes available. You can probably think of other useful states, but these initial five make a good core set.

This finer-grained classification offers a more accurate picture of each variation's status, and clearly identifies those that are impacted by defects. But it still has some weaknesses. It doesn't distinguish between a variation that takes three minutes to execute and one that takes three days. All are treated equally, so the true effort levels aren't reflected. Also, it's not obvious how to translate these classifications into a simple chart that will clearly convey the team's status trends. For example, a pie chart could show a snapshot of the current spread of variation states, but a pie chart can't give a view of progress over time. A series of graphs could be plotted week to week for each possible variation state, but multiple graphs could muddy the team's main message.

Weighting

These weaknesses can be addressed through a further refinement: assign a weight to each variation corresponding to the estimated amount of time it will take to perform. For example, you might assign weights on a scale of 1 to 10, with the higher weights associated with the more complex scenarios. Or you could define a weight of one for any scenario that will require some baseline amount of time, then assign a two to any scenario that will take twice that amount of time, and so on. If you choose this latter approach, don't worry about getting too granular. Many teams have been successful by simply assigning a value of one to any scenario that will require up to a half day, a value of two for a scenario expected to need between a half and a full day, and so on. As long as the same baseline is used for scoring all scenarios, the actual value of that baseline doesn't matter. What's important is that you capture the relative differences in effort required for the scenarios, not any absolute value.

Combining these weights, or "points," with target dates for the completion of each variation allows you to create a fairly accurate graph of expected test progress over time. Plot total cumulative points on the Y axis, and time on the X axis. As variations are completed, their points are added to the current test total. Partial points can also be claimed on a sliding scale for variations in "attempted" status. Every week (or whatever reporting interval you choose), you plot the new grand total on your graph. The result is a nice, clear chart showing testing progress over time. When scenarios are in a failed or blocked state, you can sum up the points for each of those scenarios and quickly convey the total amount of testing effort that is being delayed by the offending defects or late code deliveries. An example of this is shown in Figure 18.1.

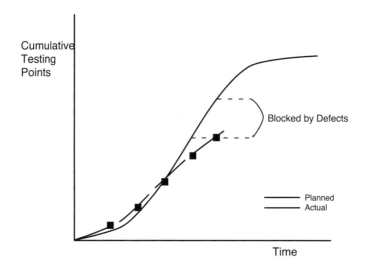

FIGURE 18.1 Actual versus projected test progress.

With these relatively simple techniques you can do a reasonable job of conveying the testing effort that's been expended, the effort remaining, and the impact of defects on testing progress. Undoubtedly, this combination does not deliver a measurement nirvana. But it does the job and requires fairly minimal effort, so more time can be spent on testing than tracking. For many testers, that's close enough.

Measurements as a Weapon

Testers are sometimes annoyed by the need to track their progress and link bugs to variations, even when the effort required to do so is minimal. They shouldn't be. In fact, testers should *love* tracking this information, because it's a weapon they can use to ensure that bugs are fixed.

When testing is behind schedule, the test team leader becomes a natural target at project status review meetings. All eyes are on him as he defends his team. He can panic. Or, he can display a simple graph that clearly shows actual versus projected test progress, with the difference representing a realistic, effort-based gap. On the same chart he can include an indicator showing what percentage of that gap is due to unresolved defects. Next, he can show a chart listing all outstanding defects, ordered by the amount of testing progress each is blocking. At this point, all attention will shift from the test team leader to the development leads. The burden suddenly falls on them to explain why development is behind in fixing defects, and what *they* are going to do to catch up. The result is that the most critical bugs get the prompt attention they deserve, and maybe testing has a good chance to finish on time.

The Most Important Measurement

Despite all of this discussion about metrics, don't lose sight of the most important measurement of them all: impact to customers. Always ensure the defects with the highest potential for derailing customers are fixed first, regardless of what the test progress chart happens to show. Fortunately, once such defects are clearly described, getting them fixed is usually an easy sell. Just don't let fancy measurements get in the way of protecting customers from harm.

REMOVING DEFECTS VERSUS MEETING SCHEDULES

It's the rare test project that finishes with time to spare. Instead, the final stages of most tests seem more like a mad dash for the finish line. As the end date nears and defect reports continue to mount, nervous project managers start to look for ways to, well, manage. Hopefully yours won't go so far as to order you to stop finding bugs so the code can ship.

It's not necessary to spend long in test before you come face to face with a simple reality: code ships before it's perfect. That fact is clear from the number of fix packs that supersede almost all complex commercial software. Testers don't like this reality too much. They'd rather see the code they're testing be defect-free before it goes out the door, but that isn't realistic. As we've noted elsewhere, all complex software has bugs. Combine that with another popular testing axiom, namely that you can't test quality into a product, and the conclusion is inescapable: testers will never be happy with what ships. They'll always wish another bug could have been removed. The trick is to get beyond the desire for perfection to be able to see the difference between software that is ready to go, and software that is truly in trouble. Good exit criteria can help here. But even when it's clear the software isn't ready, the challenge is figuring out what to do and convincing decision makers to do it.

Downstream Effects if Testing Ends Prematurely

If pressure to exit a test is intense even though the job isn't finished, one of the most persuasive arguments for restraint involves the potential for disastrous downstream effects.

Risks

First, identify the risks. Are there known defects that have not been fixed? The answer to this is frequently "yes." How severe are they, both singly and cumulatively? For example, a single bug that causes the corruption of critical data is devastating. Other bugs may not be overly troubling when looked at individually, but when viewed as a group clustered in a particular function they may be crippling.

Are there major functional areas that have not been fully tested, perhaps because scenarios are blocked by open defects? Are those areas optional, or are they central to the software's operation? Try to project worst-case and probable-case failure scenarios for those areas, based on defect trends the testing has revealed so far.

Impacts

Once the risks are identified, assess their potential impact on the software's next consumer. If another test phase is due to receive the code, how likely are they to be affected by the risk? Is it even worth their while to start in light of known deficiencies, or will those problems cause so much redundant error discovery and debug that starting now will actually lengthen the project's overall timeline? Are areas that have yet to be tested critical to the next test phase's planned activities? Can their entry criteria be met?

If the software is due to ship to customers, how will they react to the identified risks? Will they be warned about them? If so, will they refuse to install it? If not, what happens when they put the code into production and those risks manifest themselves? Will their business be seriously impacted? Will their confidence in the product be permanently shaken? Will their satisfaction level drop off a cliff? Will they denounce your product at user group conferences or in Web chat rooms?

By coolly articulating both the potential risks and likely impacts of prematurely ending a test, you can remove the hysteria surrounding an approaching end date, both from testers who want a perfect product and project managers under pressure to release it. The team can then focus on devising realistic solutions.

The End Date Arrives and Testing Isn't Finished: Now What?

Despite Herculean efforts by the test and development teams, you've reached the end of the line. The end date has come, and the test team has not achieved its exit criteria. Major bugs remain unresolved, significant chunks of testing are not complete, or both. You recognize the code may never be perfect, but as a tester and the software's first real user, you can't sign off on releasing it as is. It's decision time.

First, a reality check: as a tester, the choice of whether or not to ship a product isn't yours to make. It's a business decision to be made by senior managers who will take into account many factors, only one of which is test status. However, it's likely the test team will have an opinion on what that decision should be. What solutions might you recommend? How can you convey your opinion in a way that's convincing? There are several possibilities.

Delay Shipment

This one is every tester's favorite, and sometimes it's the best answer. If problems in the software are serious and pervasive or testing is far behind in major functional areas, there may be little choice but to extend the end date. That choice is rarely made lightly, however. If the test team feels strongly that a delay is required, they must present their rationale to the decision makers in a precise and powerful way.

In such situations, data talks. Your problem tracking and test measurement charts should provide a solid base, but may not be enough. Look for ways to strip out extraneous information and present your core message in a compelling way. For example, if you want to convey that many areas of test are blocked, that story may not come through clearly in a standard "S" curve showing overall test progress. Consider creating a bar chart, with each bar representing a major functional area of the software and showing its planned versus actual accumulation of testing points. If many bars register a low score, the true state of the situation becomes obvious.

Withdraw or Fence a Function

If the trouble is focused in one or two distinct areas of the software, another solution might be to keep the end date intact but pull those specific functions from the package. Sometimes this is easy to accomplish, sometimes it isn't. If the function is intertwined with the rest of the offering, pulling it may not be realistic. In that case, it is sometimes possible to *fence off* the function, leaving it in place but disabling it. In fact, if testers are involved during the code design phase, they can sometimes sway the development team to create code that is easily disabled in case it becomes necessary.

Either way, well-presented data can help you make your case. The bar chart for test progress by function can work here as well, but this time it will show only one or two areas as dramatically behind the others. Pair that with a similar bar chart showing open defects by function, backed up with a detailed list of defects, and others should quickly see your point.

Restrictions List

If the broken areas can be bypassed by the user, then it may be enough to simply provide a warning. Create a *restrictions list* describing functions to avoid until further notice. This may be particularly useful if the next consumer of the software is another test team. If that team is able to stage its testing in such a way as to avoid the problem areas initially, that will give your team and development a chance to clean them up. This approach may also work with beta customers, particularly if there are only a handful of them and they are well-known and can be robustly supported. Even in that case, be aware that users have a tendency to ignore restrictions lists, and then complain loudly when functions don't work.

A restrictions list is usually an easy sell, sometimes too easy. It's often tempting to try to document your way out of a tough spot that really requires more direct action. If the restrictions list is longer than the working functions list, or the broken areas are too embedded in mainline function for a user to avoid them, it's probably best to consider an alternative.

Gamble with Overlap

Most commercial products have a window between the date that testing is supposed to finish and the date the software is shipped to customers. This time is often used to press the software onto CD-ROMs, finish documentation, etc. Another approach is to exploit this window to finish any remaining testing, resolve outstanding defects, and create a plan to ship a package of fixes at the same time as the product. Obviously, this is a risky proposition. There's no guarantee that all critical issues will be fixed in time. As with Russian roulette, teams that decide to go this route may win the gamble and live to fight another day. Or they might not. It's probably best to consider other options before accepting this one.

SUMMARY

Day-to-day, down-in-the-trenches software testing is a fun but often chaotic adventure. By taking some basic steps to take control of the chaos you have a good chance of keeping the testing on track. Run logs allow you to document the test as you go, creating a diary of activities that is useful for later reference during debugging and problem re-creates, for information sharing among team members, and for providing proof of test execution to auditors. An end-of-day checklist can keep you from forgetting tasks that you might later wish you had performed. Reporting defect impacts as well as severities can help get the right focus on the hottest bugs. Remaining diligent about tracking test progress using simple, yet sufficient methods, offers an important and powerful tool for fixing bugs. Finally, when despite your best efforts the test doesn't finish on time, you can leverage data to slice through any hysteria and offer workable solutions.

No matter how much testing you do, it will probably never be enough. Chapter 19, "The Customer's Role in Testing," looks at why customers may need to do some testing of their own.

Part
VI

The Final Stages

The day your software ships to its first customer can be very satisfying, but also a little worrisome. You've done your best, toiling away for hours on end to detect and destroy all the bugs that matter. But was it enough? Will the users' experiences be smooth and satisfying, or troubled and disappointing? Is there anything you could have done better?

The concluding two chapters look at the final aspects of testing. We'll start with what customers tend to do with new software, and what you should expect to gain from their experience. We'll examine the kinds of defects that early customer testing (often called beta testing) is expected to extract, and why it complements your own efforts. But defect removal isn't the whole story—you'll see other benefits that beta testing can offer as well. You'll also learn why customers do their own testing of most new software before putting it into production, and why there's a whole class of defects that are beyond the scope of what you can find.

The experiences of your early customers may suggest areas where your testing can be strengthened. But there are other ways to probe for opportunities to enhance your work. We'll review a variety of avenues a test team can pursue on the road to continuous improvement—because as rewarding as it can be to wring the bugs out of a complex package of software, there's always another test on the horizon.

19 The Customer's Role in Testing

In This Chapter

■ The value of a beta test
■ Why customers should test generally available software

New software in a new environment is a new experiment. Even with the best laid plans and flawless execution of tests in your environment, new software will benefit from an early, controlled introduction into a variety of real user environments. Once a customer has their hands on the software, regardless of whether it's an early release or generally available, it's unlikely they will trust it enough to throw it blindly into production. Nor should they. A customer will first want to spend some time assessing its behavior in their unique environment. Software customers have an explicit role in its testing.

CONTROLLED EARLY INTRODUCTION PROGRAMS

It is very common in the computer software industry to send software to a subset of customers prior to releasing it on the open market. This activity is often referred to as a beta test. It's typically assumed that these beta tests are put in place to augment internal testing to see what bugs are reported by early users. That's certainly a key value, but there are additional benefits that a strictly controlled early introduction program can provide to the software development organization. It also offers an opportunity for testers to work closely with the customers.

Objectives of a Controlled Beta

At a high level, the basic objective of a controlled beta test is to determine that the software is ready for prime time. In other words, is it ready to handle the strenuous demands of complex production environments? At a more detailed level, there are a number of proof points that should be demonstrated by the software. Let's examine a few.

Order Process and Ease of Installation

Just as the software itself and the production environments in which it will operate are complex, the ordering process of sophisticated, general purpose software is not trivial. There may be many choices to make from a smorgasbord of available options. A large software stack can have entitled pieces and separately priced features. There may be conditional dependencies on other software already installed or requirements on some hardware. While the ordering process for some betas involves little more than clicking the "download" button on a Web page, others go much further. There is a benefit to running a trial of the actual ordering process. You can obtain excellent feedback from the beta test participants on the ease of navigating the menu of ordering choices. You can also obtain timely feedback on the fulfillment of the orders. Was the order processed accurately? Was the experience positive? The order process is the first experience customers will have with the new software and you'll want it to be a positive one.

The next step is to install the software. This is also a prime area for feedback on such questions as:

- Was the install smooth?
- Did the documentation clearly guide the installer, or did the installation wizard achieve its goal?
- Were all the prerequisites properly identified?

- Were prerequisite products available and installable themselves?
- Was the makeup of the software package correct?

Information on the installation itself is not all you can glean from this activity. You'll also want to learn about the experiences of the initial setup and customization that occurs as a final step of the install process. Also, some of the software documentation will get a good workout during both the install and set up activities. Customer feedback may indicate updates to the documentation are warranted. You may also be able to determine if any additional test scenarios should be executed prior to the general software release.

Exposure to Multiple Environments

By having multiple customers involved in the beta test, you can increase the number of environments into which the software will be exposed. You'll get much broader coverage with respect to its integration with many software and hardware components than you can ever hope to achieve with internal testing. The software will need to slip smoothly into these robust, heterogeneous environments. It may have to interface with various hardware components manufactured by different suppliers and coexist with all kinds of commercial software. It can also get initial exposure to home grown applications and real, live end users.

Software testers can play a role in the selection of the beta customers. You'll have a good understanding of the strengths and weaknesses of your test environments. By reviewing the environments of potential beta customers, you can provide input on which of them would best augment your work. This helps hone the candidate list based on educated decisions and increases the potential for an effective beta test.

Validation of the Solution

The new software will be packed with new functions. Those functions were developed to meet certain requirements. Included in the list of beta customers should be some that have an explicit interest in those new functions. Although it may be easy to find customers who are willing to participate in the beta test, it's best to find some who have a recognized business need for the new function. These customers will be driven by their own requirements to implement the solution aggressively. They won't be bashful about describing how well the software addressed their needs. You'll get a good sense of how ready your software is for customers and how well the new functions will succeed.

Regression

It's almost a certainty that the new software will be introduced into an IT environment that is already supporting the customer's business needs. One objective for a beta test is to ensure that the introduction of new software doesn't adversely affect existing applications and systems. You'll want to identify any unforeseen, disruptive intersections with other software components or applications. This may lead to adjustments to the software to remove or reduce the need for customers to make changes in their own applications in order to deploy it.

Can the Software be Serviced?

It's typical for commercial software to be serviced by different people, even a different organization, than those who developed it. The beta test is a good time to ensure that service capability is ready for action. Are the service personnel up to speed on the new functions? Is the support infrastructure in place to handle incoming calls? The service team can gain early experience with diagnosing problems with the new functions during the beta window. This way they'll be much better prepared to interact with customers during the general release of the software. Consider it a dry run for servicing the product.

Were Any Defects Missed?

Difficult though it may be to believe, there might be a few bugs that you missed during your testing. One obvious objective of a beta test is to find those bugs. This is a good reason why you should be intimately involved in the execution of a beta test. You can get direct knowledge of the types of problems that escaped. You can identify trends from the defect data and determine what additional tests you may wish to execute prior to general release. It also gives you a good reason to work directly with customers and expand your customer insight and knowledge. That insight can help you improve your testing the next time around.

In addition to customer insight, some of the problems found during a beta test will also suggest future enhancements and improvements for testing. Others may fall into the category of defects that internal testing shouldn't be expected to find. Let's look at a real life example of a problem that escaped internal testing but was found during a beta test.

Case Study: The Escape of a Defect

IBM itself is a big user of the software it develops, including z/OS. Many IBM sites rely on it for aspects of their daily operations. The z/OS team likes to take advantage of this fact by supplying early versions of new releases to a select set of these internal sites at some point during the SVT cycle for them to try out. Just as with any beta test, this activity broadens the test coverage through early production usage.

Prior to providing software to external customers, consider running an internal beta under controlled conditions on your company's own systems.

During the development cycle for a predecessor of z/OS, a handful of these internal beta test accounts had been selected and were anxiously awaiting the new code. Schedules were put in place, as were specific milestones for the SVT team to meet before shipping the new release to these internal customers. The SVT team put the new software through a battery of tests to ensure it was stable enough for their colleagues to trust in production. Finally, the milestones were achieved. The SVT team celebrated, and with a flourish the code was sent off to IBM sites around the country.

Trouble in Paradise

The celebration didn't last long. When one of the sites attempted to boot the new release, the system froze, dropping into what's called a disabled wait state. This was unacceptable. The SVT team was shocked. The software was stable. It had been booted over and over again during SVT without any problems. It had survived a series of load/stress and other tests. None of the other beta sites were experiencing this problem. What had happened? The site experiencing the failure captured a full system memory dump on tape and rushed it to the development laboratory. Eagerly, the SVT team began to examine it. Quickly, the problem became apparent.

The Culprit

Installed at the IBM location in question was something called an IBM 3850 Mass Storage System (MSS). Akin to a modern tape robot, the MSS was a monster. Consisting of 8 cabinets, it was 3 feet wide and 20 feet long with a series of honeycombed chambers inside that held some 2000 data cartridges. A mechanical hand fetched cartridges and brought them to a central read/write unit as needed for processing, then returned them when finished.

The bug was simple. During boot processing, a change in the operating system unrelated to the MSS was conflicting with the support for that device. This conflict forced the operating system into a position where it could not safely continue, and so it triggered the disabled wait state.

Some software bugs, even ones with devastating consequences, will only surface under specific environmental conditions.

Any system with an MSS installed would have seen this failure during boot processing. However, at the time of this incident the MSS was nearing its end of life. While technically still supported by the operating system, it was no longer widely used. None of the other beta test sites had one. Neither, unfortunately, did the SVT team. That's how the defect escaped.

There was nothing wrong with *how* the SVT team had done its testing. The flaw was with what had been *missing* when that testing was done. This example illustrates how even the most thorough set of test scenarios can be foiled by environmental gaps. It also shows the testing value to be achieved by exposing a new software offering to a variety of different environments to attain a level of diversity that no single test team could hope to match.

If you can choose your beta test environments, pick ones that offer the greatest exposure to diverse hardware and other software to increase the odds of finding subtle defects.

Learning from the Escape

Chapter 20, "The Testing End Game," will go into more detail about how a test team can focus on continuous improvement via many means, including performing analysis of escaped defects. The MSS example represents an interesting challenge for the test team. A quick, easy solution to address this escape would be to purchase and install an MSS device into the SVT environment. But that may not necessarily be the best option. As mentioned, the MSS device was old technology and no longer pervasively used. Would it really be the best use of money to purchase the device? Additional options could be considered first. The team should investigate what other ways the failing code path could be driven. Could a specific, focused, automated test case be written to drive this path? Could the device and its interactions with the software be simulated is some way? Can the problem be generalized somehow so that a test to cover it will be more broadly applicable? Do any other ideas surface? The team can then make an educated decision from a list of options. The important point is to *do something* about the escape and to turn the negative of a defect into a positive set of actions.

PREPRODUCTION TESTING

Most businesses depend on information technology. Some have a very critical dependence on IT, even to the point where they are literally out of business without it. Because of this dependence, they continually need to squeeze more and more out of their computer investments and implement solutions that give them advantages. However, any change made to the IT environment brings with it a certain amount of risk. The risks need to be mitigated. One mitigation action customers can take is to test.

Why Customers Should Test

Customers detest problems in their production environments. They go to great lengths to avoid them. Yet their environments are growing in complexity as each day passes. In addition to this, many industries are getting more and more competitive, requiring extreme levels of flexibility and very fast reaction to all kinds of events. There have been merges and acquisitions, multicompany partnerships, and globalization activities. The Internet's role as a sales channel that reaches directly into the homes of consumers has taken IT performance and behavior out from the back office and exposed it to the masses. The result is not only a need for full application availability 24 hours a day, 7 days a week, but also for ever more aggressive deployments of new technology.

This evolution of IT environments has caused an explosion in complexity. In Chapter 6, "Coping with Complexity through Teaming," the complexity of a large software stack was illustrated with the simplified picture shown in Figure 19.1. In fact, that figure illustrates only a sliver of typical large enterprise environments. When that software stack is introduced into production environments, it must interface with a myriad of additional technologies, as summarized in Figure 19.2. Much of that additional technology is unique to each enterprise. It's not easy or even possible to replicate exactly such complexity in any software test lab.

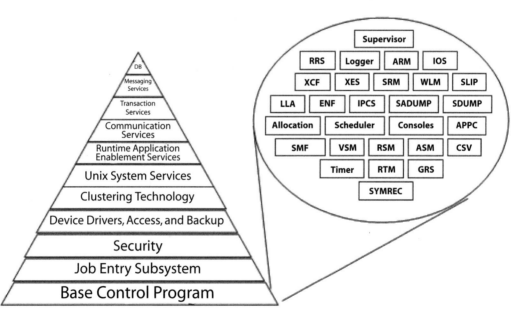

FIGURE 19.1 z/OS components.

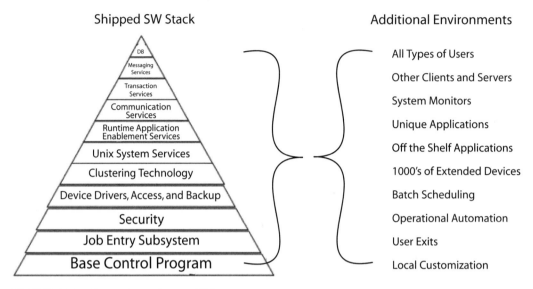

FIGURE 19.2 Enterprise-unique additions.

With so much riding on an enterprise's production environment, it's little surprise that before changes can be introduced they require some amount of validation. A publicly held company has an unwritten obligation to its shareholders to mitigate any risk to the business that such changes might impose. In other words, they need to test. But are these tests a duplication of effort with the internal testing of software suppliers? No, the focuses are different.

A Shift in Focus

The target of customer testing is the integration of all the disparate pieces that make up the production environment. The customer can examine the effects of the proposed changes on the total environment, with particular attention paid to their unique components.

User Exits and Local Customization

It is not unusual for software to provide various ways for users to alter the default behavior of a subset of its functions. One approach that has existed for many years is the notion of exit points. At very strategically placed spots in the software, the ability to pass control to an *exit* is provided that optionally allows the customer to alter how the software works. This exit is a program written by the user. The exit may have to follow some strict rules, but it offers users a degree of freedom for customizing the software's processing to meet their needs. However, whenever the software containing the exit points is upgraded, any exits tied to those exit points need to be tested to ensure they still work without any undesired side effects.

Of course, there's more to customization than just exit points. Most software offers many other ways for users to alter default behavior. Many knobs and switches may be provided. A large number of adjustments by any customer may create a combination that forces the execution of unique code paths. Experimenting with that combination of adjustments first in a test environment is another step customers can take to reduce the risk of change.

Operational Automation

Computer technology has improved and developed tremendously over the years. The speed and volume of processing that current technology allows makes it very difficult to manage and operate within human reaction times. To address this challenge, customers often automate many operational tasks. Several vendors offer software products that allow a user to specify system events to watch for, and actions to take in response to each event. The automation hovers in the background, monitoring system activity. When it detects a targeted event, such as a log file filling up, it responds with an appropriate action, eliminating the need for human intervention.

This technique is very effective, but it quickly fosters a dependence on correct operation of the automation, since automation miscues in the production environment can be very disruptive and difficult to work around. As a result, any proposed changes that may effect the automation processing, including adding or upgrading software, should be validated. For example, many automation packages are triggered by messages that the software presents. So software upgrades that might have changed message content or format demand special attention.

System Monitors

In addition to automation, programmatic monitoring of systems is typically a key part of production. The monitors become the eyes and ears of the system administrators grappling with massive amounts of processing. Many times, it is a monitor's alerts that give the system's human operators their first indication that there is an issue that requires action. As with automation, reliance on the correct operation of monitors is widespread. Where do the monitors get their information and data? Normally, it's from other components of the system. Some monitors even are dependent on the internal control structures of other software—structures which of course may change with a new release. Customers will want to demonstrate correct operation of monitors after changes are applied to the system, but before introducing those changes into production. In other words, they'll need to test.

Applications

Although lots of attention is paid to a production environment's infrastructure, it's applications that provide the most visible value to the business. However, most applications rely heavily on the services of the infrastructure. Also, production environments do not simply include one application, but many. And, it's typical for them to have dependencies on, interface with, or pass data among each other. The combination of all these applications is most likely unique to the enterprise that runs them. It cannot be assumed that a software supplier or vendor has experimented with this exact combination. Changes to any of these parts should be validated prior to putting them in a position that may hurt the enterprise.

End Users

Servicing the end users of production environments is almost always the main reason those environments exist. End users may range from the CEO of the company, to the warehouse worker filling orders, to the busy mom sitting in her kitchen browsing the Web. A business cannot afford to let its end users be thwarted by changes introduced to production. If the warehouse must delay filling orders because the inventory system is down, or the busy mom can't place an order and so hops to a different Web site, it's a direct hit to the bottom line. Validating the changes in a test environment from the view of an end user is an important step in testing. One way this can be accomplished is to have the application development and system support communities act as the end users. As a group they can simultaneously invoke the most important or often used areas of the applications. This can be done on a robust test environment if it exists, or during the change window in production prior to when the bulk of the real users start using the system. It's a relatively cheap way to do some functional validation, but may not drive the same amount of activity as will occur during peak times in production. Customers concerned about this can invest in the same load driving, user simulation test tools used by software development organizations.

Smooth Production Roll Out

The objective of the testing by customers is to ensure new software works according to their expectations, in their environment, with their complete software stack. It helps ensure a very smooth introduction of those changes into the production environment. Many times it can be a thankless job. If it is done well, no one may notice. In fact, the goal is to create a nonevent. It may take some time for the advantages provided by new software or other changes to be generally recognized by the user community. But it won't take long for problems to be noticed. System support can celebrate among themselves when no one else is even aware that a change occurred.

SUMMARY

Industrial-strength software has an unimaginable number of code paths. No matter how much testing or how many test phases new software is put through, it can always benefit from exposure to additional environments and users. At the point in the development cycle when the new software has stabilized, a controlled release to some customers can provide coverage not easily performed in the development labs. This beta test can also be the fastest way to get new solutions into the hands of the customers most interested in them. They'll provide very timely feedback, and testers can learn a lot from them. You should be intimately involved in many aspects of beta tests in order to investigate problems that escaped your testing and to become more familiar with your customers.

Even customers of generally available software will want to spend time testing it. Their focus is not specifically tied to the new software itself, but to the effects it has on all the other technology that may be unique to their environment. Their goal is to stay current with new technology and implement solutions that provide value, while at the same time not subjecting their enterprise to unnecessary risk. Both the software supplier and the customer IT support staff can celebrate successful deployments of changes into production. With luck, they may be the only ones that noticed that anything changed.

As a tester, you have traveled the long, tiring road. You've successfully used a variety of means to put the software through its paces, challenged it, and helped get it ready for its customers. You've even assisted the customers during their first experiences with the software. But you can't go home yet. They are some things left to do. Chapter 20 discusses what remains and shows you the path home.

20 The Testing End Game

In This Chapter

- Continuous improvement
- The big picture

Y ou've maneuvered your way through the test of an entire software product. You may have escaped with only cuts and bruises, but it's not time to go home just yet. A few tasks remain. As we've noted before, successful software is rarely produced once and then forgotten. There's always another version on the way. How can you prevent any mishaps encountered during this test from occurring on the next? Are there ways to improve the technical approach and processes used? Let's examine several techniques.

CONTINUOUS IMPROVEMENT

Continuous improvement means solving problems that bit you in the past so you can avoid them in the future. As we have previously discussed, activities such as component assessments help identify potential process improvements. It's important not to ignore or lose sight of any shortcomings. How do you address them head on?

Closing the Loop: Postmortems

Test teams should consider performing a periodic self-evaluation or postmortem to close the loop on the project. These are reviews targeted at identifying what worked well and what didn't. The results can lead to adjustments in testing techniques and processes. The review can be done once at the conclusion of a project, or iteratively throughout. Let's examine both approaches.

Comprehensive Postmortems

At the end of a complex project, the test team needs to look back at where they've been. Invite everyone on the team to a meeting. Start by discussing things that worked well and should be retained for future tests. Then brainstorm on areas for improvement. There are several questions to ask and topics to consider:

Test Strategy: Was there anything good or bad about the overall strategy used?

Tools: How well did the chosen tools work? Should you have selected a different set? If new niche tools were invented, did they work out well? Is everyone on the team aware of them as possible candidates for reuse in future tests? Have they been added to the team's tool list?

Test Plans: Could the checklists, consideration lists, and test plans have been improved?

Workloads: Were workloads representative of those used by customers, or stressful and complex enough to squeeze out defects?

Environment: Were enough resources available or did the configurations allow problems to escape?

Test Flow: Could communication with the testing phases before or after yours have been improved?

Education: Was the team technically prepared to perform the tasks of the test? Did everyone understand the items they were assigned?

Clarity: Were test scenarios documented well enough for others to execute them in the future?

Documentation: Was all of the necessary technical and operational information available for the test team to use?

Problem Data: Did you find the types of problems you expected? Were there trends in the data? Problematic components or functions?

The above set of questions and topics is definitely not complete, but it offers a starting roadmap. Keep in mind that the objective of the initial postmortem meeting is only to identify areas of strength and weakness, not to devise actions. Once you have a list of possibilities, then various participants can later investigate possible next steps and report back to the team.

Iterative Postmortems

Just as there are iterative development techniques, there can also be iterative postmortem reviews. Simply because the entire project is not yet completed doesn't mean that a review of what's happened so far shouldn't be considered. In fact, interim reviews will capture ideas while they're fresh in your mind. Consider carving out time during a busy test to step back and review.

Postplanning Reviews

After your test plan has been developed, test cases have been written, and execution has begun, you may wish to pull together the team for a review of the planning and preparation activities. This will help outline what to pay attention to the next time through the planning cycle. Additionally, it might also identify short-term actions that the team can take to enhance the test. When a group of testers get together they're bound to generate new ideas on how to tackle test planning and preparation.

A review of the current schedule and whether modifications are needed is often a good area to explore. The end date may be beyond the test team's control, but internal checkpoints owned by the team can often be adjusted. Perhaps now that test execution is underway, some assumptions made during planning are dubious and should be revisited. By stepping back to take a fresh look, you might see an adjustment to testing order or overlap that can help the overall efficiency of the test. A few such tweaks might actually improve the end date, or at least make it achievable.

Interim Execution Reviews

Performing a review of successes and failures while the test is underway is also an effective way to identify gaps "on-the-fly." What if the set of scenarios developed during test planning aren't finding the anticipated volume of important defects? Should you use a different technique for driving out the bugs or shift attention to another feature of the software? Likewise, if one new technique is uncovering lots of defects, should it be expanded to other areas? These interim execution reviews help with early identification of the weaknesses in the test, but also help point out methods that have been unusually fruitful.

Many test teams get hung up on continuing to execute the original plan of record. If it isn't exposing important defects, does sticking with it even make sense? Test teams should make their test plans dynamic so that they can rapidly change their approach. If the need to shift strategies becomes clear, the test team must be able to dynamically change the execution plan *and* have management's support in doing so. To enact a dynamic plan change, you may need to have a rapid review and approval process in place. Alternatively, you can anticipate the need for dynamic adjustments up front and make provisions for them by including time for artistic testing in your plan. The important thing is to find a way to keep your testing flexible. Move quickly and be nimble—change your plan to find those bugs.

Interim Defect Reviews

Even while you are still deep in the throes of a test, it can be useful to look for trends in the defects found thus far. An interim defect review of an entire software package or any of its components can point out soft spots. This certainly doesn't have to be a formal event. It can be as easy as scanning the list of bugs and identifying the affected areas. Based on that, the development and test teams may decide to take additional actions, such as adding code inspections, revisiting earlier tests, or expanding stress testing.

The characteristics of the defects can also relay a message to the team. Are the problems in mainline function, recovery processing, or installation? Each unique area can yield unique actions. For example if it's recovery processing that's unstable, then a review of the various resource serialization points within the code could produce a new set of error injection scenarios that were previously overlooked. A higher-than-normal volume of installation-related defects might imply a lack of attention to factors surrounding product introduction. This could push the development team to enhance their migration and installation documentation, and lead the test team to execute tasks identified by the documentation to ensure that it holds up.

Postmortems

Is all this reviewing worthwhile? Well, to tell you the truth, yes! If you don't recognize the problem, it's tough to fix it. Whether done at the end of a test or at logical checkpoints along the way, some simple reviews can really pay off. They may lead to testing modifications that will increase your efficiency and effectiveness at hunting down bugs—and what could be more worthwhile than that?

Escape Analysis

No matter how comprehensive a test plan is, there will inevitably be problems that escape from one test phase to the next. Unfortunately, some problems will slip out to customers as well. Escapes are likely in any environment, but steps can be taken to limit them. One important technique is for testers to perform an analysis of the ones that got away.

Postproject and in-process escape analysis activities are critical means for driving test improvements. It's important to review the problems with some specific goals in mind. How can you attack that analysis? First and foremost, look at the function that's in error. Also, examine the type of defect. For example, is the error in a simple API, a complex serialization method, or a user interface?

Which Test Phase Allowed the Escape?

Which test phase should have logically removed the defect? Was it a simple function verification test that was overlooked? Or was it a multithreaded test missing from the system verification plan? Was a performance problem missed? This is where each test team needs to swallow their pride and learn from experience. Looking at each defect objectively will help the test team improve the next time around.

Escape analysis is important across all testing phases. How many defects that could have been caught during unit test instead leaked through to FVT? How many did the beta test customers find that could have been extracted earlier? These analyses drive improvements. The test team will identify actions they can take so that these specific problems don't sneak through.

Looking for Trends

One missed defect in a particular functional area of the software might not be something to lose sleep over. But if there are trends in a component or a type of defect, that may be a different story. A trend can provide much more information than a lone defect. It can help pinpoint soft spots. Once identified, these soft spots are where the test team should emphasize their efforts for improvement.

Trends are very telling. Customers seem to identify trends at a much higher level than testers do. They might point out that an entire function or component is error prone. If a customer gets a bad taste in their mouth from problems, it will take a long time for them to get rid of it. Testers need to have that same perspective. If the test team can identify trends while the software is still in the development cycle, they can shield customers from ever seeing them. Identify trends as early as possible and focus on them quickly.

Sources of Escapes

The escape trends you just identified can now become important feedback for the test team. The team can map these into their test cases, tools, environments, processes, and methods to see what can be done differently the next time to prevent not only the defects that did escape, but others in the same class.

Yes, this may be a painful exercise. On the other hand, if the analysis identifies bugs that escaped because the team was missing some key hardware, that can create a powerful argument for additional test equipment the next time around. Take advantage of the findings.

Customer Involvement

An excellent way to understand the shortcomings of your test efforts is to share them directly with actual customers. Customers are often amenable to discussions of improvements in the vendor's testing.

If the problems encountered by customers are significant, they will expect action by the software vendor to address the apparent lack of test coverage. But experience shows that customers also tend to be helpful in identifying specific gaps and helping to create solutions. In fact, a close working relationship with a particular customer can help not only them, but also the industry of which they are a member, or even the entire customer community. Analysis of a customer's environment and their exploitation of the software will help both to identify what exposed the problem, and to formulate an action to take in response.

As we discussed Chapter 2, "Industrial-Strength Software—It's Not a Science Project," customer environments have a wide combination of system software, middleware applications, different hardware devices, and end-user clients. These integrated environments challenge the test team to keep up with state-of-the-art testing techniques to simulate them. Understanding customers is a critical first step.

Conference calls, executive briefings, and on-site meetings with customers can help pave the way for a relationship that can continue to improve the effectiveness of both your test team and the customer. Being able to meet directly with their leading information technology specialists allows you to hear directly from the folks who feel the satisfaction or pain. This environment encourages building more comprehensive test scenarios and programs at both the vendor and the customer.

Communication between Test Teams

Continuous improvement is a byproduct of continuous communication. When different teams stay close in touch, they can build an ongoing improvement plan as the product is created.

In particular, test teams whose activities overlap should consider frequent communication sessions, especially during an active product development cycle, to ensure that they are passing observations, concerns, and solutions to one another. These sessions could be as casual as a mutual coffee break, or as formal as a weekly status meeting. Regardless of the venue, such talks help break down the wall between test teams so they can feel comfortable leaning on one another. Some give-and-take between camps goes a long way toward promoting teamwork, and teamwork drives improvements in the product's test.

Examining Best Practices

Another mechanism that helps a test team to improve is the implementation of testing best practices. These practices could be anything from tools to processes to automation. Gather a list of possibilities, and then see how your team's approaches compare. Mature software organizations usually have test teams that maintain a list of best practices. They may exist at the corporate level and at the local level as well. Less mature platforms and technologies may not yet have accumulated a significant number, or any, best practices. How can they determine some?

Research studies are a good place to start. Ram Chillarege identifies a set that includes functional specifications, formal entry and exit criteria, automated test execution, and "nightly" builds [IBM99]. Individual computing providers or test consultants may have practices that they promote. We've recommended many others in this book. There are also a number of other sources for best testing practices. Teams can attend testing conferences, such as STAR (Software Testing Analysis & Review), and learn from a wide range of industry professionals.

What about talking? Just stepping out of your office and talking to sister groups can provide you with a set of ideas that you can benefit from almost immediately. The creation of test communities to identify and share best practices is definitely a recommended action.

Another approach is to "benchmark" your test techniques and methodologies against other companies. This may require involvement from your management team for orchestration with the other company. Sitting down with folks from four or five other companies, at one time, and comparing notes in a cross-section of areas can highlight where your team stands.

A self-examination of how your team measures up to the state-of-the-art, or to *anything* different, might prove to be beneficial. In fact, you may find that some of your own methodologies should be considered "best" practices. You never know. What about starting your own set and sharing it with others?

Getting Out of the Groove

Change, though sometimes painful, is necessary for improvement. Many teams and the tests for which they are responsible become *grooved*. Grooved tests are those that simply repeat the same activity against a target product from cycle to cycle. By its nature, regression testing tends to fall into this category. Pure regression testing is an important activity. But by supplementing it with new techniques for exercising the "same-ol'-code," you might expose fresh paths where business-critical defects are lurking.

Teams that get into a groove can have difficulty getting out of it. Force the issue. Combine a critical look at the way you are operating today with a discussion of possible changes. You may be surprised at the number of great ideas that appear once someone expects them.

So What's the Big Deal?

Continuous improvement means continuous investment. If you look at a test organization's overall priorities, you might not see improvements at the top of the list. Meeting tight schedules and resolving critical situations with customers often get in the way of maintaining a focus on constant improvement.

Investment in making the team more effective must be a stated goal of the folks holding the checkbook. The team needs the time and resources to make the improvements they identify a reality. Test teams can build subteams that implement specific enhancements. These subteams, if given the chance, can drive significant change into the test team's tools, techniques, and approaches for removing defects. But without such special effort, the enhancements will die on the vine. Management and test teams must be invested in the mutual goal of producing high-quality software to satisfy the end-users' needs and expectations.

THE FINAL LESSON—BUGS: YOU'LL NEVER FIND THEM ALL

We have covered much information. What message should you walk away with?

Defects That Matter

The number of defects in software is seemingly infinite. As long as you continue to test, you *will* continue to find problems. This is especially true for sophisticated products that operate in complex environments, where customers combine packages from multiple software and hardware vendors to create a solution to a business problem.

You will never find all possible bugs. But you must ensure that included in the subset you do find are the defects that matter to your customers. Impact, impact, impact!! Customers grudgingly tolerate minor problems—they know software defects are an unfortunate reality. But they are unwilling to accept bugs that can cripple their business.

The Big Picture

There are so many methods, techniques, and actions that you can explore to help you target these important defects. We have outlined a variety of ways for your test team to focus on the prize. So, one more time . . .

Find the Best Process

Remember to find the development model that fits your organization's objectives. There are many to choose from and you may be able to borrow the strengths from one to enhance another.

Target specific phases of testing. Identify the areas of focus within each one and the types of defects that each is most effective at removing. Don't overload any individual test team. Spread the wealth. Don't skip test phases. This can be disastrous because the crippling defects that the "skipped" phase was supposed to remove will lie in wait to bite the customers.

Teamwork and Objectivity

Development and test teams must work together, but testers should stay at an arm's length to maintain objectivity. Developers and testers need to recognize and align with their respective strengths: makers versus breakers. Building an organization that allows for teamwork, yet also provides the necessary wall between development and test, is important in reinforcing each person's role in the software development process.

Testers must work to build and maintain their technical credibility. This helps them to get their voices heard and their defects addressed—as well as being a potent force for career growth.

Finding Information to Build Your Test Roadmap

Knowing what you test will help you build a test approach and execution plan that leaves customers smiling. Be relentless in the search for information that will make up your test roadmap. Don't act like a traveler who refuses to ask for directions. Make use of all the resources you can find. Talk to development experts and your test team members. Everyone will have something to contribute.

Understanding the problem that your software is designed to solve is about as important as delving into vast volumes of information on the software itself. First create the problem, and then apply the solution. Does it fix the original issue? Who are the customers who might be interested in this solution? How do they operate? The answers will shape your plan to probe for the defects that matter.

Conquering Complexity

Industrial-strength software is complex. A test team must disassemble that complexity through a number of techniques. Once the complexity is conquered, the team can identify the most strategic test approach.

Complexity can be conquered through technical assessments of the software's components—which has the byproduct of building the testers' expertise. It can also be handled by pulling together knowledgeable testers with various types of expertise to construct a comprehensive test approach that will address all areas of the product.

Test Plans and Their Focus

A test plan is the blueprint for validating software. Its areas of focus provide the framework for finding the problems that customers dread. Interfaces, limits, mainline function, regression, migration, load/stress, recoverability, usability, reliability—all are important elements of a complete plan of attack. A test plan review is something every tester should embrace. A good one will steer you away from unnecessary work and toward new opportunities for fruitful bug hunting.

Will Anything Go Wrong?

Of course, it will! With trouble a near certainty, you need to plan for it. Build your testing schedule so that when something does go awry, there's time to react. This contingency gives the team a chance to survive and live to test another day.

Precise entry and exit criteria are a great aid in managing the handoffs between teams. If a certain test phase is still uncovering high-impact problems, is the software really ready to move forward? The criteria can help guide you. Maybe the code itself can be designed and developed with an eye toward aiding beleaguered testers. A little forethought might transform untestable software into a target-rich environment.

Hammer the Door Shut on Those Defects

To extract the right defects you need the right tools. Those tools can be purchased on the open market or developed in the back room. Regardless, tools don't make the tester, but no tester is complete without them.

Before you search, know your requirements. Common ones can probably be best filled by a tool vendor. Ones unique to your specific situation may require an investment in your own custom development. Whichever approach you take, make sure you're taking full advantage of the tools you already have before looking for more.

Same Test Case, Different Phase

Look to recycle tests, scenarios, and test cases across testing phases. The same test case can be reused in a different context to find new bugs. FVT might use a test case to validate basic function, while SVT might combine it with many others to drive the system to extreme levels of stress.

Enforce a set of standards that will make test cases portable and streamable. Also consider taking test programs and "stealing" their framework or foundation to create your own twist on it. Artistically modify them to force out fresh defects.

What about Brand New Software?

Reuse is wonderful, but it often isn't enough. You'll need to develop new test cases to attack new features and functions in the target software. Make sure that whichever test phase they are targeted for, the test cases are built efficiently and with all of the necessary infrastructure and diagnostic capability they need. Don't forget that in the future someone is likely to reuse them. Ensure they meet all of those reusable characteristics as well.

We Don't Need Bad Data!

Mission-critical software revolves around its data. Flaws that lead to the corruption of that data are some of software's most insidious defects. Data integrity monitors are one means for unearthing these gremlins before they can escape. Look at any software that adds to or alters its approach for manipulating data with a very suspicious eye.

Know Your Customers to Emulate Them

Customers want testers to find bugs first. Will all of your scenarios, test cases, and tools zero-in on the right defects? There are many techniques for understanding how the customers will use software. Take advantage of them. Leverage that knowledge to build workloads and tests that will mimic your customers. Put the customer first and listen to their feedback. Find ways to work directly with them to improve your testing.

It's Test Time

When it comes time to test, be relentless. Use a variety of methods—each targeting a unique class of defects. Maybe today's iterative approach is tomorrow's artistic, traditional or load/stress method. Each approach has its own strengths that can help you squash bugs where they sleep.

Learn how the software works so you can either diagnose the defects yourself or provide all of the information your debugging specialists will require to track them down. Keep your eyes on the software's behavior to detect less-than-obvious problems too. And ensure that the documentation is accurate, because bad documentation can cause users as much trouble as bad code.

You Don't Have the Hardware

Many software projects begin without enough machines to run on. That puts you in a bind. But there are options. Virtualization, prototypes, and simulators may allow you to get going. They also offer tremendous advantages for such things as injecting errors, debugging, saving test environments, rapid system provisioning, and automation.

These cool tools can be as simple as a small program that changes a bit mask in the system to masquerade as something else, or as complex as one entire operating system emulating another. See if you can leverage the power of virtualized environments to your advantage.

This Is Chaos

Uncontrolled testing can quickly spin out of control. But it doesn't have to be that way. The test team can utilize a large range of techniques to get things back in line. Run logs and checklists can help generate a script of testing activities, so that you don't miss those subtle or not so subtle problems that customers will somehow spot immediately.

What if the test end date nears but you aren't done? How close are you? Have you uncovered all the crippling defects, so all that remains are minor problems? Simple yet accurate status tracking can help testers get the critical bugs they identify promptly fixed. But what if you haven't even attempted all of your tests yet?

Options include delaying the product, including some code that disables the new function, or shipping it with restrictions. The project management team needs to understand all of the risks and available options. This means that the test team better have a handle on it. Keep an eye on how you are tracking against your plan and how the product is holding up.

What Will the Customers Do?

Once customers have the code in their hands, they most likely will not drop it directly into a production environment. They will want to test it as well.

Every customer environment is unique. They all have their own application combinations that can reveal previously hidden bugs. They also must ensure their local exits and automation are compatible with the new software. This leads them to check out the new software before placing their trust in it. Many customers build environments comparable to their production shop for testing. Others rush tests through on weekends. In any case, the added coverage they may provide during a beta test can help to produce an excellent software product.

Don't Forget to Review

Your test is finished and you think you did a good job. But, could you have done anything better? Absolutely! Look over what you've done, what problems have escaped to your fellow testers and customers, and what others think of your product. Continuous improvement requires communication and effort, but it pays big dividends.

SUMMARY

The defects that matter, really do. Your customers will be the first to tell you that. Focus your test on finding the problems that impact enterprises and *their* customers. Drive your test team toward processes, practices, and technical expertise that will make you all successful and envied. Don't be timid—take control of your testing objectives.

Now go find some bugs!

References

[ANSI/IEEE792] ANSI/IEEE Standard Glossary of Software Engineering Terminology, ANSI/IEEE Std 792.1983.

[Bach99] Bach, James, "Heuristic Risk-Based Testing," *Software Testing and Quality Engineering* magazine, November 1999. Available online at *http://www.satisfice.com/articles/hrbt.pdf.*

[Bach03] Bach, James "Exploratory Testing Explained," available online at *http://www.satisfice.com/articles/et-article.pdf,* April 2003.

[Bassett97] Bassett, Paul, *Framing Software Reuse: Lessons From the Real World.* Prentice Hall PTR, 1996.

[Baumeister02] Baumeister, Hubert, et al., "Applying Test-First Programming and Iterative Development in Building an E-Business Application," *International Conference on Advances in Infrastructure for e-Business, e-Education, e-Science, and e-Medicine on the Internet, SSGRR 2002,* L'Aquila, Italy, January 2002.

[Boehm88] Boehm, Barry, "A Spiral Model of Software Development and Enhancement," *IEEE Computer 21, 5, 61-72. 1988.* © 1992 IEEE, figure reprinted with permission.

[Bothwell01] Bothwell, F., "Comparative Large System Capabilities and Attributes," Enabling Technologies Group, Inc., available online at *http://www.etginc.com/services/publications/index.shtml,* February, 2001.

[Creasy81] Creasy, R.J., "The Origin of the VM/370 Time-Sharing System," *IBM Journal of Research and Development* 25, No. 5, 1981.

[Dike01] Dike, Jeff, "User Mode Linux: Running Linux on Linux," *Linux Magazine,* April 2001.

[FUND] "FLEX-ES Technical Overview," Fundamental Software, Inc., available online at *http://www.funsoft.com/technical-body.html.*

[GCC] The GNU Compiler Collection home page can be found at *http://gcc.gnu.org/.*

[Gupta94] Gupta, Sinha, "Improving Software Testability by Observability and Controllability Measures," in Proc. 13th World Computer Congress, IFIP Congress '94, Hamburg, Germany, August–September 1994.

[Hulme03] Hulme, George, "Global Watch: Attacks Come From Just About Anywhere," *InformationWeek,* September 1, 2003.

[IBM99] "Software Testing Best Practices," International Business Machines Corporation, IBM Research Report RC 21457, Log 96856, 1999.

[IBM03] Developer Guidelines: Software Accessibility, International Business Machines Corporation, available online at *http://www-3.ibm.com/able/guidelines/software/accesssoftware.html,* 2003.

[IBMZOS03] "IBM z/OS Integration Test: Error-Injection Tool," International Business Machines Corporation, available online at *http://www-1.ibm.com/servers/eserver/zseries/zos/integtst/injerror.html,* 2003.

[IEEE610.12] IEEE Standard Glossary of Software Engineering Terminology, IEEE Std 610.12.1990.

[IEEE829] IEEE Standard for Software Test Documentation, IEEE Std 829.1998.

[Kan02] Kan, Stephen, Metrics and Models in Software Quality Engineering, 2nd edition, Addison-Wesley, 2002.

[Kaner99] Kaner, Falk, et al., *Testing Computer Software,* second edition, John Wiley and Sons, 1999.

[Kaner03] Kaner, Cem, "What IS a Good Test Case?" Proceedings from STAR East conference, May 2003.

[Kenney92] Kenney, Vouk, "Measuring the Field Quality of Wide-Distribution Commercial Software," Proceedings, Third Annual International Symposium on Software Reliability Engineering, IEEE, 1992.

[Kidder81] Kidder, Tracy, *The Soul of a New Machine,* Little, Brown & Company, 1981.

[Loveland02] Loveland, Miller, et al., "Testing z/OS: The premier operating system for IBM's zSeries server," *IBM Systems Journal* 41, No. 1, 2002. © 2002 by International Business Machines Corporation. Reprinted with permission.

[Mandelbrot83] Mandelbrot, Benoit, *The Fractal Geometry of Nature,* W. H. Freeman and Company, 1983.

[May96] May, Zimmer, "The Evolutionary Development Model for Software," Hewlett Packard Journal Online, *http://www.hpl.hp.com/hpjournal/96aug/aug96a4.htm,* Article 4, August 1996.

[Nick97] Nick, Moore, et al., "S/390 cluster technology: Parallel Sysplex," *IBM Systems Journal* 36, No. 2, 1997.

[Reis00] Reis, Christian, "A Commentary on the Extreme Programming Development Process," Async Free Software, Inc., Sao Carlos, Brazil, June 18, 2000.

[Rothman02] Rothman, Johanna, "What Does It Cost You To Fix A Defect?, available online at *http://www.stickminds.com,* February 13, 2002.

[Scalzi89] Scalzi, Ganek, et al., "Enterprise Systems Architecture/370: An architecture for multiple virtual space access and authorization," *IBM Systems Journal* 28, No. 1, 1989.

[Schoch00] Schoch, Russell, "Q&A—A Conversation with Chalmers Johnson," *California Monthly,* Volume 111, No. 1, September 2000, available online at *http://alumni.berkeley.edu/Alumni/Cal_Monthly/September_2000/main.asp.*

[SPEC04] Standard Performance Evaluation Corporation, available online at *http://www.specbench.org,* 2004.

[STAF] "Software Testing Automation Framework," available online at *http://www.sourceforge.net/projects/staf/.*

[Sugerman01] Sugerman, Venkitachalam, et al., "Virtualizing I/O Devices on VMware Workstation's Hosted Virtual Machine Monitor," Proceedings of the 2001 USENIX Annual Technical Conference, June 2001.

[TPC04] Transaction Processing Performance Council, available online at *http://www.tpc.org/,* 2004.

[Turk02] Turk, Dan, et al., "Limitations of Agile Software Processes," Third International Conference on eXtreme Programming and Agile Processes in Software Engineering, 2002.

[USGOV1] "Software Accessibility Checklist," United States of America Department of Justice, available online at *http://www.usdoj.gov/crt/508/archive/oldsoftware.html,* 2000.

[Varian97] Varian, Melinda, "VM and the VM Community: Past, Present and Future," available online at *http://pucc.princeton.edu/~melinda/,* August 1997.

[Weyuker98] Weyuker, Elaine, "Testing Component-Based Software: A Cautionary Tale," *IEEE Software* magazine, September/October 1998.

[Williams03] Williams, Laurie and Alistair Cockburn, "Agile Software Development: It's about Feedback and Change." *Computer* magazine, June 2003 (Vol. 36, No. 6).

[Whittaker03] Whittaker, Thompson, *How to Break Software Security: Effective Techniques for Security Testing,* Pearson Addison Wesley, 2003.

Glossary

ABEND   ABnormal END, a mainframe term for a program crash. It is always associated with a failure code, known as an ABEND code.

Accessibility Testing   Testing that determines if the software will be usable by people with disabilities.

Address Space   A z/OS construct, analogous to a UNIX process, that provides a range of virtual memory within which work executes. Each interactive time-sharing user, started task, or batch job is given its own address space. Multiple tasks, analogous to a UNIX thread, can run within a single address space.

Agile Software Development   Processes used to develop software with the goal of early and often code delivery.

Algorithm Verification Testing   A software development and test phase focused on the validation and tuning of key algorithms using an iterative experimentation process.

Artistic Testing   Testing that takes early experiences gained with the software and uses them to devise new tests not imagined during initial planning. It is often guided by the intuition and investigative instincts of the tester. Also known as *Exploratory Testing*.

Automation   Software that watches for specific system events and takes predefined actions in response to each event.

Batch Job   A class of software program that does not interact directly with the user. It is submitted by the user to the system, eventually executes (when system resources permit), and returns a result. May be defined to run automatically at a specific time.

Batch Window   A time period, usually at night, used to perform database consolidation and reconciliation activities or other disruptive tasks, often by running streams of specialized *batch jobs*.

Beta Test   Testing done by customers on a prerelease version of the software.

Black-box Testing   A technique that assumes little, if any, understanding of software's internals, but rather relies on a comprehensive view of its inputs and associated external behaviors.

Boundary Condition Testing   See *Limits Testing.*

Breakpoint   A function provided by interactive development environments, debugging tools, and hypervisors in which a specific instruction in a program is marked, such that when that instruction is reached the program or system is suspended to allow a person to observe its status information. Also known on some systems as a *trap.*

Bucket   A collection of executable test cases.

Bug   See *Defect.*

Capture-replay Tools   Tools that give testers the ability to move some Graphical User Interface (GUI) testing away from manual execution by "capturing" mouse clicks and keyboard strokes into a script, and then "replaying" that script to re-create the same sequence of inputs and responses on subsequent tests.

Channel   A dedicated, specialized processor that completely offloads I/O work from the CPU on a mainframe computer.

Clear-box Testing   See *White-box Testing.*

Cluster   A collection of computer servers that operate together as a single unit to process work.

Coexistence Testing   Testing that checks to see if a new version of software interoperates successfully with older versions of that same software.

Compatibility Testing   Ensuring an updated product can still interact properly with other older products.

Component Spy   A tester who explores an entire software component with the goal of becoming a technical resource within the test team for anything having to do with that area.

Considerations List   A list of key areas of concern that should be focused on during a test. The descriptions are brief and are used during early test planning. They also typically feed into the formulation of a variation list.

Contingency Factor   A percentage of the total amount of time or resources required for the test. This factor represents the estimated time required for reacting to problems, waiting for fixes, handing test machine failures, and so on. It is added to the overall projected schedule as a safety cushion. See *Task Contingency* and *Methodology Contingency.*

Cookbook Scenario   A test scenario description that provides complete, step-by-step details about how the scenario should be performed. It leaves nothing to chance.

Coupling Facility (CF)   Licensed internal code running in a special type of logical partition in certain mainframe processors that provides a shared storage medium used in a Parallel Sysplex cluster.

Coupling Facility Rebuild   The act of moving coupling facility structures from one CF to another.

Coupling Facility Structures   Hardware assists within a coupling facility to enable multisystem data-sharing support. These assists support global locking, caching features, and a set of queuing constructs. Unique structures can be allocated for different software exploiters.

Database Administrator   Someone who manages database optimization, backup, and recovery.

Data Corruption   What occurs when data is incorrectly modified by some outside source and the user is not notified.

Data Integrity   The completeness and correctness of data that has not been corrupted.

Data Integrity Monitor   A small test program that creates specific conditions in which data corruption might occur, and then checks to see if it does. See *Thrasher*.

Debug   Find the source of an error in a computer program.

Defect   An error in a computer program.

Emulator   A software application that emulates a hardware platform different from the one it is actually executing on. It runs as an application on a host operating system, but unlike the *software partitioning* approach, the emulated environment is not tied to a particular operating system. Any operating system that can run on the hardware being emulated can also run under the emulator.

Enterprise   A business or government entity.

Escape Analysis   A thorough, technical review of the defects found in a following test phase or by customers with the goal of identifying technical modifications to the test processes so that these types of defects no longer escape.

Evolutionary Software Development   Software creation process based on the waterfall development model but exploits feedback loops to ensure improvements are continually made.

Exploiter   Other software that makes use of the target software's services.

Exploratory Testing   See *Artistic Testing*.

eXtreme Programming   Software development process with the goal of reacting quickly to changing requirements. Quick customer feedback is a critical trait of eXtreme programming and is achieved through shared test creation with customers and execution by development. See *Agile Software Development*.

First Failure Data Capture (FFDC)   The ability for software to automatically collect and save enough status information at the time of its failure to enable the error's root cause to be determined later by a human. Software with this trait eliminates the need to turn on special traces or other diagnostic aides and then re-create the problem in order to diagnose it.

Fix Testing   Rerunning of a test that previously found a bug in order to see if a supplied fix works.

Framework Scenario   A test scenario definition that provides only enough high-level information to remind the tester of everything that needs to be covered for that scenario. The description captures the activity's essence, but trusts the tester to work through the specific steps required.

Function Verification Test (FVT)   Testing of a complete, yet containable functional area or component within the overall software package. Normally occurs immediately after Unit Test. Also known as *Integration Test* (though not in this book).

Grooved Tests   Tests that simply repeat the same activity against a target product from cycle to cycle.

Guest   See *Virtual Machine.*

Hard Dependency   Something that is absolutely required in order for the dependent software to work correctly.

Heterogeneous Environment   Infrastructure that consists of multiple classes of computing systems.

Host Hypervisor   A hypervisor that coexists with a host operating system on the same machine.

Hypervisor   Software for providing virtualization which runs the virtual computer natively, suspends it any time it executes an operation that would affect the state of the real CPU, and emulates that operation before returning control to the virtual computer. Also known as a *Virtual Machine Monitor*. See *Virtualization.*

Incident   See *Defect.*

Information Technology (IT)   Computer hardware, software, and related equipment.

Integration Test   A test that looks at an entire solution as a whole. It moves beyond the single-product domain of system verification test and tries to *integrate* the new software into a simulated customer environment. It takes a big picture view, with the new software as merely one of many elements in that picture—just as if it had been thrown into production. Also known as *Acceptance Testing* (but not in this book).

Internationalization Testing   Validates that a program which has been translated for sale in other countries continues to operate properly. Also known as *Translation Testing.*

Iterative Software Development   Software creation processes that are focused on providing frequent feedback in all phases.

Limits Testing   Testing a piece of code to its defined limits and then a little bit more. Also known as *Boundary Condition Testing.*

Load/Stress   High levels of activity applied to software in order to put it under extreme pressure to see what limits it can endure.

Logical Partition (LPAR)   One subdivision of a physical computer that has been divided into a number of smaller, logical computers. The number of CPUs, memory, and I/O paths defined for each LPAR image is adjustable. Each LPAR is independent and capable of running a different operating system instance.

Longevity Testing   See *Reliability Testing.*

Long-haul Testing   See *Reliability Testing.*

Mainframe   A class of large computer systems architected to address the needs of commercial computing, designed to handle the constant movement of data between the processor and external storage, very large amounts of data, processor resource consumed in short bursts for each transaction or read/write operation, and large pools of simultaneous users and tasks competing for resources.

Mainline Function   The primary job a software program is designed to perform.

Memory Leak   A type of software defect. Typically occurs when memory is repeatedly obtained and released, but the amount released is inadvertently less than what was obtained, causing memory consumption to gradually accumulate.

Message-Digest 5 (MD5)   An algorithm for creating a digital fingerprint of a file. Commonly used for ensuring that files were not changed or corrupted during transmission.

Methodology Contingency   A cushion of time or resource added to the schedule based on test phase or the execution environment.

Middleware   Software that provides infrastructure services upon which applications depend.

Migration Testing   Testing to see if a customer will be able to transition smoothly from a prior version of the software to a new one.

Mission-critical   Describes software and computing systems deemed so vital that without them, the enterprise simply can not operate.

Native   Describes a nonvirtualized environment, with no emulation or hypervisor layer between the processor hardware and the operating system.

Native Hypervisor   A hypervisor that runs directly on the server hardware.

Operator   Someone who handles the day-to-day monitoring of the production systems.

Outage   A slowdown or complete shutdown of the availability of an application, subsystem, full system, or system cluster.

Penetration Testing   See *Security Testing.*

Performance Verification Test (PVT)   Determines software's maximum throughput and/or response-time characteristics. Also identifies inhibitors to software achieving its performance goals.

Physical Partitioning   Electrically splitting a single physical computer into two separate computers.

Postmortem   Self-analysis of interim or fully completed testing activities with the goal of creating improvements to be used in the future.

Pressure Points   Areas of software that have the toughest demands placed upon them.

Privileged Instructions   A carefully grouped subset of the CPU instructions that can only be executed when the CPU is in a specially authorized state.

Problem   See *Defect.*

Production   The running of some portion of an enterprise's business.

Production Systems   Computing platforms and environments on which an enterprise's business is deployed.

Program Listing   Output that shows the low-level assembly and machine language instructions that make up a compiled program, along with the offset of each such instruction from the program's beginning. Can usually be generated by a compiler when it is invoked with the appropriate options.

Provisioning   Populating a computer with an operating system and associated middleware and applications such that it is a fully functional system.

Race Condition   See *Timing and Serialization Problems.*

Reactionary Iterative Model   Software development process that makes use of quick and iterative reactions to issues that arise.

Real Memory   Memory that is physically installed on a computer. See *Virtual Memory.*

Recovery Routine   A chunk of software code that is automatically given control if an unexpected failure occurs so it can perform any needed cleanup activities and allow the software module it is protecting to resume operating normally.

Regression Testing   Testing that determines if new code has broken, or "regressed" old functions.

Reliability Testing   Determines if software can continue running significant load/stress for an extended period. Also known as *Longevity Testing* or *Long-haul Testing.*

Restartability   The capability of a software product to be restarted without error after a failure.

Scaffolding   Bits of code that surround a module to prop it up during early testing by receiving invocations from the module and responding to them according to an expected protocol. See *Stub Routines.*

Scenario   A series of discrete events, performed in a particular order, designed to generate a specific result.

Security Testing   The art of validating software security mechanisms by attempting to penetrate them. Also known as *Penetration Testing or Vulnerability Testing.*

Serialization   A software construct (such as a lock or mutex) used to coordinate the actions of multiple software entities executing concurrently on the same computing system. It is used to force a serial order in the use of resources they all share, such as control structures in common memory areas.

Service Level Agreement (SLA)   A contract between the provider of information technology services for the enterprise (typically the company's own I/T department, or an outsourcing vendor), and the users of those services.

Service Test   Tests software fixes, both individually and bundled together, for software that is already in use by customers.

Sniff Test   A quick check to see if any major abnormalities are evident in the software.

Soft Dependency   Something required in order for the dependent software to work a certain way.

Software Partitioning   An approach to subdividing a computer system which employs control software that works in concert with a specific operating system to subdivide its resources.

Software Stack   The layers of software necessary to allow an application to execute. Typically includes an operating system, one or more middleware products, and the application itself.

Spiral Development   Iterative software creation process focused on performing risk review and assessment throughout the iterations of the test cycles to influence the improvements for the next phase of testing.

Streamable Test Cases   Test cases which are able to run together as part of a large group.

Stub Routines   Tiny routines that stand in for actual modules by imitating their responses when invoked. See *Scaffolding.*

Subsystem   Software that provides critical supporting services to an operating system, such as job submission control or security management.

Symmetrical Multiprocessor (SMP)   A server that contains multiple tightly coupled processors, each of which can independently accept work.

Sympathy Sickness   A situation where one system's difficulties cause a chain reaction in which other systems it is in contact with also get sick in "sympathy."

System Administrator   Someone who supports a server at a departmental level.

System Programmer   Someone who installs, sets up, configures, customizes, and maintains system software. The term programmer is included in the title due to their typical tasks of writing scripts, customization exits, etc.

System Verification Test (SVT)   Testing of an entire software package for the first time, with all components working together to deliver the project's intended purpose on supported hardware platforms.

Task Contingency   A cushion of time or resources added to the schedule for each set of activities performed during a test.

Test Case   A software program that, when executed, will exercise one or more facets of the software under test, and then self-verify its actual results against what is expected.

Testability   An attribute of software describing how well it lends itself to being tested.

Testability Hooks   Those functions, integrated in the software that can be invoked through primarily undocumented interfaces to drive specific processing which would otherwise be difficult to exercise.

Thrasher   A type of program used to test for data integrity errors on mainframe systems. The name is derived from the first such program, which deliberately generated memory thrashing (the overuse of large amounts of memory, leading to heavy paging or swapping) while monitoring for corruption. See *Data Integrity Monitor*.

Timing and Serialization Problems   A class of software defect, usually in multithreaded code, in which two or more tasks attempt to alter a shared software resource without properly coordinating their actions. Also known as *Race Conditions*.

Transaction   A class of software program that is designed to respond immediately to requests from users. They are typically atomic, meaning that either the transaction successfully completes all actions it was asked to perform, or it completes none of them. A request to move money from one bank account to another would be an example of a transaction. Transactions run under the control of a *Transaction Monitor*.

Transaction Monitor   Middleware that coordinates the processing of transactions. If a transaction doesn't complete successfully, the transaction monitor will typically ensure any changes it made to data are fully backed out. See *Transaction*.

Translation Testing   See *Internationalization Testing*.

Trap   A debugging aid ability offered by some operating systems and hypervisors that allows a user to request that a particular action happens when some event occurs on a live system. The event could be the crash of the given program, the invocation of a particular module, or even the execution of a specific line of code. The action could be to force a memory dump, write a record to a log, or even freeze the entire system. This is different from the use of the same term on some systems as a means of describing a crash or ABEND. See *Breakpoint*.

Unit Test (UT)   Testing done by software developers of their own code prior to merging it into the overall development stream which exercises all of its new and changed paths.

Usability Testing   Ensures that software's human interfaces are intuitive and easy to follow.

Variation   A single test to be performed. Similar to the IEEE definition of a test case.

Virtualization   A technique that creates one or more simulated (or virtual) computers within a single physical computer. Each virtual computer appears to the software running inside it to have all of the resources that are available on a real computer. The virtual computer may also have the ability to emulate hardware that does not actually exist on the underlying physical machine.

Virtual Machine   One of the virtual computers created by a hypervisor. See *Hypervisor* and *Virtualization*.

Virtual Machine Monitor   See *Hypervisor*.

Virtual Memory   An illusion created by computer operating systems to make it appear to applications that they have more memory available for use than may be actually installed on the physical computer. This is done by creating a virtual memory space, and mapping the portions of that space that are actually in use to the computer's installed, or *real*, memory. When real memory becomes scarce, chunks of it are freed up by moving them out to a page or swap file on a hard disk. The next time a program tries to access one of those chunks, it is copied back into real memory from disk. All of this is managed by the operating system, making it transparent to the application program. See *Real Memory*.

Virtual Network   Support provided by a hypervisor to allow that virtual machines on the same physical computer can communicate with each other at memory speeds as if they are on a physical network. See *Hypervisor* and *Virtualization*.

Vulnerability Testing   See *Security Testing*.

Wall-clock Performance Measurement   Observing obvious performance problems in software through measuring its response to external stimuli via a clock on the wall.

Waterfall Model   A linear and sequential approach to developing software that depends on one phase completing before the next can begin.

Waterwheel Model   A modification of the waterfall software development model that retains its up front activities of requirements collection, specification development, and product design. However, it stages the development and testing phases by shipping code in logical groupings so that testing can occur on one chunk of code while the next chunk is being created. It also implements a form of continuous feedback between the development and test phases to enable ongoing adjustment to the software's operation.

White-box Testing   A technique where an understanding of the software internals is key to creating the test plan and approach. Also known as *Clear-box Testing*. See *Black-box Testing*.

Wild Store   When a program modifies memory at an incorrect location, thereby corrupting it.

Zap   The dynamic alteration of computer memory. Usually intended to bypass a problem or force software to take a particular action.

Index